Although the celebrated friendship be
France and the United States may be
historical myth, in a certain sense it has also
been a reality. In spite of many frictions and
controversies the two nations have always
managed to restore the kind of harmony and
understanding characteristic of close diplomatic
associates. As Charles de Gaulle has put it, in
a rare conciliatory gesture, " . . . there is
always one of our two countries whose instinct
inclines it to moderation when the other tends
to abandon moderation."

This is the first thorough appraisal of
Franco-American diplomatic relations in their
historical perspective, from the beginning of
the American republic in 1789 to the outbreak
of World War I in 1914. In his discussion of
political, economic, and ideological questions
Mr. Blumenthal emphasizes the period since
1870, and in his analysis of expansionism,
colonialism, imperialism, and political strategy
he relates French-American diplomacy to the
interactions of Great Britain, Russia, Germany,
Japan, and other powers. De Gaulle's attitudes
toward the United States are shown to have
deep roots, and in this respect the book may
be considered an introduction to the former
French president's intellectual ancestors and an
invaluable aid to an understanding of
contemporary Franco-American relations.

d detailed, the
ject is even
it works of
dy is based upon
riginal sources,
An intelligent
eaders, it contains
ns, and insights.
or of history,
Rutgers, The State University, Newark, New
Jersey. He is the author of *A Reappraisal of
Franco-American Relations, 1830-1871,* and is
currently working on a broad study of French-
American cultural relations during the
nineteenth century that will complement this
volume.

France and the United States
Their Diplomatic Relations
1789-1914

FRANCE
and the
UNITED STATES

Their Diplomatic Relations, 1789–1914

by HENRY BLUMENTHAL

The University of North Carolina Press
Chapel Hill

To My Teachers

Preface

In the past, historians have written about limited aspects and periods of the diplomatic relations between France and the United States. Franco-American foreign affairs for the entire period from 1789 to 1914 have heretofore not been discussed in their total historical perspective. This is strange because France, after all, has been one of the most important countries with which the United States has maintained active and significant ties. It is doubtful that the United States could have won its independence without French assistance. Throughout the nineteenth century the two nations recognized the mutual benefits they derived from their cultural and commercial exchanges. Even in international questions involving the interests of France and the United States respectively they exercised considerable indirect influence on each other.

Throughout the century it was the stated policy of the United States to remain aloof from strictly European issues, as if it could operate in an international vacuum. In fact, not only was its own security related to the balance of power on the European continent, America's attitudes and policies with respect to major European developments usually reflected its awareness of the interdependence of the Old World and the New. Its Monroe Doctrine indirectly helped to channel Europe's expansion to other continents. As a matter of record, all major powers felt the economic and political impact of the United States especially from the later part of the nineteenth century on. Throughout the period under consideration, moreover, the accomplishments and shortcomings of the model republic were of conscious concern to European monarchists and republicans alike. At no time did the French people and their monarchical and republican governments lose sight of this major aspect of the age. The shadow of the United States seemed to be ever present on the European continent. America's policy of aloofness was thus more an impossibility than a failure. Various French attempts, on the other hand, to stop the territorial growth of the United States ended in failure on the American continent as well as overseas. Ill-disguised discrimination against American agricultural products in the final decades of the century was also ill conceived. The United States naturally resented these obstructionist policies which resulted in long periods of strained political relations.

But if the celebrated friendship between France and the United States has been a historical myth, in a certain measure it has also been a reality. In his conciliatory gesture on the occasion of Ambassador Charles E. Bohlen's farewell luncheon, former President de Gaulle admirably interpreted nearly two centuries of Franco-American history. ". . . there is always," he commented, "one of our two countries whose instinct inclines it to moderation when the other tends to abandon moderation. At the various times when France was choosing to lead a hazardous life, she did not unfailingly have the United States' support. Today, when the latter in its turn is particularly susceptible to the impulses of power, it is true that France does not always approve it. Perhaps, after all, these divergencies, under such circumstances, have contributed to world equilibrium. But if formerly, and if now, there results from this certain differences in attitudes, certain frictions in feelings, the capital of mutual interest, attraction and admiration common to both our peoples, and which on various decisive occasions has weighed so fortunately and so heavily in the destiny of the world, must not be diminished because of it."[1]

It is indeed noteworthy that in spite of many frictions and controversies France and the United States have always managed to restore the kind of harmony and understanding characteristic of close members of an occasionally quarrelling family. Tradition and interest no doubt facilitated these rapprochements. The numerous personal contacts, particularly between educated Americans and Frenchmen, helped to keep traditional sentiments alive. Although relatively few Frenchmen visited the United States during the last century, thousands of American sightseers toured France and admired its natural beauty and artistic creations. In the first half of the nineteenth century many American doctors received their advanced medical training in France and proudly added to their names the initials

1. Ambassade de France, *Speeches & Press Conferences,* No. 281, New York, January 31, 1968.

"M.D.P.," "Doctor of Medicine, Paris." By the end of the century literally thousands of American art and music students made France their second home. Unlike regular tourists who had almost no personal contacts with French families, eminent American scientists and other creative minds found the hospitality of French homes and the intellectual stimulation and generosity of their hosts most gratifying. To be sure, the occasional immorality of French literature and art and the superficiality of the French people's "religion" shocked American puritans. But somehow, with typical French shoulder-shrugging, many of them seem to have been willing to make allowances for these French weaknesses. Similarly, Frenchmen who were appalled by the excessive materialistic outlook of the United States nevertheless admired the results of the American people's industry and ingenuity. On balance, the intimate cultural connections between French and American citizens clearly took the sting out of the all too frequent political differences between their respective governments.

Though it does not ignore public opinion, this study focuses on policies and developments. The image of the United States in France, largely based on oral and written reports rather than on personal visits, underwent frequent changes. The very passage of time, as well as the political and economic evolution in both countries, affected these fluctuations and modifications. Despite a noticeable disenchantment, particularly since the July Revolution and the Jackson period, the two nations nevertheless felt attached to each other. The United States did not turn out to be the kind of ideal society French intellectuals had envisioned during the late eighteenth century. And since the third decade of the nineteenth century the rising middle class of France began increasingly to apprehend the economic and political competition of the rising middle class of the United States. It was only at the end of the nineteenth century that some French and American leaders drew from their political analyses the rational conclusion that sensible cooperation rather than militant competition would serve their two countries best. In an international political sense, they needed and supplemented each other. In their respective spheres of superiority—in cultural and socioeconomic respects—both nations found much to admire in the other.

Studying these 125 years of Franco-American relations, one cannot help but be reminded of the old French saying, "The more things change, the more they remain the same." Though the period since 1914 has produced its own contemporary problems and shifts, at crucial moments in history France and the United States have joined forces in defense of common interests. Their differences of opinion after the two World Wars must of course be seen in the light of the observation that these wars accelerated the historical evolution as a result of which the United States emerged with its position in the world phenomenally strengthened while that of France had diminished. Since the Restoration an ever-increasing number of Frenchmen were concerned about this prospect. At first they sensed it; then they began to be dismayed by it; and finally it haunted and hurt them.

As far as Franco-American relations are concerned, former President de Gaulle's views have deep historical roots. Adapted to the current world situation, the towering French statesman sees the United States in relation to France and the rest of Europe in a light similar to that of Jules Cambon. There is indeed a remarkable historical continuity in French thought concerning America. François Guizot, Jules Cambon, and Charles de Gaulle have frankly articulated viewpoints about the United States as concerned Frenchmen and Europeans. Understandably, Guizot expressed his apprehensions in a milder and more diplomatic form than either Cambon or de Gaulle. Guizot anticipated the overpowering effect of an unusually powerful country. Cambon and de Gaulle were already being confronted with the existence of the American giant. If security was to be found in a balance of power, then power had to be balanced. For independent European states to survive individually in the presence of giant powers called for the formation of a combination of independent European states. It was not so much economic and political rivalry with the United States that worried Frenchmen as their fear that France and Europe might be overwhelmed by it. In this respect, this book introduces the reader to de Gaulle's intellectual ancestors.

This study deals with the diplomatic relations between France and the United States in the nineteenth century. To gain a fuller picture, the years 1789 and 1914 seemed to be less arbitrary as start-

ing and terminal points than the turns of the centuries. In an effort
to avoid, as far as possible, the tedious restatement of well-known
facts, the author has not only striven to present the earlier relations
in meaningful perspective, he has also emphasized Franco-American
history since the last third of the century. It may be of interest to
some readers to know that a second volume, dealing in considerable
detail with Franco-American cultural aspects and mutual influences
in the arts and sciences, is slated to be published in the not-too-dis-
tant future.

I am greatly indebted for the courtesies extended to me by the
libraries of many institutions and their staffs. Prominent among
them are the Archives de France, the Archives du Ministère des Affaires Étrangères, the Bibliothèque Nationale, the Institut de France,
and the Sorbonne (all in Paris); the Library of Congress, the
Massachusetts State Historical Society, the National Archives, the
Newark Public Library, the New York Historical Society, the New
York Public Library, the Pennsylvania Historical Society, and the
Philosophical Society (Philadelphia); Columbia, Duke, Georgetown,
Harvard, Johns Hopkins, Princeton, Rutgers, Tulane, and Yale Uni-
versities; Louisiana State University Archives; and the Universities
of California (Berkeley), North Carolina (at Chapel Hill), and
Pennsylvania. I wish to express my special appreciation to the *At-
lanta Constitution* for having granted me access to its private index.

To the readers of my manuscript I am indebted for valuable criticism and helpful suggestions. To Mrs. Elizabeth Nankivell I owe a
debt of gratitude for her cheerful readiness to type this manuscript
with her customary skill. I wish to thank also Miss Filomena Guar-
ino for having typed my final revisions and additions. And finally, I
wish to acknowledge the financial assistance I received from the
Rutgers Research Council. Its generous support, stretching over several years, enabled me to travel to far-away sources and to concentrate on the writing of this book.

HENRY BLUMENTHAL

Rutgers University
Newark, New Jersey
May, 1969.

Contents

Tables

Abbreviations

AHR	*American Historical Review*
AMAE	Archives du Ministère des Affaires Étrangères
CP	Correspondance politique
CPEU	Correspondence politique—États-Unis (AMAE)
DDCDS	Diplomatic dispatches from U.S. ministers in China to the Department of State
DDEDS	Diplomatic dispatches from U.S. ministers in England to the Department of State
DDFDS	Diplomatic dispatches from U.S. ministers in France to the Department of State
DDGDS	Diplomatic dispatches from U.S. ministers in Germany to the Department of State
DDRDS	Diplomatic dispatches from U.S. ministers in Russia to the Department of State
DDSDS	Diplomatic dispatches from U.S. ministers in Spain to the Department of State
DS	Department of State
FIDS	Instructions from the Department of State to U.S. ministers in France
FNFDS	Notes from the Department of State to the French Legation
FNTDS	Notes from the French Legation to the Department of State
LC	Library of Congress
NS	New Series
RDDM	*Revue des deux mondes*
RIDS	Instructions from the Department of State to U.S. ministers in Russia

I
Franco-American Diplomatic Relations
1789–1871

1. The Federalist Period

Historians are fond of pointing out that the past is the prelude to the future. If this observation merits being taken seriously, then a microscopic look at Franco-American problems and trends during the previous century should enlighten us about the elements of continuity and change in the contacts between these two nations. In view of France's fundamentally European orientation, it is striking but not surprising that throughout almost the entire nineteenth century the diplomatic relations between France and the United States occupied a more central place in the history of the United States than in that of France. Despite many cultural and political differences, however, both peoples were drawn to each other by strange emotional bonds which often led to expectations that clashed with the realities of existing situations.

The essential contribution of the Franco-American alliance of 1778 to American independence and the participation of the United States in the First World War as an "associate" of the allied powers have helped to perpetuate the myth of the traditionally close political association between France and the United States. Actually public opinion in both countries with respect to the other ranged at any given time from admiration to contempt. And their respective policies regarding each other produced more frictions than mere diplomatic pleasantries could hope to minimize, much less resolve.

Historically the Franco-American alliance of 1778 was the by-product of the struggle for world leadership in which France and Britain had been engaged for ages.[1] The humilia-

1. For this early period, see Samuel Flagg Bemis, *The Diplomacy of the American Revolution* (New York, 1935); Richard B. Morris, *The Peacemakers—The Great Powers and American Independence* (New York, 1965); Gerald Stourzh, *Benjamin Franklin and American Foreign Policy* (Chicago, 1954); Ralph L. Ketcham, "France and American Politics, 1763-1793," *Political Science Quarterly*, LXXVIII (1963), 198-223; and

tion France had suffered as a result of the Seven Years' War, which ended in 1763 with its expulsion from North America, in time aided the revolutionary cause of the English colonies in America in two major respects: it predisposed France to encourage sentiments of independence in the colonies and it emboldened the colonists to defy their mother country now that they no longer needed its protection against the French in Canada. Until 1776 this defiance was aimed at achieving greater autonomy rather than independence. The English colonists in America, including Benjamin Franklin, were skeptical of French intentions. This "intriguing nation," they feared, according to Joseph Galloway, one of their leaders, would help them to gain their independence from England "only to become the slave of arbitrary power, of popish bigotry, and superstition."

But as the Anglo-American colonial crisis deepened, even before the Declaration of Independence in 1776, and more so after this revolutionary step, the independent United States needed the material aid and political support of a powerful and prestigious country such as France. Without it, it would have lacked the means of defying England effectively. On her part, France was motivated by defensive and offensive considerations in her support of the American independence movement. Count de Vergennes, the French foreign minister from 1774 to 1787, advocated this policy on competitive grounds: "We shall humiliate our natural enemy, a perfidious enemy who never knows how to respect either treaties or the right of nations; we shall divert to our profit one of the principal sources of her opulence . . . we shall extend our commerce, our shipping, our fisheries; we shall ensure the possession of our islands, and finally, we shall re-establish our reputation,

---

Claude H. Van Tyne, "Influences Which Determined the French Government to Make the Treaty with America, 1778," *AHR*, XXI (1916), 528-41.

and shall resume amongst the Powers of Europe the place which belongs to us."

When the revolutionary government of the United States sent Benjamin Franklin to Paris, it did not originally instruct him to seek a military alliance with France. Material and financial aid, it thought, would be sufficient to meet its most urgent needs. This limited assistance had the great merit of not compromising the independence of the young United States. France was expected to extend this aid for its political reasons, and Franklin, the venerated archrebel, skillfully pointed to the great economic gains France would enjoy as a future reward from America. While these French-aid discussions were going on, a military development occurred that influenced French policy decisively. The defeat of General Burgoyne's British army in the Battle of Saratoga (October, 1777) demonstrated to the French the ability of the Americans to defeat the British on the field of battle and prompted the British to offer the English colonists in America home rule within the British empire. The possibility of such an Anglo-American accommodation alarmed France sufficiently for it to promise official recognition of the United States without waiting for Spain to join it in such a move. By now, however, home rule no longer satisfied the Americans. They desired independence and, when asked what France could do to assure it, Franklin was ready with his reply: "We want a treaty and an alliance."

On February 6, 1778, the two countries concluded two historic treaties, a mutually advantageous commercial treaty and a treaty of alliance. The alliance was of a conditional and defensive nature, essentially providing that in case war should break out between France and Great Britain, France and the United States would fight until American independence had been gained; that neither would make a separate peace or truce without the consent of the other; and that each guaranteed the other's possessions in the Western hemisphere. Unlike the Franco-American Treaty of Amity and Commerce, the treaty of alliance was to be kept secret, but its existence was divulged by Franklin's secretary, Dr. Edward Bancroft, who turned out to be a spy in the service of the well-informed British government.

By the summer of 1778 France and Great Britain had drifted into an undeclared war. When Britain refused to yield Gibraltar, among other islands and territories, to Spain as a price for the latter's mediation of the Anglo-French war, Spain concluded an alliance with France and declared war against England on June 21, 1779. Through the Franco-Spanish alliance, embodied in the convention of Aranjuez of April 12, 1779, these two continental powers pledged to fight until Gibraltar had been returned to Spain. Even more than France, Spain had its own objectives in mind when it joined its forces against England. Not wishing to encourage its colonies to break away from their mother country, Spain rendered primarily indirect aid to the American cause by preventing Britain from concentrating its resources in the North American theater of operations. Soon the Dutch were also at war with Great Britain, and Catherine the Great of Russia headed the Armed Neutrality, a weak combination of powers trying to protect their rights as neutrals. Thus the American Revolution, originally an internal Anglo-American controversy which had degenerated into a limited war, gradually became merely a phase in a war of international scope.

This unexpected turn of events obviously benefited the United States from a military point of view, but it also foreshadowed the possibility of undesirable political entanglements and intrigues. The failure of the Franco-Spanish alliance to wrest Gibraltar from Britain led to attempts to compensate Spain with vast territories east of the Mississippi. And France itself, while supporting the independence of the United States, wanted it to be a country of a size small enough to be politically dependent on France and large enough to be economically beneficial to it.

Once aware of these designs, the American peace commissioners, John Adams, Benjamin Franklin, and John Jay, felt no longer obliged to be absolutely bound by their instruction not to conclude a peace without being in close consultation with their French ally. Though it is true that the government of the United States believed it was morally obligated to issue these instructions on its own initiative, it must also be remembered that the French ministers to the United States during the Revolutionary War, Alexandre Conrad Gérard and his successor, Chevalier Anne César de La Luzerne, exercised a dominant social and political influence in America. Unexposed to such pressures, the American peace commissioners in Europe were not only better informed about the latest developments, they were also freer agents than their leading compatriots at home. Britain of course had an interest in driving a wedge between the Franco-American allies and it succeeded in doing so by ultimately granting peace terms that met the American condition of leaving detailed arrangements to negotiations while recognizing the independence of the United States as the *sine qua non* for any negotiations.

In the final phase of the war and peace negotiations neither France nor the United States lived up to the spirit of the alliance of 1778. Both had independently approached the British in an effort to gain the most favorable terms for themselves. Although Vergennes expressed his surprise at Dr. Franklin's apparent indiscretion in concluding peace terms without first consulting France, Franklin assured the French foreign minister that "nothing has been agreed in the preliminaries contrary to the interests of France." In a masterfully disarming manner Franklin reiterated his country's eternal gratitude to France and said he could think of no more sincere way of expressing America's undiminished friendship than by asking France for another loan. Despite Britain's generous peace treaty and France's less-than-generous attitude regarding an American peace treaty, the United States continued to do business with both countries without being really close to either.

This brief sketch of early Franco-American relations clearly shows that realistically defined self-interest, at times calling for dubious diplomatic maneuvers, guided both countries from the start. The young American republic was determined not to be a weak puppet in the hands of French manipulators, whether the concern was trans-Appalachian territory, as in the 1780's, or trade and neutral rights, as in the 1790's. The common roots of the Enlightenment notwithstanding, the American and French Revolutions obviously did not merge French and American national interests. These revolutions disturbed the existing political and social order of the Western world and temporarily evoked sentiments of fraternity. But when in the final years of the eighteenth century their independent interests diverged, France and the United States found themselves in quarrelsome controversies which ultimately engulfed them in an undeclared naval war.

There were both underlying and immediate reasons for this limited confrontation. Basically, the French felt that their alliance with the United States entitled them to preferential treatment. If they could not realize their ancient dream of a French empire stretching from Canada, via the Mississippi Valley, to the Gulf of Mexico, preferably limiting the boundary of the United States to the Alleghenies, French statesmen of the last quarter of the eighteenth century desired to exercise at least a dominant influence in American foreign affairs. In the pursuit of their national ambitions, particularly in regard to the restitution of Louisiana to France and the transformation of the Gulf of Mexico into a French Lake, they made expediency their chief guide. To accomplish their objectives, they would ally themselves with Spain or against it and they would support the independence of the United States as long as it did not become strong enough to be too independent.[2] The acquisition of sizable possessions in North America would of course have been the most direct way for France to assure itself of dependable political control in America. Having been unsuccessful in acquiring such territories, French statesmen regarded favorable trade and shipping arrangements with the United States as the next best approach in defending French interests. The outbreak of the French Revolution, however, was anything but helpful in this respect. The execution of Louis XVI; the revolting violence and terror in France; and the declaration of war, in February, 1793, against England, Holland, and Spain produced profound effects in the United States.[3]

Prior to these developments, American public opinion on the whole welcomed the revolutionary changes in France.[4] Unlike the domestic aspects of the French Revolution, the involvement of revoluntionary France in external wars confronted the United States with the necessity of determining the extent of its involvement or its neutrality. What obligation, if any, did the alliance of 1778 impose upon the United States during the administrations of George Washington and John Adams? If the nature of this question was essentially a legal one, the answer to it was determined by economic, ideological, and political considerations, which, in turn, contributed a great deal to the emergence of political parties in the American republic. The pro-British Hamiltonians, emphasizing the vital priority of the Anglo-American trade, opposed the

2. Frederick Jackson Turner, "The Policy of France toward the Mississippi Valley in the Period of Washington and Adams,"*AHR*, X (1905), 258, 277; Alexander De Conde, *Entangling Alliance—Politics and Diplomacy under George Washington* (Durham, N.C., 1958), pp. 199, 447; and A. L. Burt, *The United States, Great Britain and British North America —From the Revolution to the Establishment of Peace after the War of 1812* (New York, 1961), p. 169.

3. De Conde, *Entangling Alliance*, pp. 85–89, 187–89.

4. Charles D. Hazen, *Contemporary American Opinion of the French Revolution* (Gloucester, Mass., 1964), pp. 288–94.

Jeffersonians, who were disposed to implement the Franco-American treaty provisions of 1778 as scrupulously as possible. President Washington's neutrality proclamation and his professed intent to observe it strictly pleased Great Britain and the Hamiltonians. Naturally, it disappointed France, which treated it as the action of an ungrateful ally. When Jeffersonian critics went so far as to label their president's neutrality proclamation a "violation of solemn treaties," French government leaders of the middle 1790's began to make a distinction between the views of the American people and the policies of the American government. To draw such a sharp and inaccurate line between the people and the government of the United States led the revolutionary leaders of France to a series of misjudgments and miscalculations. It was clearly unrealistic to assume that the differences between the Hamiltonians and the Jeffersonians, to the extent that they affected France, could be resolved in favor of France because the Federalist government disregarded the preferences of the American people. Whatever genuine sense of obligation the American people felt toward France for its assistance during the American Revolution, Washington's defense of the necessity of peace and the benefits of neutral trade found strong popular support, even though it appealed more to residents of the Northeast than to those of the South and Southwest.

The possible consequences of the European war with respect to the future of liberty in America caused legitimate differences of opinion in the United States. The Republicans feared that the defeat of the French republic would encourage the European monarchists to do what they could to destroy republicanism in the United States also. Interpreting events differently, the Federalists looked upon the French revolutionary version of liberty as "a delusion and a sham." France could hardly derive any satisfaction from this divergence of views because, upon reflection, it was quite obvious that both Republicans and Federalists were united in their overriding desire to preserve liberty in the United States. They might interpret the meaning of liberty differently, but their ideological arguments were primarily concerned with the United States, not France. Still, this preoccupation with liberty at home was not entirely divorced from foreign-policy attitudes. For the Jeffersonians considered the Federalists to be believers in monarchical institutions who felt a strong ideological kinship with British legitimists, while the Hamiltonians looked upon the Republicans' sympathy with French republicanism, which they regarded as a danger to society everywhere, as confirmation of the Republicans' menace to American society.[5]

Faced with the complex challenges of war, the revolutionary governments of France expected a great deal from the United States, an ally and a sister republic. President Washington's neutrality policy therefore ran counter to their expectations and almost nullified the value of the alliance of 1778 and the Franco-American Treaty of Amity and Commerce. The privileges this treaty accorded to French warships and privateers during times of war embarrassingly conflicted with the principles of strict neutrality that guided the Washington administration. To complicate matters immeasurably, the Mistress of the Sea invoked rules and regulations governing maritime questions in a manner as highly objectionable to belligerent France as to the neutral United States. Great Britain's unilateral Rule of 1756, for instance, forbidding trade not open during times of peace to be extended during times of war, cut into American profits and deprived France of a vitally needed carrier service. With respect to this regulation, France and the United States developed a common interest in liberal maritime principles. The Americans, however, did not pursue the totally anti-British policy advocated by some

5. Albert Hall Bowman, "The Struggle for Neutrality—A History of the Diplomatic Relations Between the United States and France, 1790–1801" (Unpublished Ph.D. dissertation, Columbia University, 1954) , p. 455.

French sympathizers in the United States, as succinctly expressed in a popular paraphrase of "Yankee Doodle":

> Yankee Doodle! sing Ça Ira!
> Keep it up for ever.
> Drive the Tories far away—
> Now's our time or never.

The leaders of the young American nation, predominantly Federalist in the executive branch and the Senate, did not yield to sympathies or prejudices when they deliberated about what course to follow during the raging international storm. Weighing their facts very carefully, they noted that both belligerents were guilty of costly interferences with American shipping but that, unlike the French government, the British at least paid for the confiscated goods. The fact, however, that influenced American statesmen decisively in their final determination of policy was the unmatched volume and value of Anglo-American trade. In the circumstances in which they and their country found themselves, this trade and the preservation of peace seemed to justify some temporary concessions to Britain, regardless of French reactions.[6]

The leaders of the French government had different ideas. Early in 1793 they sent Edmond Genêt to negotiate a new treaty with the United States aimed at political and commercial coooperation between the two countries that would go beyond the treaties of 1778. In disregard of President Washington's neutrality proclamation, Genêt's instructions authorized him to enlist the American people's support for the cause of the French Revolution and to issue military and naval commissions to Americans and others willing to fight for France. The French diplomat's arrogant and indiscreet conduct compelled Washington to request his recall, which brought the serious differences between the governments in Paris and Phila-

---

6. De Conde, *Entangling Alliance*, pp. 99–100.

delphia into the open.[7] If divergent policies drove the two governments increasingly apart, their respective choices of diplomats promoted further ill-feeling and suspicion. Gouverneur Morris, the "insolent and vile man" who represented the United States in France, made no secret of his hostility toward republican France. According to Thomas Jefferson, Morris poisoned President Washington's mind with his prejudiced interpretations of events in France. In June, 1792, for instance, Morris wrote to Jefferson: "The best picture I can give of the French nation is that of cattle before a thunderstorm. And as to the government, every member of it is engaged in the defense of himself or the attack of his neighbor."[8] Genêt's fate in America finally afforded the Jacobin government of France the longed-for opportunity of requesting the recall from France of this disdainful and aristocratic American.

When, in 1794, to head off a war, the United States concluded the Jay Treaty with Great Britain, Franco-American relations deteriorated very rapidly. Although the agreement settled some of the problems growing out of the Peace Treaty of 1783 and indeed failed to assert some of America's maritime principles, to France it was an infamous treaty. The very fact that the United States, bound to France by contractual agreements and solemn assurances, negotiated the Jay Treaty with the archenemy of France led to angry charges of betrayal and perfidy. It put James Monroe, Gouverneur Morris's successor, in the rather embarrassing position of unwittingly serving as a friendly republican decoy in Paris while John Jay carried on his negotiations in London. Worse than that, as the result of the treaty any French notion of involving the United States in the war against Britain had to be given up. Speaking

7. *Ibid.*, pp. 197-201.
8. Anne Cary Morris (ed.) , *The Diary and Letters of Gouverneur Morris* (New York, 1888) , I, 542; see also Bowman, "The Struggle for Neutrality," pp. 145 ff.

for the Directory, Foreign Minister Delacroix advised Monroe in July, 1796, that in view of America's breach of the treaties of 1778, France regarded certain neutrality provisions in the commercial treaty of 1778 "as altered and suspended."[9] Henceforth the Federalists endeavored to free the United States from the obligations of these treaties as soon as they could legally do so.[10]

In an effort to calm the French government, Monroe indiscreetly alluded to the presidential election of 1796 and the anticipated political changes that would restore the ancient amity between the two nations. In the meantime, Pierre Adet, the French envoy who assumed his extraordinary duties in Philadelphia in June, 1795, did his best, in accordance with the instructions of the Directory, to bring about "the right kind of revolution in the United States" by "campaigning" in the election of 1796 against President Washington.[11] Although this intolerable interference in America's domestic affairs did not prevent the election of John Adams, another Federalist, it caused bitter resentment in the United States and prompted President Washington to warn the American people in his Farewell Address against "the insidious wiles of foreign influence" and permanent, as distinguished from temporary, alliances.

Monroe's recent indiscretion left President Washington little choice but to recall him. But Adet continued to exercise his unwholesome influence on Franco-American relations and on his advice, the French Directory refused to receive the new American envoy, the moderate South Carolina Federalist Charles Cotesworth Pinckney.[12] Indignant about this latest

9. De Conde, *Entangling Alliance*, pp. 372–78.

10. By 1795 the United States had already liquidated its financial debt to France. See Howard C. Rice, "James Swan: Agent of the French Republic, 1794–1796," *New England Quarterly*, X (1937), 477–78.

11. S. F. Bemis, "Washington's Farewell Address: A Foreign Policy of Independence," *AHR*, XXXIX (1934), 250–68.

12. E. Wilson Lyon, "The Directory and the United States," *AHR*, XLIII (1938), 516–17.

French insult, Pinckney's government instructed him to leave for the Netherlands. His departure from French soil late in January, 1797, signaled a complete rupture between France and the United States. Soon other events enveloped the two countries in a crisis having ominous overtones. The Directory was evidently so outraged by the Jay Treaty and the election of another Federalist that on March 2, 1797, it issued a decree authorizing, among other provocative provisions, the seizure of enemy goods on neutral ships.[13] And, adding insult to injury, the French government refused to deal with a special commission headed by John Marshall and including Elbridge Gerry and Charles C. Pinckney, three distinguished Americans who had been charged to resolve existing French-American misunderstandings. The Directory's conditions for an official reception of this American Commission, tactlessly transmitted by the obscure XYZ agents, namely, a sizable loan and a bribe, insulted the dignity of the commissioners and their country. When the news of this offensive treatment reached the American shore of the Atlantic, the patriotic pride of the American people was manifested spontaneously. On June 13, 1798, Congress suspended all commercial transactions with France. In July, it authorized the capture of armed French ships and declared the Franco-American treaties of 1778 null and void by virtue of the fact that the French government had already violated them.[14]

The ensuing undeclared naval war taxed the resources and nerves of both nations for about two and a half years.[15] The

13. As a result of various French decrees, American shippers lost about twelve million dollars between 1793 and 1800. *Ibid*, p. 518.

14. General Washington was recalled from his retirement to head the American army that was being raised. French policy-makers played right into the hands of Alexander Hamilton, who was to be in command of the army. The XYZ episode transformed many American supporters of peace and neutrality into advocates of war. *Ibid.*, p. 456.

15. For a detailed account of this conflict, see Alexander De Conde, *The Quasi War—The Politics and Diplomacy of the Undeclared War with France, 1797–1801* (New York, 1966) .

France, particularly after the sale of Louisiana and the disastrous defeat of the French fleet. This view did not obscure his innermost belief, however, that if France and Britain "can so far worry one another as to destroy their power of tyrannizing, the one over the earth, the other over the waters, the world may perhaps enjoy peace, till they can recruit again."[1] On balance, though, the arrogant way in which Britain used its enormous commercial and sea power constituted in Jefferson's judgment a combination of factors that could be most harmful to the United States. His foreign policy was as much influenced by these thoughts as by his earlier experiences and observations in Europe.

An ardent believer in peace, Thomas Jefferson preferred to follow the wise course of his predecessors and not become entangled in European affairs in any way. When the belligerents, however, interfered with the neutral trade of the United States, Jefferson and his compatriots realized that their policy of nonintervention and nonentanglement could not be realistically implemented without the fullest cooperation of the Europeans. Even then, the protracted war between Britain and France was inevitably destined to affect the United States in its economic development and future relationship with Europe. For a change of the balance of power in Europe, as Jefferson was fully aware, would ultimately be felt by the United States. The duration of the war, the final identity of the victor, or an eventual stalemate were of direct and immediate consequence to the United States, regardless of how aloof it might remain from the conflict. Without becoming militarily involved in the rivalries of the Old World powers, President Jefferson decided to take advantage of their very existence. By doing so he recognized the important difference in American foreign affairs between active and passive entanglement. He

1. Quoted in Lawrence S. Kaplan, *Jefferson and France—An Essay on Politics and Political Ideas* (New Haven, Conn., 1967) , p. 164; see also pp. 122, 135, 145, 165, and 222.

used Europe's preoccupation with its own affairs to strengthen the security of the United States by expanding its frontiers in North America. It is idle to speculate whether Napoleon would have sold Louisiana had there been no war, or whether he would have attempted to recover it had he been victorious. The fact remains that Jefferson saw his opportunity and he made the most of it, in spite of the many scruples he had about violating some of his guiding principles. Although he tried to duplicate the Louisiana feat in the Floridas, Napoleon this time merely held out the hope of assistance as a bait for America's participation in his still-undecided struggle against Britain.[2] When the emperor realized that neither President Jefferson nor his successor was willing to pay this price, Franco-American relations deteriorated rapidly.[3]

The arrogance Napoleon displayed in his dealings with the United States and its representatives in France showed a lack of understanding of the American republic, its people, and president that backfired badly.[4] Instead of effectively exploiting the resentment Americans harbored against Britain because of its harassment of American ships and its impressment of American sailors, Napoleon provoked the wrath of the American nation against himself. His arbitrary treatment of American ships did a great deal more than arouse the ire of American shippers and traders. By causing Jefferson to play into the hands of the Federalists, it undermined the president's political position at home and limited his options with respect to his policies vis-à-vis France and Great Britain. Subsequently, President Madison was of course confronted

2. Lawrence S. Kaplan, "Jefferson, the Napoleonic Wars, and the Balance of Power," *William & Mary Quarterly*, 3rd ser., XIV (1957), 198-203.

3. "Du système continental et de ses effets sur les relations entre la France et l'Amérique du Nord," *Revue Américaine*, III (Paris, 1827), 344-62.

4. Bradford Perkins, *Prologue to War: England and the United States, 1805-1812* (Berkeley, Calif., 1963), p. 68.

with the same situation.[5] But as important as this internal American problem was, the strategic ramifications of the various French and British decrees, which amounted to a declaration of war against the trade of neutrals, and the American responses to them, from Jefferson's embargo to Macon's Bill No. 2, transcended every other consideration.

Evidently neither Napoleon nor the leading American statesmen fully appreciated the importance of the neutral United States as a perhaps decisive factor in the outcome of the European war. Whatever long-range commercial objectives the French emperor had in mind when he initiated the Continental System, its purpose as a war measure was to close the European market to British commerce. Unable to defeat Britain militarily, he logically tried the more promising alternative of destroying it through economic strangulation. To make certain that Britain's economic ruin would be so complete as to compel it to sue for peace, Napoleon had no choice but to bring the United States into his over-all schemes. Without its cooperation he could not hope to prevent Anglo-American trade, a safety valve for Britain, and to close the Baltic gate in the Continental System through which American ships carried British and American goods to the Continent.[6] Ideally, Napoleon should have sought Jefferson's voluntary cooperation to accomplish these two objectives, so vital to France to be worth a compensatory sacrifice adequate enough to cover American losses. But such a deal would have run counter to American principles of the freedom of the seas and the rights of neutrals. Ideally, the United States wanted more trade, not less. It also wanted to maintain its neutrality and not to be drawn into the war, directly or indirectly. The em-

5. Consult the standard works by Irving Brant, *James Madison, Secretary of State, 1800-1809* (Indianapolis, 1953) and *James Madison The President 1809-1812* (Indianapolis, 1956) .

6. Edward L. Andrews, *Napoleon and America* (New York, 1909) , pp. 33-42, 52-55; see also Perkins, *Prologue to War*, p. 70.

bargo made America's priority quite clear: For the sake of peace it would temporarily sacrifice its profits from neutral trade, hoping, however, that in due course both belligerents would respect the rights of neutrals. After the enactment of the embargo, in December, 1807, Napoleon and Jefferson worked at cross-purposes and accomplished the opposite of what either of them desired. That a longer test of the embargo might have resulted in British concessions to the United States is quite conceivable. In fact, however, neither France nor Great Britain yielded to the pressures the embargo was intended to bring to bear against them. On the contrary, its ruinous effects on the American economy and its divisive political consequences led to its relatively early repeal. Jefferson frankly admitted another ironic aspect of the embargo by agreeing that, in effect, it favored France over Britain.[7] In other words, the president not only sacrificed America's rights as a neutral trader, but to some degree its neutrality as well, evidently quite trustingly assuming that the perfidious emperor would treat the United States in a respectful manner once he had succeeded in humbling the Leviathan of the Seas.

To compound the ironies surrounding the history of the embargo, Napoleon probably spared Jefferson any future disappointments by his incredible failure to grasp the extraordinary opportunity the embargo afforded him. Since, in effect, it closed the existing gap in the Continental System, the emperor had every reason to persuade the United States to keep the embargo in force. Its crucial importance to France would have justified whatever reciprocal consideration was called for. Instead, Napoleon insulted and angered Americans with his cynical sequestration of American ships in European waters at the time of the enactment of the embargo.[8] Instead of

7. Kaplan, *Jefferson and France*, pp. 125–29.
8. See Archibald H. Stockder, "The Legality of the Blockades Instituted by Napoleon's Decrees, and the British Orders in Council, 1806–1813," *American Journal of International Law*, X (1916), 503–4.

coaxing the United States into further voluntary cooperation
with France by all means short of war, he forcibly tried to
drag it into an offensive alliance against England, as evidenced by his letter to General Armstrong from Champagny,
dated January 5, 1808.[9] In this letter he stated, with reference
to England's decrees of November 11, 1807: "War exists then
in fact, between England and the United States, and His Majesty considers it as declared from the day on which England
published her decrees. In that persuasion, His Majesty, ready
to consider the United States as associated with the cause of
all the powers who have to defend themselves against England, has not taken any definitive measures towards the American vessels which may have been brought into our ports."

Napoleon's provocative methods and aims did not basically
change during Madison's administration, during which other
neutrality measures replaced the Embargo Act. The renewed
seizure of American ships ordered by the Rambouillet Decree
of March 13, 1810, and the deviously phrased Cadore Letter a
few months later typically reflected Napoleon's unscrupulous
and insensitive handling of American affairs. Exasperated by
these developments, President Madison confided to Jefferson:
"The late confiscations by Bonaparte comprize robbery, theft,
and breach of trust, and exceed in turpitude any of his enorm-
ities, not wasting human blood."[10] Despite his awareness of
the conditional nature of the Cadore Letter, however, Madison accepted the declaration of the revocation of the French

9. Robert Walsh, *An Inquiry into the Past and Present Relations of
France and the United States* (London, 1811), pp. 33–34, 82. Until 1812
France tried to bring about "an intimate alliance" with the United States
to defeat England with the help of another continent, "that of Europe
being insufficient to defeat it." "Examen des rapports entre la France et les
États-Unis en 1812," CPEU, LXIX, pp. 80–89. On the other hand, Napoleon rejected a plot in 1810 to bring about peace by an agreement on the
part of England and France "to repossess themselves of North America."
Andrews, *Napoleon and America*, pp. 33–42.

10. Perkins, *Prologue to War*, pp. 244–46.

decrees at face value, searching, as he was, for at least a tolerably acceptable way out of the American dilemma.[11]

Unfortunately, Napoleon's successes in Europe made him even more unresponsive to trans-Atlantic pleadings not to seize or burn American merchant vessels. As a consequence, the longer his regime lasted, the greater became the number of his American detractors, some of whom had at one time or another admired his *élan,* his genius, and some of his more lasting domestic accomplishments. They became disgusted with the emperor's "monstrous system of fraud and rapine." In New England the clergy took the lead in condemning the capricious and merciless mind of the greatest military conqueror in modern times. Supported by Federalist business interests, clergymen used the pulpit to denounce the very thought of alliance with the totally untrustworthy and unreliable French. "From England," one of them warned, moreover, "we have nothing to fear as a friend, but much as a foe."[12] Generally, Americans who watched Napoleon's apparently insatiable appetite for conquest with growing concern looked to England as the only power capable of stopping him in his tracks.[13]

This, then, was the dilemma the Madison administration faced in 1812: economically, the United States was caught between two desperate belligerents, both of whom victimized

11. Madison has been severely criticized for falling into Napoleon's "crude and clumsy trap." Burt, *The United States, Great Britain and British North America,* p. 283. When the Duc de Cadore declared that "the decrees of Berlin and Milan are revoked," he added, "it being understood that, in consequence of this declaration, the English shall revoke their orders in council . . . or that the United States . . . shall cause their rights to be respected by the English."

12. See Isaac Braman, "Union with France a Greater Evil than Union with Britain," sermon, Rowley, Mass., April 5, 1810; and William Ellery Channing, "Sermon Preached in Boston, April 5, 1810" (Boston, 1810) .

13. Alfred Schalck de la Faverie, *Napoléon et l'Amérique* (Paris, 1917) , pp. 294–95; see also Paul H. Giddens, "Contemporary Opinion of Napoleon," *Journal of American History,* XXVI (1932) , 189–204.

American interests; politically, the government's inability to compel respect for its neutral rights and differences of opinion concerning how to cope with the disgraceful conduct of the two maritime foes created such a disruptive atmosphere at home that it constituted a potential danger to the survival of the federal union and its republican institutions;[14] and ideologically, the choice between support of an autocratic and ruthless aggressor who might want to control, and perhaps conquer, the world, and a country with liberal tendencies, but intolerably domineering and bent on a comparatively more subtle domination, appeared to be a choice between the devil and the deep blue sea. Tempted to go to war against both violators of American neutral rights, and officially considering such a policy, the political leaders of the United States were also motivated by the desire to add Florida and Canada to the American domain when in June, 1812, they declared war against Great Britain. By reaching out for these objectives, they intended not only to deprive Britain of acquiring Florida for itself, but of finally expelling it from North America. In the process, they also hoped to put an end once and for all to the collusion between the British and the Indians in the Northwest and to unsettled conditions in the Southwest. Unprepared and underestimating the efforts required for that "little excursion" into Britain's North American possession, the Madison administration embarked upon an enterprise of incalculable consequences.

Writing from St. Petersburg before he knew of the outbreak of hostilities between his country and Great Britain, John Quincy Adams pleaded until the last moment for patience to delay, and, he hoped, prevent, the "plunge into the fatal vortex of European wars."[15] As a keen political observer, he saw

14. Roger H. Brown, *The Republic in Peril: 1812* (New York, 1964), p. 189.

15. John Quincy Adams to Jonathan Russell (U.S. chargé d'affaires in Paris), St. Petersburg, July 28, 1812, Jonathan Russell Papers (Brown University MS).

the popular spirit in America and the legislative temper rush-
ing the country into an unnecessary war, without facing up to
the perils and risks involved in a conflict against a powerful
enemy. If neutrality is essentially a euphemism for war by
other than military means, as Philip C. Jessup contends, then
the exhaustion of both European belligerents held out the richest rewards to the neutral United States, as President Jefferson had originally suggested and John Quincy Adams still
maintained as late as August, 1812.[16]

The coincidence of the three major developments during
the last two weeks of June, 1812—the revocation of the British
Orders in Council, the outbreak of the Anglo-American war,
and Napoleon's invasion of Russia—shaped the course of
American and European history in an extraordinary fashion.
When Congress enacted a state of war between Great Britain
and the United States, it did not know that the British Parliament had at last set in motion the repeal of the troublesome
Orders in Council. It seems reasonable to assume that had
Congress known of this step, its already unusually divided war
vote might instead have preserved the precarious peace.[17] Five
days after America's belligerent involvement, Napoleon's
army crossed the Niemen. Would the French emperor have
considered it necessary to invade Russia at that particular
time had he known of the American decision against England, which was likely to have a crippling effect on the British
economy? And conversely, would the United States have made
this decision had it known that only six months later the "in-
vincible" emperor would be in hasty retreat from Russia? Although historians obviously cannot answer these hypothetical
questions, each one of them illustrates the complexities and
hazards of the art of timing major decisions.

The sequence of events, and particularly Napoleon's disas-

16. *Ibid.*, August 11, 1812.
17. The House voted 79 to 49 and the Senate 19 to 13 in support of the
resolution declaring that a state of war existed.

trous invasion of Russia suddenly changed the international picture and seriously affected the strategic situation in which the United States unexpectedly found itself.[18] If Napoleon was too preoccupied with his Russian campaign to bother about or boost the American war effort, no excuse could be made for the continuing French harassment of American ships. Although Britain was now the common enemy of France and the United States, the latter were neither allies nor associates in this war; nor did they coordinate their war plans.[19] They were cobelligerents whose relations were so strained during the first year of the war that a break between them was in the realm of the possible and, at times, under active consideration in Washington. The emperor exposed Joel Barlow, the American poet-diplomat who pleaded his country's cause, to many personal indignities. It was bad enough that Napoleon would hardly give Barlow a few moments to present his requests for the arms the American forces needed immediately but worse that little French aid was forthcoming, although the Duke de Bassano, among other high French officials, recommended it.[20] The one area in which France rendered valuable assistance involved arrangements by which French port facilities were made available to the United States. These arrangements enabled the Americans to bring captured ships and cargoes into the ports of the empire and to use French ports as a base for operations against British shipping.[21] In this connection, the

18. Lawrence S. Kaplan, "France and Madison's Decision for War, 1812," *Mississippi Valley Historical Review*, L (1964), 658–61.

19. *National Intelligencer*, August 4, 1812.

20. "Rapport à Sa Majesté" by Bassano, Wilna, October 15, 1812, CPEU, LXIX, pt. 4, pp. 258–65; see also Barlow to the Duke of Bassano, Wilna, November 28, 1812, and December 4, 1812, CPEU, LXVIII, p. 464, and LXIX, p. 397.

21. See Ulane Bonnel, *La France, les États-Unis et al guerre de course (1797–1815)* (Paris, 1961), p. 304. Occasionally American captains transferred British prisoners to homeward-bound French ships. By the time the war ended, the American Congress had not yet reciprocated these various French maritime services. See Monroe to Sérurier, Washing-

True Blooded Yankee, originally equipped at Brest, was credited with a remarkable number of captures. Such activities took their toll of British shipping, but as important as they were they certainly were not sufficient to decide the outcome of the war in America. It would have been of great help to the United States if Napoleon, whose naval power had grown considerably by 1813, had shared with it his heavier class of warships. This, however, Napoleon was not prepared to do, although the United States lacked this type of naval equipment.[22]

As in the years prior to 1812 President Madison refused to make an alliance with Bonaparte on terms the emperor would have liked to dictate; he also decided against a close connection with him in the war against Britain. The emperor had not inspired the confidence that alone could have generated the necessary trust between allies. As in the past, the United States had no intention of becoming another satellite of France, and of possibly being compelled by the victorious emperor to acquiesce in the transfer of Canada from Britain to France.[23] This possibility, by the way, Madison's war aims attempted to head off. Above all else, however, the American government preferred to be merely a cobelligerent because it wished to confine its war to Britain only and to avoid the eventuality of being drawn into hostilities against any other enemy of France.[24] This applied particularly to Russia, should

ton, D.C., October 18 and November 2, 1813, and January 31, 1814, FNFDS. See also Charles S. Hyneman, *The First American Neutrality—A Study of the American Understanding of Neutral Obligations* (Urbana, Ill., 1934) , pp. 28–29.

22. A. T. Mahan, *Sea Power in Its Relations to the War of 1812* (London, 1905) , I, 382, and II, 224–25, 253–55.

23. Richard Glover, "The French Fleet, 1807–1814; Britain's Problem; and Madison's Opportunity," *Journal of Modern History,* XXXIX (1967) , 251.

24. Allan Nevins (ed.) , *The Diary of John Quincy Adams, 1794-1845* (New York, 1951) , pp. 101–6.

it become locked in battle with Bonaparte. Napoleon's invasion of Russia created serious complications for both Tsar Alexander I and President Madison, the heads of state of two friendly countries. Alexander deplored the outbreak of Anglo-American hostilities, which could not but weaken the two powers on whose assistance he liked to think he could count in his defense of Russia.[25] His eagerness to mediate the Anglo-American war was therefore prompted by a sound determination of Russian needs. Britain's rejection of his offer kept alive the likelihood of embarrassments that both St. Petersburg and Washington would have preferred to avoid. Secretary of State James Monroe regretted, for instance, that "by availing Great Britain of the services of the Russion fleet, tho' confined to Europe, the British Government is enabled to detach an equal number of British ships to our Coast."[26] But Chancellor Romanzoff convinced John Quincy Adams, the skillful and alert American minister, that Russo-American relations would not be badly disturbed. In a quite conciliatory manner, Count Romanzoff raised the flattering and well-remembered question; "How happens it that you are constantly beating at sea the English, who beat all the rest of the world?"[27] Both Russia and the United States realized that it was Napoleon's invasion, after all, that had created many circumstances beyond their control.

As gifted a military leader as Napoleon I was, he made his grand-strategy decisions with respect to Russia too hastily to explore alternatives to the invasion of this Eurasian country. In the last analysis, the invasion was not an end in itself, but merely a means toward his primary goal of defeating Great

---

25. In 1811, for instance, very much to Napleon's annoyance, the United States exported to Russia goods valued at $6,137,657. See Alexandre Tarsaidzé, *Czars and Presidents* (New York, 1958), pp. 46, 51.

26. Hyneman, pp. 27–28; see also F. A. Golder, "The Russian Offer of Mediation in the War of 1812," *Political Science Quarterly*, XXXI (1916), 380–82.

27. Nevins, *John Quincy Adams*, p. 106.

Britain. To make sure that Britain would be cut off from Russian resources, to deprive it of Russian military assistance, and to tighten the Continental System, the emperor deemed it necessary to bring Russia under his control before he could launch the final attack against his unyielding archenemy. Although he was the undisputed master of the Continent, Napoleon had so far failed to beat Britain because of its superior sea power. The emperor had gradually come to understand his weakness in this respect, but his conceit and impatience now contributed greatly to his final undoing. As has already been noted, through a more apt and tactful treatment of the United States and through intelligent exploitation of American policies he could have achieved some of the major objectives that took him to Moscow. Had he not been as sure of himself, moreover, he would not have dismissed Robert Fulton as a charlatan whose naval gimmicks he considered to be probably just another of those American moneymaking schemes.[28] But if the emperor missed in this instance a genuine and timely opportunity to develop decisive naval power, convincing evidence has recently been presented that as a result of an extraordinary shipbuilding program the French fleet would by 1815 have been powerful enough to be more than a match for the British navy.[29] If Napoleon did not invade Russia unnecessarily, he at least precipitated his defeat prematurely.

Since his debacle in Russia coincided with the early phase of the War of 1812, the United States was left more to its own resources than it had anticipated. And the collapse of the First Empire during 1814 confronted President Madison with a potentially disastrous situation. Previously France had at

28. Jacques Philippe Mérigon de Montgéry, *Notice sur la vie et les travaux de Robert Fulton* (Paris, 1825) , pp. 14–21.

29. Glover, "The French Fleet," p. 248. Since Glover's conclusion is based on thorough recent research, it carries more weight than the opinion expressed in O. Troude, *Batailles Navales de la France* (Paris, 1868) , p. 177.

least pinned British forces down in Europe. As Albert Gallatin, then one of the distinguished American peace commissioners, noted with grave concern, Britain would henceforth
be free to throw its full might into the war in America.[30] Napoleon's downfall suddenly put the very existence of the
United States in jeopardy, had Britain insisted on punishing
the Americans. And Britain was the more tempted to do so because it firmly believed the Americans had opportunistically
concerted with Bonaparte at a time when they thought him
triumphant and Britain about to be subdued. Having read
and decoded John Quincy Adams' mail illicitly, however, the
Russians were fortunately in a position to disabuse the British of the notion that the United States had been a close ally
of France.[31] If William H. Crawford's information was correct, and the United States minister to France, a prominent
southern and national politician, believed it was, then the
government of Louis XVIII had also convinced the British
government, very much to its surprise, of the virtual alienation between France and the United States. After the peace of
May 30, 1814, the royal government of France advised the administration in Washington that henceforth it must be neutral and could no longer permit American warships access to
French port facilities.[32] According to Crawford's intelligence,
the Bourbon government actually considered participating in
the war against the United States. However, "after neutrality
had been decided upon," he reported to James Monroe, "the
instructions given to the maritime prefects were to favor the

30. Count Gallatin (ed.), *The Diary of James Gallatin, Secretary to Albert Gallatin—A Great Peacemaker, 1823–27* (New York, 1924), pp. 16–17.
   31. See Golder, "The Russian Offer of Mediation," pp. 382–83; and
Mahan, *Sea Power*, I, 389–90.
   32. Instructions to Sérurier, Paris, September 8 and November 8, 1814,
CPEU, LXXI. On its part, the United States government directed the
public and private armed vessels of the United States to observe scrupulously the neutral rights of other nations.

English in every case, as far as it was practicable."[33] Unwittingly the government of the Restoration thus rendered the United States a service by demonstrating that Franco-American relations were not as friendly as the British had imagined them. Tired of war, motivated by long-range commercial and political considerations, and realistically evaluating the existing military stalemate, the British government granted the United States a generous peace, restoring the status quo ante bellum. Paris welcomed the conclusion of the Anglo-American war with a sigh of relief; the end of hostilities removed the uncomfortable uneasiness that had cast a shadow on Franco-American relations in recent years.

During the brief interlude between Napoleon's return from Elba and his final banishment to St. Helena both Bonaparte and Louis XVIII vied for America's acceptance and friendship. Napoleon now regretted the situation in which his first abdication had left the United States. If in the past occasional clouds had darkened the Franco-American horizon, he apologetically attributed them to unprecedented circumstances.[34] France and the United States, he pleaded, must ban any jealousy and ill will from their mutually beneficial relations.

Crawford was intrigued by the enthusiastic reception the population of Paris gave Napoleon on his return. He was especially impressed that the masses mingled cries of "Vive l'Empereur" with "À bas les prêtres." In his judgment, it did not speak well for the future of the Bourbon regime that it permitted aristocratic refugees and the clergy to restore their former influence. "The great mass of talents, wealth and enterprise," he commented, "are opposed to them. . . He who in the nineteenth century is determined to govern France by

33. William H. Crawford to James Monroe, Paris, April 15, 1815, DDFDS.
34. "Projet de lettre de créance pour Mr. Sérurier," Paris, April 19, 1815, CPEU, LXXII.

divine right must trust to Heaven and Priesthood for support."[35]

In contrast to Crawford's skepticism about the latest developments in France, Louis Sérurier, the French envoy, told
Prince Talleyrand that the United States had emerged from
the late war as a greatly strengthened manufacturing country.[36] As an independent nation, it had passed the test of possible disunion and demonstrated its ability to make sacrifices for
the sake of the republic. Not least important, he noted the
brilliant reputation of the American navy, which in the future would have to be treated as an imporant element in the
maintenance of the balance of power in the world. More than
ever before the 1808 prophecy of Hyde de Neuville, one of
Sérurier's successors, seemed to be justified: "In thirty or forty
years the dynamic American giant will exercise great influence in the Old World and the New. He is destined to be the
balance among the great powers."[37]

The age that closed with the Congress of Vienna had a profound and lasting effect on modern civilization. The American and French Revolutions established a new social order,
which in a relatively short time broke down centuries-old barriers to the realization of egalitarian and democratic principles. To be sure, the "people" soon learned that the substance
of their progress was relative and limited, always subject to
never-ending struggles for more equality, though extraordinary strides were made, following the trail blazed by the British. But the American and French Revolutions accelerated
the pace of the historical evolution from legal equality to political, social, and economic equality to which modern nations
have been increasingly aspiring. Two of the major legacies of

35. Crawford to Monroe, Paris, March 21, 1815, DDFDS.
36. Sérurier to Talleyrand, Washington, February 21, 1815, CPEU,
LXXII.
37. Jean Guillaume Hyde de Neuville, *Mémoires et Souvenirs* (Paris,
1892), I, 466–67.

these revolutions—the growing emphasis on national independence, and nationalism—also provided a sense of direction in
the nineteenth century.

It was of historical significance that during this era France
and the United States usually found themselves allied in a
common front against Britain. It was this opposition that
formed the main basis of their original alliance and often parallel policies. Though the roots of this opposition were inter-
twined, its aims were not exactly the same. To France, Great
Britain was the great Anglo-Saxon rival competing with it for
world leadership; to the United States, it was the parent country that used its superior economic and naval power in an an-
noyingly controlling way. France wanted to wrest leadership
from Britain; the United States merely wanted it to be exercised more wisely, with more restraint and less greed. As the
weaker naval powers, France and the United States had, ever
since the American Revolutionary War, found a common interest in the defense of liberal navigation principles above
and beyond the combination of their naval forces as a potential means of balancing those of Britain.[38] These maritime
links influenced Franco-American relations throughout the
nineteenth century and, significantly, England too did not ignore frequent references to the even larger potential combination of American, French, and Russian naval forces.

The twenty-five years of war and revolution in Europe gave
the young American republic time to develop its resources;
and the exhaustion caused by this long period of destructive
and disruptive warfare further diminished the chances of
European military adventures in the Western hemisphere for
some time to come. And finally, the experiences of Americans

38. Richard Rush to Mr. Ingersoll, London, February 14, 1824, Richard
Rush Papers, "Family Letters," 1824–25 (Princeton University MS), Box
12. These principles included the propositions that free ships make free
goods and that neutral ships may carry noncontraband goods between
ports of a belligerent. They furthermore strove to define what constitutes
contraband and an effective blockade.

before 1814 produced at least one other noteworthy effect: the Anglophobes and Francophiles among them lost both ardor and ground. Better than any contemporaries, the prophets of the past overlooking the whole century can now see how this gradual change developed into a trend.

3. *France and Latin American Independence*

Having lost the war against the coalition headed by Great Britain, France emerged from the final peace settlement remarkably intact. Under the leadership of Talleyrand, French diplomats succeeded in exploiting the principles of legitimacy and balance of power to the utmost. Nevertheless, faced with the opposition of the reactionary Holy Alliance, France had to keep fighting for the preservation of the basic principles of the French Revolution. Under these circumstances, even the Jeffersonians were willing to accept Britain as the moderating influence between American republicanism and the militant conservative statesmen of Europe.[1] Eager to recover its lost prestige and rank in the family of nations, France watched the extent of postwar Anglo-American cooperation very closely. In his capacity as foreign minister, the Duke de Richelieu, on July 11, 1816, took the unusual step of actually inquiring about this, only to receive confirmation that there had been an almost unbelievable improvement in the contacts between London and Washington.[2] French agreement to the then fairly progressive Franco-American Commercial Treaty of 1822 was in part a measure designed to meet England's competition in the American market. But the

1. Kaplan, *Jefferson and France*, p. 131.
2. Gallatin to Monroe, Paris, July 12, 1816, DDFDS.

major concern of the Restoration government centered around the Latin American independence movements and Anglo-American policies with respect to them.

From the French point of view there was much more at stake in Latin America than keeping pace with England and the United States in that region, or securing economic advantages. Favored by cultural affinities, French leaders saw there a long-range opportunity for grandeur that would lift the morale of the French people and permit it to again envision a glorious future. These psychological aspects were of immense importance to contemporary Frenchmen. In fact, the cumulative effects of the frustrations Frenchmen suffered in their foreign and domestic policies between 1815 and 1852 ultimately found their expressions in two revolutions and one coup d'état. For what was *gloire* to France, was bad business and potential danger to England and the United States, and the Anglo-Americans let France know it.

Acting independently in the spring of 1822, the United States recognized the independence of the Spanish-American provinces, causing official France to worry about the "moral" effect of this action on the revolutionary spirit of Europe.[3] France was too deeply involved in Spain not to be also concerned about the effect of this recognition on its own prospects in Latin America. Having been authorized by the Holy Alliance to restore the throne of Ferdinand VII, by the middle of 1823 France occupied nearly all of Spain. Faced with an overseas disaster, the Spanish king hoped that France would also assist him in suppressing the Latin American revolutions.[4] But any talk of French military intervention in the Western hemisphere was enough for Britain and the United States to block it. They genuinely sympathized with the Latin Americans for political as well as for economic reasons. With

3. Gallatin to John Quincy Adams, Paris, April 26, 1822, DDFDS.
4. A. Debidour, *Histoire diplomatique de l'Europe (1814–1878)* (Paris, 1891) , I, 202–3.

a little ingenuity, however, the French hoped they could extend their influence in Latin America without resort to force. Foreign Minister Châteaubriand devised a scheme whereby Spain would establish autonomous kingdoms in its American colonies and ask princes of the House of Bourbon, including those of the French branch, to govern them. Albert Gallatin, evidently aware of these French ambitions, bluntly warned Châteaubriand that any French interference in the affairs of the emancipated colonies or any attempt to take possession of them "might force them [the U.S.] into an alliance with Great Britain." In his explicit response, the foreign minister assured the American envoy that "France would not make any attempt whatever of that kind or in any manner interfere with the American questions."[5]

That the Polignac Memorandum of October, 1823, by which Great Britain practically compelled France to renounce any designs on Latin America, followed Châteaubriand's assurance and preceded Monroe's historic message of December 2, 1823, is a chronological matter of considerable substantive meaning.[6] By the time Monroe declared that the Western hemisphere would be closed to all further European colonization, France had already yielded to firm British pressures and American warnings directed to it alone. As far as the French government was concerned, Anglo-American diplomacy aimed at the same objective and succeeded in "persuading" France to lower its Latin American sights. Simon Bolivar was grateful to Britain and the United States for having taken a stand favoring the cause of Latin American independence. He and his friends fully realized the crucially important part Britain

5. Gallatin to John Quincy Adams, New York, June 24, 1823, DDFDS. In spite of this assurance, however, the United States remained suspicious about French intentions with respect to Cuba and Porto Rico. For details, see James Brown to Henry Clay, Paris, July 15, 1825, and January 10, 1826, DDFDS.

6. D. Sheldon, Jr. to John Quincy Adams, Paris, November 29, 1823; DDFDS.

played in preventing repressive military intervention. But as an American, Bolivar dreamed of one big American family organized in an American Union. Bolivar's vision was incomparably greater than that of the contemporary leaders of the United States who, in foreign affairs, thought essentially in defensive terms when areas beyond the North American continent were involved. Their sense of mission, however, knew no geographical frontiers in the propagation of republican principles. To France and Britain, the concept of an American Union of Western hemispheric republics constituted a multiple threat to their interests. French diplomats in Washington took the lead in recommending a combination of all great European powers, including Britain, to prevent the coalition of republican America against monarchical Europe.[7] The purpose of the alliance would not be to make war against the United States but to oppose a monolithic republican structure in America by helping to organize, perhaps with the approval of Bolivar, a number of independent monarchies in Central and South America. For surely, these Frenchmen contended, the United States would dominate such an American Union and, sooner or later, try to dominate Europe as well.[8]

The republican and mercantilistic tendencies of the United States, further accentuated by Henry Clay's famous speech in the Congress on March 30, 1824, in which the concept of a large and independent American market was developed, seemed too alarming to be dismissed as being inconsequential. The least that France could do now was to recognize some of the Latin American states. Urged by the French press and interested parties to protect the mercantile and strategic interests of France in the Western hemisphere, in 1826, the French

7. Marneuil to Damar, Washington, October 28, 1826, and March 25, 1827, CPEU, LXXXII and LXXXIII; see also Hyde de Neuville to Richelieu, Washington, December 20, 1818, CPEU, LXXVI.

8. Menou to Châteaubriand, Washington, December 11, 1823, CPEU, LXXX. See also Pierre Renouvin, *Histoire des relations internationales, 1815–1871* (Paris, 1954), V, 95–97.

government recognized the independence of Brazil, previously a part of Portugal's empire. By concluding a treaty of amity, navigation, and commerce with the Brazilian Empire, France hoped to strengthen the monarchical principle in America and to lay the foundation for a profitable commercial future. Two years later, the withdrawal of French troops from Spain helped to clear the air for the normalization of relations between France and the Spanish-American republics.[9]

4. American Expansionism, the July Revolution, and the Spoliation Claims

Looking at the first six decades of American expansionism in its totality one discovers elements of continuity that a detailed step-by-step approach tends to obscure. When Jefferson thought it wise and proper to pay "a decent respect to the opinions of mankind" and when the young American nation and its leaders were fully conscious that "the eyes of the world are upon us," they acknowledged certain moral responsibilities towards the family of nations. Just as the domestic policies of the young republic had their international ramifications, developments abroad could not be without impact on the United States. The intensification of nationalism and the political realities growing out of the Napoleonic wars profoundly affected American foreign policy. The jealous competition between France and Britain, the rivalry between Russia and Britain, and the developing friendship between Russia and the United States led the European governments to include the United States as a potentially active political power

9. William Spence Robertson, *France and Latin-American Independence* (Baltimore, 1939), pp. 402, 424–25, 440.

in their general policy deliberations. On its part, the United States wished to limit its relationships with the European governments to a quite passive role, unless its own cultural, commercial, and political interests were at stake. The resulting contradictions were as confusing then as they are now enlightening.

The United States did not wish to become entangled in European politics, but it was always ready to exploit Europe's preoccupation with its many divisive problems. It did not intervene in strictly European affairs so as to be in a stronger position to discourage European intervention in American affairs. And though it stayed aloof from European rivalries, it tried to maintain friendly relations with all European rivals. Similarly, after 1815 France and Britain attempted to block America's rising power in the Western hemisphere because they feared the threatening scope and pace of American expansionism. But, separately, they and other European powers were eager to take advantage of America's material and naval resources to promote their respective national interests in Europe and elsewhere. At least ever since the enunciation of the Monroe Doctrine, "Europe" anticipated with growing apprehension America's eventual challenge, but in the meantime each European power found it profitable to do business with the United States, both in a commercial and geopolitical sense. Seeing the greatest measure of security in a complex balance of power, each individual European power and Europe as a whole found it convenient to think in terms of adjusting the balance of the Old World by adding as a further balancing factor at least the resources of the New World. Continental powers, for instance, counted customarily on America's cooperation in their efforts to check Britain's naval supremacy.

Although the United States too had an interest in preserving this European balance of power so that no single power or combination of powers might effectively interfere with its destiny, it rejected François Guizot's notion of an American balance of power. This French statesman and historian, on whom Louis Philippe relied heavily, argued that the unchecked expansion of the United States in the Western hemisphere could in time upset the world balance of power and thus become a threat to the security and prosperity of Europe and, therefore, of France. Britain, he noted, checked Russia's penetration of Asia, and the United States balanced the expanding power of Britain and Russia. But who, he asked, was checking the United States in America? Why should it alone be permitted to monopolize power in a world governed by competition among powers? Combining questions of ideology with those of hegemony, Guizot contended furthermore, in defense of his American-balance concept that "what is not good for the universal monarchy, is not good for the universal republic."[1] Though his intention was by no means unfriendly, by taking this stand, he echoed President Jefferson's earlier reaction to Napoleon's ambitions: "It cannot be to our interest that all Europe should be reduced to a single monarchy."[2] Jefferson was well aware that any monolithic power structure destroys the roots of freedom and diversity.

By and large, the relevant historical details substantiate these general observations. Like the Bourbons, who intended to increase their relative power in Europe by decreasing that of England in America at the time of the War of Independence, Napoleon agreed to double the American Republic's

1. For a more detailed discussion of Franco-American relations of this period, see Henry Blumenthal, *A Reappraisal of Franco-American Relations, 1830–1871* (Chapel Hill, N.C., 1959), pp. 33–52, 73–77. See also Alfred Vagts, "The United States and the Balance of Power," *The Journal of Politics,* III (1941), 401–49; and Frederick Merk, *The Monroe Doctrine and American Expansionism, 1843–1849* (New York, 1966), pp. 88–90. As far back as 1827 a French diplomat deplored that Europe did not realistically face the ideological threat of the American republics. Marneuil to Danar, Washington, March 11, 1827, CPEU, LXXXIII.

2. Vagts, "The United States and the Balance of Power," p. 416.

domain toward the long-range goal of strengthening the future challenger of Britain's naval and commercial supremacy. This interrelationship between Europe and America in the first quarter of the nineteenth century was furthermore demonstrated by Britain's recognition of the former colonies of Spain in America. That the parallel action of the United States also had the effect of frustrating France's ascendency in the Western hemisphere pleased England as much as it reminded France of the wisdom of not counting on gratitude in international politics. Britain's generous terms at the end of the Revolutionary War and in 1814 had already foreshadowed its desire to loosen the ties between France and the United States. Since the Treaty of Ghent the French government indeed noted a lessening of hostility between England and the United States which, in turn, alerted it to the necessity of exercising a prudent caution in its dealings with these two members of the Anglo-Saxon family. For a long time to come, however, distrust and subdued hostility still continued to characterize Anglo-American relations and, for that matter, those between France and England.

From the correspondence between President Jefferson and his friend Pierre Samuel du Pont de Nemours we know how disturbed the president was when he learned of the secret Franco-Spanish deal, embodied in the Treaty of San Ildefonso of October 1, 1800, enabling France once again to be a neighbor of the United States. In view of this potential threat to the future safety of the United States, he asked Du Pont "to impress on the government of France the inevitable consequences of their taking possession of Louisiana." This "embryo of a tornado," he thought, might reluctantly throw the United States into the arms of Britain and involve the otherwise friendly French and American nations in a most unfortunate war. Du Pont's sound advice to purchase Louisiana from France appealed to Jefferson as a desirable alternative if it were feasible. Du Pont thought it was, for the same reason that, among others, influenced Napoleon when he agreed to sell Louisiana: "Only France," he wrote to the president, "wishes you to become a sea power. Only England fears it."[3] Napoleon's decision to conclude the Louisiana Purchase Treaty with the United States was unquestionably facilitated by his need for money and the fiasco of his troops in Santo Domingo. But according to Barbé-Marbois, Napoleon's finance minister, the emperor was influenced by a more far-reaching consideration. Taking a long view, he concluded that only a strong commercial sea power, closely collaborating with France, a continental power, could "some day . . . . break England's commercial tyranny."[4] French contemporaries also assumed that in a cultural and strategic sense Louisiana would always remain French. Should military necessity ever compel France to disembark its forces in Louisiana, Hyde de Neuville wrote in 1817, they would not find it to be a hostile territory.[5]

Also in the case of the Floridas, it was not expansion for its own sake but geopolitical necessity that pointed toward their acquisition by the United States. American control of this territory would protect the western states against any attempt on the part of the maritime powers of Europe to close the vital outlet of the Mississippi River.[6] The American government preferred to accomplish this objective, too, through negotiations rather than war, as evidenced by the discussions carried on between Secretary of State John Quincy Adams and Luis de Onis, the Spanish envoy.[7]

Hyde de Neuville, the French minister to the United States,

3. Dumas Malone (ed.), *Correspondence Between Thomas Jefferson and Pierre Samuel du Pont de Nemours, 1798–1817* (Boston, 1930), pp. 48, 58.

4. F. Barbé-Marbois, *Histoire de la Louisiane* (Paris, 1829), p. 282.

5. Hyde de Neuville, *Mémoires*, II, 267–68.

6. Malone, *Thomas Jefferson and Pierre Samuel du Pont de Nemours*, pp. 106–13.

7. S. F. Bemis, *John Quincy Adams and the Foundations of American Foreign Policy* (New York, 1950), pp. 300–40.

realized at the time that France had an interest in a peaceful arrangement between Spain and the United States because a war between them over Florida would risk an invasion of Cuba by either England or the United States. On August 9, 1818, John Quincy Adams had confided to the French minister that the United States would occupy Cuba should England make the slightest move designed to acquire the Pearl of the Antilles.[8] The French foreign ministry consequently exercised its influence in Madrid as well as in Washington to keep the Spanish-American negotiations going, in spite of General Andrew Jackson's unjustifiable invasion of Florida. Basically, though, the French government felt confident that England would not push Spain into a war with the United States because "the situation in Europe is too delicate."[9] More far-reaching than the peaceful disposition of the Florida question in 1819 was the subsequent dissolution of the Spanish empire in the Western hemisphere. It changed the distribution of power in the world. Just as geography played a major role in the making of American foreign policy, in the interplay of the European powers, the significance of American sea power was never overlooked. In a memorandum to the members of the British government Foreign Secretary George Canning speculated on November 30, 1824, that "sooner or later we shall probably have to contend with the combined maritime power of France and the United States."[10] In anticipation of such an active combination he therefore proposed close cooperation with the new Latin American states as "a fair counterpoise." As the course of history unfolded, the assumption of close Franco-American ties proved time and again to be as much an oversimplification as that of the traditional Anglo-American enmity.

8. Hyde de Neuville to Richelieu, Washington, August 10, 1818, CPEU, LXXVI.
9. Richelieu to Hyde de Neuville, Paris, September 1, 1818, *ibid.*
10. Frederick Merk, *The Oregon Question—Essays in Anglo-American Diplomacy and Politics* (Cambridge, Mass., 1967) , p. 149.

The spoliation claims episode in the early 1830's demonstrated, after all, the tenuousness of the Franco-American friendship when offended national pride and personal vanity seemed for a moment capable of plunging the two nations into a war.[11] When the French Chamber of Deputies failed to implement the Treaty of 1831, by which the French government had agreed to pay certain claims to the United States, dating back to damages suffered at the time of the Napoleonic wars, President Jackson treated this action as an insult to the United States as well as a breach of contract. In turn, Jackson's intimation that France was acting in bad faith offended the French sense of honor. And his determination to retaliate if France should fail to meet its obligations temporarily involved the two nations in a serious crisis. In spite of much talk of war, however, William C. Rives, America's minister to France, sized up the situation in an encouraging fashion: "Unless the French Government is vastly more silly . . . than I suppose . . . there can be no difficulty in closing the breach."[12] Desiring the maintenance of peace, Great Britain offered its good offices to head off a calamity that would have disrupted the world economy. Lord Palmerston was also very much concerned about the disruptive consequences of a Franco-American war on his grandiose scheme of organizing Europe against Russia's designs on the Ottoman Empire. Through his tactful unofficial mediation efforts Palmerston helped to preserve a common-sense atmosphere which in the end made a diplomatic settlement of this episode possible.

French reaction to American expansionism in the middle

11. For this episode, consult R. A. McLemore, *Franco-American Diplomatic Relations, 1816–1836* (Baton Rouge, La., 1941). John C. Calhoun, President Jackson's irreconcilable political opponent, warned on the floor of the Senate, on January 18, 1836: "The capacity of France to inflict injury upon us is ten times greater than ours to inflict injuries on her. . . . A war with France will be among the greatest calamities."

12. William C. Rives to Niles, Castle Hill, June 5, 1835, Nathaniel Niles Papers (LCMS), Vol. II.

part of the nineteenth century depended to a certain degree as much on ideological and cultural outlook as on questions of power and trade. If the wheels of progress in democratizing public life turned more slowly in France than in the United States, the difference could be accounted for to a large extent by divergent backgrounds and temperaments. It was hardly a coincidence, however, that the Jacksonian Revolution, the Great Reform movement in England, and the July Revolution occurred at about the same time. What Frenchmen thought about American institutions and what Americans thought about constitutional developments in France were in many ways reflected in their respective attitudes toward strictly foreign political issues.

Once Europe had been freed from what the sage of Monticello described as "the atrocious caprices of Bonaparte,"[13] such qualified judges as Presidents Jefferson and Monroe expected France to rise again to a position of leadership on the European continent, provided it finally acquired the "habits of order." With this condition in mind, Jefferson believed that a constitutional monarchy would suit the French temperament better than a democratic republic.[14] Evidently recognizing their own limitations, in those days educated Frenchmen clearly acknowledged the avant-garde character of the republican institutions of the United States. Intellectually, they could applaud the American experiment; but practically they were skeptical about its applicability to France where the sense of individual responsibility had not been sufficiently cultivated.[15]

13. Thomas Jefferson to Hyde de Neuville, Monticello, December 13, 1818 (copy), CPEU, LXXVI.

14. William H. Carr, *The Du Ponts of Delaware* (London, 1965), p. 105; see also George Ticknor, *Life, Letters and Journals* (Boston, 1876), I, p. 129.

15. John de Witt McBride, Jr., "America in the French Mind During the Bourbon Restoration" (Unpublished Ph.D. dissertation, Syracuse University, 1954), pp. 243–48, 276.

Unfortunately, when Charles X became king of France in 1824, his ultraroyalist and clerical inclinations contributed to the rapid loss of the popularity he enjoyed initially.[16] By comparison with 1790, conditions in France had notably improved by the late 1820's, particularly in such areas as agriculture, commerce, and manufacturing. The number of proprietors was now much greater and numerous abuses had been corrected. Still, there was discontent. In a report to Henry Clay, for instance, the United States minister in Paris observed in 1827 that "the republicans, if there are any in France, are few in number and can have no hope of success. And the family of the late Emperor has now no avowed adherents." But the growing influence of the clergy, the opulence of religious foundations, and the intolerance of missionaries gave rise to much dissatisfaction. Law and medical students were prominent in leading the opposition to ecclesiastical tyranny. Their experiences had taught them the desirability of representative government better than any ideological exhortations.[17] Blindly refusing to liberalize political life in France, Charles X moved toward greater absolutism. In 1829 he stubbornly asserted, "I would rather saw wood than be a king of the English type." When just before the July Revolution the king made radical changes in the existing election system, depriving three-fourths of the electors of the right of suffrage, abolishing the secret vote, and reducing the number of deputies from 430 to 258, he misjudged the temper of his time. His suppression of all opposition journals and his suspension of the freedom of the press finally ignited the popular fuse.[18] The July Revolution of 1830 was thus not only directed against the newly regained power of the Papists, it also condemned the unpopular misrule of a king who failed to grasp the politi-

16. James Brown to Col. Aspenwale, Paris, December 25, 1824, James Brown Papers (Louisiana State University MS).
17. James Brown to Henry Clay, Paris, April 27, 1827. DDFDS.
18. William C. Rives to Van Buren, Paris, July 30, 1830, DDFDS.

cal aspirations of his people.[19] More was at stake in the July Revolution than a change in domestic institutions. The time had come, so it appeared to enlightened French nationalists, for France to assume leadership in the political liberalization of Europe. The conservative spirit of the treaties of 1815 and the status quo they had been designed to maintain no longer accorded with the conditions of 1830.[20] Men like the banker Lafitte and Adolphe Thiers, who used the liberal daily paper *Le National,* founded in 1830, to support the Duke of Orleans, were convinced that they were advancing the national interest of France. Having been in principle opposed to a republic, they advocated a constitutional monarchy. As Thiers phrased it then, "We must either cross the Channel or cross the Atlantic."[21]

For a short time General Lafayette and his closest friends weighed the possibility of the establishment of a republic. But the conservative element of French bourgeois society, unwilling to yield its power and influence to the government, prevailed in the final decision to establish a constitutional monarchy. Presenting himself as a republican king, Louis Philippe convinced Lafayette that the French people were not ready for a republic.

Throughout the United States, and particularly in the South, Americans hailed this "glorious revolution" as an indication of "the firm footing which the principles of liberty are obtaining throughout the world." Carried away by their enthusiasm, the members of the Louisiana House of Representatives confidently expressed the hope that the rest of Europe

19. Mary Lesley Ames (ed.), *Life and Letters of Peter and Susan Lesley* (New York, 1909), pp. 48–50.

20. Jacques Droz, *Europe Between Revolutions, 1815–1848* (New York, 1967), pp. 112, 215–31.

21. Gordon Wright, *France in Modern Times: 1760 to the Present* (Chicago, 1960), pp. 139–42. At this time Adolphe Thiers did not yet believe in the "chimera" of a republic. Arnaud to Eyma, October 14, 1830, Eyma Correspondance (Bibliothèque Nationale MS).

would follow the revolutionary lead of France and emancipate its peoples without seriously upsetting the public order.[22] Louis Philippe promised to be an ideal constitutional monarch in whom the French people could put their trust.

Although the United States too originally had high hopes that it would get along well with the reputedly fairly liberal French king, the unfortunate spoliation claims episode showed how quickly the two countries could be brought to the brink of war. The passions aroused by this incident and the indications of cynical illiberality on the part of Louis Philippe's government did not create an ideal atmosphere for discussions concerning Texas and California. Although both Great Britain and France recognized the independence of Texas and opposed the further westward movement of the United States, France showed more verbal hostility to American expansion than Britain. Both had in principle also agreed to Lord Aberdeen's plan of guaranteeing the independence of Texas and the boundary between it and Mexico. They thought that such a joint diplomatic action would be sufficient to deter the United States from going ahead with its annexation plans.[23] It is very doubtful that the maritime powers ever intended to implement their policy by more forceful methods. In any case, the French king's indiscretion of July 4, 1844, almost put an end to joint Anglo-French action of any kind as soon as its substance had traveled across the English Channel. On that day Louis Philippe politely assured William R. King, the United States minister to France, that in regard to Texas his government would take no steps "in the slightest degree hostile" to the United States. Late in May,

22. See "Address by House of Representatives of Louisiana to the People of France, New Orleans, March 24, 1831," in *Louisiana Historical Quarterly*, III (1920), 399–402. Originally President Jackson fully shared the enthusiasm about Louis Philippe. Russell M. Jones, "The Flowering of a Legend: Lafayette and the Americans, 1825–1834," *French Historical Studies*, IV (1966), 401. See also *La Révolution*, August 9 and 17, 1830.

23. Merk, *American Expansionism*, pp. 30–31, 40–47.

Guizot had already disappointed Alphonse Pageot, who represented France in the United States, by refusing to take any stronger measures than Britain had suggested.[24] But after Louis Philippe's unguarded statement Britain began to question France's reliability altogether. In any military intervention in America distance and cost usually prompted second thoughts. Also the possibility that the people of Texas might genuinely desire to join the federal union restrained Lord Aberdeen from taking any action. By December, 1844, Guizot had made up his mind that France must not go to war over Texas. Though he could not view American expansion with indifference, he did not see in it an immediate threat to the security of France.

Unwilling to offend England and the United States, with both of whom France carried on considerable trade, Guizot nevertheless ended by losing ground with both.[25] In this instance, he lost prestige abroad and at home when it became clear that he was not prepared to follow up his challenge of the United States with appropriate actions. Indeed, Adolphe Thiers took the French premier to task for his "Stop America" policy.[26] Opposing Guizot in foreign as well as in domestic policies, Thiers questioned the wisdom of the entente cordiale and of the American balance thesis. As he saw it, a strong and friendly United States was for France a gift from heaven, for "in the measure in which America grows, England needs us." Frenchmen who thus interpreted the expansion of the United States as a factor favoring France in its competition with Britain were at a loss to understand why Guizot had publicly enunciated a thesis to which Americans took strong exception and which ran counter to French interests. Guizot

24. Guizot to Pageot, Paris, May 28, 1844, CPEU, C.
25. Douglas Johnson, *Guizot: Aspects of French History, 1787–1874* (London, 1963), 295–96.
26. Discours de M. Thiers, 20 janvier, 1846, "Sur les relations de la France avec les États-Unis d'Amérique" (Paris, 1846).

flatly denied the main charges against him. He regarded the United States as a friend with whom France maintained excellent relations. Once Texas had opted for union, he told his critics in the French Chamber, he did not protest. And as much as he would regret an Anglo-American war over Oregon, France would certainly remain neutral in it. But he continued to insist that America's hegemony in the New World would create problems no responsible French statesman looking into the more distant future could safely ignore.[27] Alphonse Pageot had evidently duly impressed Guizot with his recommendation that the time had come to signify to the American republic Europe's disapproval of America's hegemony in the Western hemisphere. As a European, Pageot resented the arrogance with which the United States declared that "it will not *permit* any European power to interfere in the affairs of America."[28]

In his annual message of December 2, 1845, President Polk mildly criticized France for its unexpected efforts to prevent the annexation of Texas.[29] Many other French plans and actions produced the cumulative effect of deepening the roots of American suspicion. Prominent among them were the occupation of Vera Cruz in 1838 and the blockade of the Mexican coast to compel payment of debts, the Anglo-French intervention in the Rio de la Plata dispute, the various unofficial French activities in California before the Mexican War, and the project by which the Duke de Montpensier, Louis Philippe's son who had married a Spanish princess, was slated to become the ruler of Mexico.[30] All these schemes and interfer-

27. Merk, *American Expansionism,* pp. 57–58, 90.

28. Pageot to Guizot, Washington, June 12, 1845, CPEU, CI.

29. J. D. Richardson (ed.), *A Compilation of the Messages and Papers of the Presidents* (Washington, D.C., 1896), III, 2237. (December 2, 1845). Foreign Secretary Aberdeen was glad to see this "separation of France in feeling and interest from the United States." Kenneth Bourne, *Britain and the Balance of Power in North America, 1815–1908* (Berkeley, Calif., 1967), p. 151.

30. William Spence Robertson, "French Intervention in Mexico in

ences, the *New York Herald*[31] contended, were not just intended to contain the United States geographically but to erect barriers against the further spread of republicanism. This all-absorbing issue quite understandably haunted the believers in monarchical institutions. French monarchs—Louis Philippe as well as Napoleon III later on—found their freedom of action restricted whenever they contemplated intervention in the affairs of the American republic. Their fears of repercussions at home limited them at best to ineffectual hints at actions the American government did not take very seriously. The American envoy in France, William R. King, encouraged this attitude when in January, 1846, he advised Secretary of State James Buchanan "to disregard with lofty indifference French influence in American affairs. It is insignificant."

As the war between the United States and Mexico was about to get under way, the Polk administration ran the risk of a simultaneous conflict with Britain because of the Oregon question. Since France hesitated to tackle the United States without British assistance, the Anglo-American compromise settling the Oregon issue doomed Guizot's attempt to organize a European coalition against the westward march of the United States all the way to the Pacific. His impolitic neutrality declaration prior to the outbreak of an Anglo-American war, though originally designed to show how well disposed he was toward the United States, actually had the effect of convincing both the United States and Great Britain that France could not be relied upon in an emergency. In addition to other reservations contributing to the growing distrust between the partners of the entente cordiale was Prince de Joinville's exaggerated claim in 1844 that the French navy was

---

1838," *Hispanic-American Historical Review*, XXIV (1944), 222-52; John F. Cady, *Foreign Intervention in the Rio de la Plata* (Philadelphia, 1929); and Henri Lorin, "L'Évolution de la Doctrine de Monroe," *RDDM* (June 15, 1915), p. 822.

31. January 20, 1846.

superior to that of any other power.[32] Anglo-French differences over Egypt, Tahiti, and the Chusan Archipelago at the time of the Mexican War ruled out joint Anglo-French intervention in it. Furthermore, the French government had to take cognizance of that sizable number of Frenchmen who preferred to see the United States rather than Britain as the leading power in the Western hemisphere. To them, that was the only realistic choice they had. Some even went so far as to cite the genuine benefits the Mexican people would derive from an infusion of American energy. In any case, they argued, Mexico must basically defend itself.[33] France could not do more for it than Mexico did for itself. With public opinion sharply divided on the Mexican War, other Frenchmen saw in it not only a preliminary step toward the conquest of Cuba, but an illustration of the American republic's wickedness that put European monarchs to shame.[34]

5. *1848, Napoleon III, and Cuba*

Americans who rationalized their country's expansion in terms of its extension of the "area of freedom" were of course cheered by the mid-century revolutionary stirrings in Europe. Superficially seen, the intellectual and political ferment on both sides of the Atlantic encouraged the belief that parallel developments in the Old World and the New would gradually bring the two civilizations much closer together. In fact, however, Americans and Frenchmen knew too little

32. Merk, *Oregon Question*, pp. 347–60. See also J. S. Galbraith, "France as a Factor in the Oregon Negotiations," *Pacific Northwest Quarterly*, XLIV (1953), 69–70.

33. *Le National*, June 30, 1846.

34. Félix de Courmont, *Des États-Unis, de la Guerre du Mexique et de l'Île de Cube* (Paris, 1847), pp. 7–10; and H. D. Barral-Montferrat, "La doctrine de Monroe et les évolutions successives de la politique étrangère aux États-Unis," *Revue d'histoire diplomatique* (1903), p. 615.

about each other and their institutions to justify such an assumption. Their judgments were clearly colored by puzzlement, pride, and prejudice.

Most Frenchmen had to take at face value the statement that the American form of government had a direct bearing on the well-being and happiness of the masses in the United States. But whether the American experience could be duplicated in France was open to question. The *Journal des Débats*[1] summed up the widely expressed sentiment: "What is good for America is not necessarily so for France." It also remained to be demonstrated whether the relatively young American system would stand the test of time in the next fifty years. Such eminent Frenchmen as François Guizot and Alexis de Tocqueville, for instance, had already begun to see signs of instability weakening the structure on which American institutions rested. To the skeptical critics of republicanism President Jackson's attack on the United States Bank illustrated the caprices of democracy, which, to them, were capable of causing as much damage and harassment as those of autocracy. Also, the growth of the urban population cast doubt on the future stability of America's institutions.[2] Yet the silent common sense pervading the successful institutions of the American people set an example of self-government that puzzled Europeans who presumed their civilization to be superior to that of the New World.

When within the short span of a generation postrevolutionary France changed its political system three times, it bared an internal weakness that went beyond the central conflict between monarchism and republicanism. The groping of the French people for the most desirable form of government bred both admiration and contempt among Americans, just as the fairly stable constitutional processes of the United States

1. May 28 and July 31, 1832.
2. Georges Weill, "L'Idée républicaine en France pendant la Restauration," *Revue d'histoire moderne*, II (1927), 338, and Ticknor, *Life, Letters, and Journals*, II, 105.

inspired some Frenchmen and made others pray to be spared the ordeal of a republican experiment in France.[3] On the whole, French monarchists and republicans alike acknowledged the amazing political maturity of the American people. On the other hand, Americans were by and large convinced of the political immaturity of the French people and concluded therefore that an autocratic government suited the French temperament best. Americans commented time and again that the French were not morally fit for a republic and deserved despotism. They reiterated this opinion so often that, as Harriet B. Stowe noted in 1854, citizens of the model republic had become, ironically and unintentionally, the propagandists of despotism in Europe.[4] Seen in conjunction with French reaction to America's Manifest Destiny, the ideological differences between Frenchmen and Americans increased the alienation between them much more than even the annoying realities of their working relationship warranted.

It was disheartening to watch the erratic course of French history ever since the Great Revolution. Many dualistic tendencies in France bewildered observers both abroad and at home. What were they to make of the concern of the French for humanity and their unconcern for brutality, of their enlightened reform and their ruthless conquest, of their longing for order and their tolerance of disorder? How could one explain that in its rendezvous with destiny defeated France left its imprint on European civilization, on its institutions and thought, while triumphant France had failed to gain the allegiance and loyalty of the various "conquered" nations? Was it sheer restlessness and political ineptitude that drove the French people to experiment with various forms of govern-

3. Merle Curti, "The Reputation of America Overseas, 1776–1860," *American Quarterly*, I (1949), 64–65. See also George Bancroft to Richard Rush, London, August 1, 1847, Richard Rush Papers, "Family Letters" (Princeton University MS).

4. Harriet Beecher Stowe, *Sunny Memories* (Boston, 1854), II, 418. See also J. D. Osborne to Wm. C. Rives, Paris, February 23, 1852, William C. Rives Papers (LC MS).

ment in the relatively peaceful decades after the Congress of Vienna as they had previously done during the turbulent years of the French Revolution and the Napoleonic wars? Or would it be fairer and more accurate to look upon these experiments as part of the French people's prolonged struggle for liberty and social justice?

The Paris-centered upheavals between 1830 and 1870, the excesses of the revolutionary minorities in 1848 and 1871, and, above all, the tragically detrimental effect of Louis Napoleon's coup d'état on the evolution of liberal institutions in Europe made it extremely difficult for many Americans to pay France the respect the French people so ardently desired.

The disappointments of the French people, obviously not universally shared in France, found much understanding in the United States. Contrary to the expectations of great liberality, Louis Philippe's regime turned out to be "a government of bayonets tempered by the Press." Out of a population of 35,500,000 the right to vote was extended to only 250,000. Instead of granting redress to complaints, the government stubbornly persisted in efforts to bend political leaders into mere instruments of the king's will. Louis Philippe, himself an upstart among kings, and his court, inflated with pretensions, neither genuinely patrician nor democratic, were too blinded by arrogance and family ambitions to yield to the demands of the people for greater political emancipation. These demands were not made in an intellectual vacuum; they were the outgrowth of historical developments which the king and his leading advisers ignored at their own risk. Thirty years of peace had brought important changes. The acquisition of property and improved educational conditions awakened the consciousness of rights and emboldened increasing numbers of people to press for them.[5]

5. Consult John Welles, "Diaries," I, March 18 and 28, 1848 (Columbia University MS); Richard Rush to C. J. Ingersoll, Paris, May 1, 1848. (Pennsylvania Historical Society MS); and George H. Calvert, *Scenes and Thoughts in Europe* (Boston, 1863), pp. 50–51.

Students of the February Revolution of 1848 have noted that distinct class interests manifested themselves more forcefully in this revolution than in 1830. The lower-middle class and the workers felt that the upper-middle class wielded too much power and influence and demonstrated a certain callousness with regard to the social and economic needs of the masses.[6] The social problems had been aggravated by the large migrations from rural regions to the urban center. Between 1831 and 1840 alone 213,000 "immigrants" complicated the already congested housing situation in Paris.[7] The misery of workers searching for a roof over their heads, depressed economic conditions and unemployment, as well as poor crops in the months just before the revolution contributed to the causes of the quite unexpected volcanic eruption in 1848. As recently as September, 1847, the Philadelphia lawyer and experienced diplomat Richard Rush expressed the belief that the Orleans dynasty was securely established. Quite "realistically," he then asked: "Will not the middle classes, grown so numerous in agriculture under subdivided inheritances, the merchants, manufacturers, the mechanics, the artisans—so flourishing—, will not these classes be likely to rally around the dynasty rather than be subjected to the confusion and risks likely to follow its overthrow?" The Revolution of 1848 took Rush as much by surprise as it did France.

In addition to social and economic problems, popular discontent was also nourished by Louis Philippe's unspectacular foreign policy, particularly his failure to aid the Italian and

6. Paul Farmer, "Some Frenchmen Review 1848," *Journal of Modern History*, XX (1948), 320–23; Georges Duveau, *1848: The Making of a Revolution* (London, 1967), xxv-xxvi; and Jacques Droz, *Europe Between Revolutions, 1815–1848* (New York, 1967), pp. 246–51.

7. Wm. L. Langer, "The Pattern of Urban Revolution in 1848," in Evelyn M. Acomb and Marvin L. Brown, Jr. (eds.), *French Society and Culture since the Old Regime* (New York, 1966), pp. 91–92. The American minister in Paris was evidently not aware of the seriousness of this situation. See Beckles Willson, *America's Ambassadors to France 1777–1927* (New York, 1928), p. 221.

Polish independence movements.[8] As the center for European exiles, Paris was not only the most cosmopolitan city on the Continent, it was also the meeting place of many liberal and revolutionary European elements. Despite the progressive atmosphere which could be sensed in Paris, reform rather than overthrow of the constitutional monarchy was the goal of many of the king's critics.[9] Interestingly, though, the February Revolution swept Louis Philippe's regime away and spread its virus on the Continent, initially very much to the satisfaction of American sympathizers.

The French Revolution of 1848 was more than a political development. Without social and economic improvements it would have been practically worthless to the more militant revolutionaries. The provisional government's reforms with respect to the liberty of the press; universal suffrage; the abolition of capital punishment; the abolition of slavery in the colonies; and the decrees putting "an end to the long and iniquitous sufferings of the workers," shortening working hours, and establishing National Workshops substantiated the claim that this was as much a social as a political revolution.[10] Its socialist aspects frankly frightened some Americans, as well as the middle and upper classes of France.

As a political movement, however, the United States extended to it its recognition and support, first through its distinguished envoy in Paris, Richard Rush, acting alone, and later in a Senate resolution presented to the French govern-

8. Wright, *France in Modern Times*, pp. 248–49. Different temperaments and outlooks permitted just the opposite conclusion. Edward Everett, the United States minister to Britain from 1841 to 1845, for instance, praised Louis Philippe for his talent in keeping the peace and felt that the king deserved to be called "the Napoleon of Peace." Edward Everett to Rev. C. W. Upham, Florence, January 1, 1841, Edward Everett Papers (Massachusetts Historical Society MS).

9. Louis Gottschalk and Donald Lach, *The Transformation of Modern Europe* (Chicago, 1954), p. 118.

10. See *New York Times*, June 25, 1878, p. 8; and John G. Gazley, *American Opinion of German Unification, 1848–1871* (New York, 1926), pp. 244–48.

ment from the American president and transmitted by Rush. Rush felt relieved when the Polk administration retroactively approved his originally unauthorized recognition of the provisional government; he had taken this hasty action to underpin the trembling authority of the newly created republic.[11] In Paris, the American colony marched in procession to the City Hall to congratulate the revolutionary government. In nearly all major American cities hundreds of thousands demonstrated to express their solidarity with their French brethren. Nevertheless the question lingered in the minds of many American enthusiasts whether the French people, accustomed to looking up to a leading political figure, could really govern themselves and, if not, whether a fatal failure of republicanism in France would not be a severe blow to liberalism in Europe. Protestants doubted very seriously, moreover, whether the French republic could survive in a Catholic country in which "Jesuits are crushing the life and spirit of freedom."[12] To many of them, France could not function as a republic unless the Protestant religion formed its foundation.

The inadequacies of its political leaders proved to be ruinous to the Second Republic. Caught between republicans and monarchists—a relatively small number of socialist workers and the great mass of bourgeois defenders of private property —as well as between extremists on the left and the right, the Second Republic was really never given a chance.[13] The cir-

11. See Blumenthal, *Reappraisal*, pp. 7–15; Gazley, *German Unification*, pp. 233–64; Roger Soltau, *French Political Thought in the Nineteenth Century* (New Haven, Conn., 1931), pp. 93–96; and S. G. Goodrich, *Recollections of a Lifetime* (New York, 1856), II, 473.

12. Daniel C. Eddy, *Europa: Or Scenes and Society in England, France, Italy and Switzerland* (Boston, 1861), 260–61; see also Robert Scott, "American Travellers in France, 1830–1860" (Unpublished Ph.D. dissertation, Yale University, 1940), pp. 113–26. The liberal Catholic leader Comte de Montalembert did not go that far, but he did attribute the success of American democracy to its socially responsible christianity, which was less evident in Europe. Le Comte de Montalembert, *La Victoire du Nord aux États-Unis* (Paris, 1865), p. 104.

13. Wright, *France in Modern Times;* pp. 171–75; see also George W.

cumstances surrounding its establishment weakened it from the start, both politically and economically. From a functional point of view, it is essential to remember that the qualified bureaucracy on which the Second Republic had to rely was necessarily still dominated by the personnel of the recently overthrown Orleanist monarchy.[14] The government was also not fully sure of the loyalty of all echelons of the French army.[15] Americans were by and large unaware of many of these crucially important aspects of this "revolution" in France. Their basically emotional reaction to these mid-century developments oversimplified matters and made the later letdown much harder to accept.

The Second Republic was an interlude in French history during which revolution and counterrevolution followed each other in almost rythmic fashion. Moving from a revolutionary provisional government to the election of a constituent assembly, whose complexion was conservative and traditionalist, a Red Republic suddenly came into existence in June, 1848. The savage atrocities during this grim insurrection were brought under control by General Cavaignac, whom the assembly entrusted with supreme executive authority when it proclaimed a state of siege in Paris. The instability caused by the February Revolution and the subsequent socialist grasp for power frightened the bourgeois classes of France and contributed to the election of Prince Louis Napoleon Bonaparte as president of the Second Republic on December 10, 1848. When Louis Napoleon assumed this high office, he took the solemn oath: "Before God, and in the presence of the French people, represented by the National Assembly, I swear to re-

---

Fasel, "The French Election of April 23, 1848—Suggestions for a Revision," *French Historical Studies*, V (1968) , 285–98.

14. René Rémond, *La droite en France de 1815 à nos jours: continuité et diversité d'une tradition politique* (Paris, 1954) , pp. 87–103; see also Peter H. Amann, "Writings on the Second French Republic," *Journal of Modern History*, XXXIV (1962) , 411.

15. Wright, *France in Modern Times*, pp. 181–82.

main faithful to the Republic, democratic, one and indivisible; and to fulfill all the duties which the Constitution imposes on me." But, driven by his ambition to re-establish the French Empire, he ignored this oath when one year later he became, via his coup d'état of December 2, 1851, Napoleon III, Emperor of France. The popular election of the president did indeed put the fate of the Second Republic in the hands of a man who interpreted in his own way Lamartine's remark with reference to the method by which the president of the republic should be elected: "Il faut laisser quelque chose à la Providence."[16]

The anonymous author of a poem published in the *Democratic Review* in March, 1849, characteristically interpreted the election of Prince Louis Napoleon Bonaparte as president of the French republic as a warning signal:

> France and Frenchmen now rejoice
> Thou'rt proclaimed her people's choice!
> Seek thy greatness in her own—
> Dream not of a despot's throne—
> Thou must battle for the free,
> Or a curse will light on thee!

The four years of the Second Republic's precarious existence have been described as a perpetual crisis[17] that discredited and retarded the cause of republicanism in Europe. Although Russia, Prussia, and Austria did not, as originally rumored, join

16. For several American reactions to the 1848 disturbances in France, see Mrs. Avenel's letter from Paris, dated July 30, 1848, Avenel Family Papers (Tulane University MS). See also Mrs. Hincks's letters dated March 7 and April 25, 1848, Hincks Family Papers (Tulane University MS) ; and Richard Rush to George Bancroft, Paris, March 21, 1849, Richard Rush Papers, "Family Letters" (Princeton University MS). See also Richard Rush, *Recollections of the Court of Louis Philippe and the French Revolution of 1848* (London, 1872) , p. 549; and John B. Wolf, *France: 1814-1919, The Rise of a Liberal-Democratic Society* (New York, 1963) , pp. 208–9.

17. Charles de Mazade, "Cinquante années d'histoire contemporaine, M. Thiers," *RDDM* (April 15, 1881) , p. 829.

forces against the advancing democracy in Europe, the United States limited itself to giving it merely moral support and encouragement.[18] In any case, the collapse of the French republic and the establishment of the Second Empire must be traced to internal rather than external factors.

The American government went out of its way, however, to show its sympathy for the Hungarian Revolution. And though unauthorized by their government, the Young Americans, among them such relatively high officials as George N. Sanders of Kentucky and the eccentric Senator Pierre Soulé of Louisiana, were in touch with Europe's revolutionary leaders, scheming the overthrow of Europe's monarchical regimes. Their conspiracies and propaganda, particularly during the period from 1848 to 1854, concentrated heavily on the new Bonaparte, who, in the competition between monarchism and republicanism, symbolized to them illiberality and vaingloriousness. Napoleon's muzzling of the press and his persecution and imprisonment of thousands of liberal-minded Frenchmen infuriated Americans, who took their solidarity with French republicans seriously.[19] French believers in the superiority of the monarchical system responded by identifying American republicanism as the dangerous source of lawlessness and license and by holding the United States up as the *enfant terrible* in the family of civilized nations.

Regardless of whether the French people voted more against General Cavaignac than for Louis Napoleon, or whether the nephew of Napoleon I was a charlatan or a political genius, neither his coup d'état of December 2, 1851, nor the subsequent proclamation of the Second Empire would have been

18. See Anna Blackwell to Sarah Helen Whitman, England, May 26, 1849, Harris Collection (Brown University MS).

19. Blumenthal, *Reappraisal*, pp. 25–29. Napoleon gradually relaxed his authoritarian controls. However, his policies vis-à-vis the United States during the 1860's so antagonized the American people that few Americans gave the emperor credit for his liberalization of French life. Wright, *France in Modern Times*, pp. 189–90.

possible without popular approval.[20] Napoleon III was a complex phenomenon on the international scene. Taking cognizance of the receding tide of republicanism in Europe, he devised a government peculiarly adapted to the French people.[21] For all practical purposes, the emperor functioned as a republican autocrat. His effective use of the referendum attested to this apparent contradiction. Napoleon understood quite clearly what he was doing. Long before "Providence" placed him at the helm of the French nation he had come to the conclusion that in a disorganized society all components must be brought together by a "new civil order" before liberty could flourish.[22] Accustomed to regarding constitutions as sacred and the oath to support them as pledges of honor, the American public condemned President Louis Napoleon's coup d'état as an act of perjury and perfidy. The coup had admittedly been facilitated by the republicans who had devised the constitution of the Second Republic, which centralized too much power in Paris, a city of "baneful influence." The constitution-makers had also not paid enough attention to the all-important connection between the government of France and French society. They had stressed centralized institutional structure more than decentralized social function.[23]

Even more important than this structural aspect, the middle class played a key role in Napoleon's rise to imperial power. Unwilling to make concessions to the working masses and determined to regain the position it had lost as the result of universal suffrage, the French bourgeoisie saw in Napoleon III a

20. See *Daily Picayune,* New Orleans, February 22, 1852; *Messager Franco-Américain,* March 21, 1850; and Mathew Gilbert Upton, "An Experience of Personal Government (in the France of Napoleon III)" (Huntington Library MS), HM 19288, pp. 1–5.

21. See speech of Senator John Bell of Tennessee, April 13, 1852; 32d Cong. 1st sess., pp. 439–46.

22. Hans Rothfels, "1848—One Hundred Years After," *Journal of Modern History,* XX (1948), 294.

23. Goodrich, *Recollections,* II, 490, 501; see also review of Bernard Roelker's, *The Constitutions of France, Monarchical and Republican* (Boston, 1848), in *Southern Quarterly Review,* XVI (1850), 502–36.

most attractive counterrevolutionary leader.[24] But the Shop-
keeper's Emperor could not really be put into a neat anti-so-
cialist category. Through public works he secured public
peace and stability. The commercial, industrial, and agricultural prosperity of France during the relatively long life span
of his regime made even bourgeois Americans admit that
"there may be occasions in which an admixture of despotism
would be better than the semi-anarchy of so-called free
states."[25]

As monarchism was solidifying its position in Europe, the
process of democratization continued to take its natural
course in the United States. The material successes of American democracy never ceased to worry the monarchical rulers
of Europe because they made the suppression of democracy in
Europe in the long run very problematical. In their counter-
propaganda campaigns they extolled such vaunted merits of
monarchism as its superior direction of the affairs of state,
greater stability, and personal loyalties. They furthermore
tried to discredit American democracy by charging it with the
hypocrisy of advocating the expansion of individual freedom
as a smokescreen for the greedy expansion of national power.
In their frequently prejudiced reports, French ministers to the
United States[26] asserted the existence of a unique national instinct that drove Americans to violate the territorial integrity
of their neighbors by any suitable method, including conquest,
purchase, infiltration, and revolution. The observation that
what Americans "hesitate to conquer by force, they seek to
buy" applied of course especially to the Cuban question in the
1850's. In this instance the United States refused to become a
party to a tripartite agreement by which it, France, and Great

24. See "La situation politique en France," *Messager Franco-Américain*,
June 13, 1850.
25. Walter Channing, *A Physician's Vacation; or A Summer in Europe*
(Boston, 1856), pp. 506–12.
26. See, for instance, Sartiges to Drouyn de Lhuys, Washington, June
26, 1854, CPEU, CXI.

Britain would have disclaimed any intention to acquire the island. In spite of the Ostend Manifesto, however, recommending that Cuba be purchased and, in case of Spain's refusal to sell, that it be "wrested" from Spain, the United States was wise enough to respect the current political realities. Also, in dealing with the Hawaiian question and the isthmian canal question the United States kept in mind the checks and balances the two major maritime powers of Europe had invoked so frequently.

It was one thing, however, for the American government to be alert to the intentions and capabilities of these powers; it was quite a different matter to be lectured to or intimidated by them. In 1854 Lord Clarendon publicly declared, with reference to the Anglo-French alliance, that it applied to the Western hemisphere as well as to the Eastern question. In his address to the French Chamber of Deputies on December 26, 1854, Napoleon III reiterated that the same views and intentions animated the entente powers "in every corner of the globe." With this statement Napoleon aroused more animosity than he might have bargained for. Secretary of State William L. Marcy had promptly taken exception to Lord Clarendon's declaration. Now Senator Lewis Cass of Michigan took the French emperor severely to task for his assumed guardianship over all the political affairs of the New World.[27] In a speech on the Senate floor Cass said he objected to this offensive arrangement and resented the fact that the United States had neither been consulted nor advised before the public delivery of this policy statement. But it should be noted that in the last analysis the very possibility of joint European intervention produced a sobering effect on the United States. Some members of the Congress always seemed ready to take on the whole world if it threatened to interfere with America's deci-

27. *Congressional Globe*, February 20, 1855, pp. 826–33; see also Ivor D. Spencer, *The Victor and the Spoils: A Life of William L. Marcy* (Providence, R. I., 1959) , p. 290.

sions, but the executive branch strove quite consciously to avoid such tests of power. Indeed, during the nineteenth century one of the major reasons why the executive branch preferred not to engage in joint policy arrangements with the major European powers was that it did not wish to strengthen the concept of joint action. On the contrary, time and again it sought to drive a wedge between France and Britain. It did not always succeed; but it was encouraged by the supposition expressed in France that regardless of Anglo-American family quarrels, ultimately, "blood, navigation, and commerce made England the natural ally of the United States."[28]

6. The United States and the Crimean War

Although the entente between France and Great Britain was not always a cordial one, its formal existence in the mid-nineteenth century disturbed the United States and Russia. The much talked-about combination of the latter's naval forces was inferior to that of the entente powers, who had a keener appreciation of the importance of sea power in the competition among nations. Even the relative strength of the American navy in relation to the French navy alone placed the United States in such an inferior position that the French consul general in New York reassured his government in 1853 that in case of war it would have nothing to fear from the American navy.[1] Its ships, he observed, were old, its crews deficient, and congressional support of it was at a low ebb.

These conditions prevailed when hostilities began between Russia and Turkey. By the spring of 1854 Russia also faced

28. Sartiges to Drouyn de Lhuys, Washington, November 5, 1854, CPEU, CXII.
1. Consul General Lacoste to French foreign minister, New York, March 10, 1853, Correspondance Commerciale, New York, 16.

the entente powers in what came to be known as the Crimean
War. Britain and France of course had their own reasons for
coming to the Turkish sultan's assistance. Britain wanted to
protect its route to India while Napoleon III was largely motivated by his desire to enhance his prestige and to steep the
new empire in military glory.[2] Though the United States assumed a rather distant and neutral attitude in the Crimean
War, public sentiment at first favored Turkey and then
turned against Britain and France, not because of important
stakes in the Balkans or the Black Sea region but for several
political and economic reasons.

Unlike the entente powers, Russia had no ambitions in
Central and South America that might collide with those of
the United States. On the contrary, in case of conflict with
these two major maritime powers the United States could reasonably count on at least Russia's moral and diplomatic support. As so often happens in history, moreover, special interests
and prejudices that were totally unrelated to the immediate international issues shifted the pendulum of public opinion in one direction or another. Thus many Southerners
opposed France and Great Britain because they gave aid and
comfort to the antislavery movement, whereas the existence of
serfdom in Russia evoked a strange social kinship. In addition
to religious prejudices involving the confrontation of Christians and Moslems, some Americans were also influenced by
the notion that Russia represented a counterpoise to the pope,
who relied heavily on French support.[3]

In those days Americans were not preoccupied with such an
abstract concept as balance of power. They might even have
denied its existence or questioned its worth. But in a very

2. Recognizing the value of the Suez Canal to France, Napoleon later
supported Ferdinand de Lesseps' project. See Alice E. Mange, *The Near
Eastern Policy of the Emperor Napoleon III* (Urbana, Ill., 1940), pp.
141–42; and Gottschalk and Lach, *The Transformation of Modern Europe*,
p. 151.

3. Gazley, *German Unification*, pp. 94–96.

practical sense their leaders understood very well that American security would be affected by major power shifts in Europe and that as long as the Europeans were preoccupied with their own rivalries they were likely to stay out of American affairs. The French envoy in the United States, who was sure that these two major considerations guided American policymakers, observed in 1854 that his Russian colleague was making sure of American attention to them.[4] America's traditional notion of its apparent aloofness from intra-European rivalries seemed to obviate still another consideration of genuine concern to Europeans. Whether the United States understood it or not, major changes in the development of the Western hemisphere—particularly the growing strength and influence of the United States—were destined to affect European powers individually, as well as the Continent collectively. Alerted to the likelihood of impending American moves aiming at the penetration of Central and South America, Foreign Minister Drouyn de Lhuys, for instance, warned the United States that France would not be indifferent to such developments. Despite the needs of the Crimean War, Napoleon III had given the order for the formation of a special naval squadron capable of coping with unforeseen contingencies. The French government was afraid that the war in Europe might encourage American officials to seek avowedly American solutions for the Cuban and Hawaiian questions.

According to a more complex version of the Cuban question at the time of the Crimean War, France actually explored the possibility of embroiling the United States in a war with Spain in order to forestall an alliance between Russia and the United States. The Spanish envoy in Paris, the Marquis of Viluma, stated on April 27, 1854, that in the eventuality of a Spanish-American war Napoleon III had promised "the entire moral influence of France and up to a squadron

4. Sartiges to Drouyn de Lhuys, Washington, January 1 and June 26, 1854, CPEU, CX and CXI.

for the defense of the Isle of Cuba." But, aside from Britain's reluctance to participate in such a scheme, Spain herself preferred neutrality as long as the United States did not make an overt move against Cuba.[5]

Each government obviously analyzed the problems growing out of the Crimean War from the point of view of its own interests. The decisive matter that concerned the Pierce administration involved fundamental policies. If the entente powers could set themselves up as the arbiter of Europe, what would prevent them from also imposing their will upon the United States?[6] Specifically, if the combined might of these two maritime powers could police the Mediterranean and the Black Sea, could it not also decide to police the Antilles and the Pacific Ocean? Since this disquieting prospect established, at least theoretically, a community of interest between Russia and the United States, it reinforced the concept of a Russo-American entente in defense of the freedom of the seas and perhaps even as a counterpoise to the Anglo-French combination. Lord Clarendon's untimely and originally provocative statement in Parliament early in 1854, seconded by Napoleon III,[7] indicated to some American leaders that henceforth more than the expedient fiction of a Russo-American understanding might be desirable. America's official neutrality in the Crimean War notwithstanding, its government did not want to see Russia defeated, lest the victorious allies become more meddlesome in the Western hemisphere.

5. Drouyn de Lhuys to Sartiges, Paris, January 26 and May 4, 1854, CPEU, CX. France was not willing to go beyond warning the United States to leave Cuba alone. Neither France nor Great Britain would grant Spain a guarantee of Cuba in exchange for which Spain would join the allies in the war against Russia. Tarsaïdzé, *Czars and Presidents*, p. 157. See also Nancy N. Barker, *Distaff Diplomacy: The Empress Eugenie and the Foreign Policy of the Second Empire* (Austin, Texas, 1967), p. 20.

6. Boilleau to Walewski, Washington, October 8, 1855, CPEU, CXIII.

7. Spencer, *The Victor and the Spoils*, pp. 290–91. See also F. A. Golder, "Russo-American Relations during the Crimean War," *AHR*, XXXI (1926), 462–76.

The mutual benefits of closer Russo-American cooperation, clearly understood in St. Petersburg, now seemed to warrant a reappraisal in Washington as well. An agreement embodying liberal neutral-rights principles to which other nations could in time subscribe was a welcome step but too limited in scope to satisfy the extravagant expectations of the Russians. Thomas H. Seymour, the American Envoy Extraordinary and Minister Plenipotentiary to Russia, reported on the last day of March, 1854, that a considerable number of influential people in St. Petersburg thought that the United States "might possibly take sides with its old and faithful ally, the Emperor."[8] And when the tsar received the American envoy two days later, he expressed the hope that the United States would not permit France and Great Britain to interrupt its commerce. He "wanted to see more of the American flag in the Baltic and Gulf of Finland" because he expected the sight of American ships along the northern shores to confirm the inviolability of neutrals' rights, besides bringing needed supplies to Russia.[9] On the whole, Russia was disappointed that the neutral United States respected the effective allied blockade of Russian ports. And with respect to the ships Russia had ordered in the United States before the war, Napoleon III doubted that the war would last long enough for the Russian fleet to benefit in time even from unlikely deliveries.[10]

Since Seymour and others interpreted the war as an attempt on the part of France and England to destroy the trade of Russia by sea and at least to slow down the feared development of Russia's immense resources, this war appeared to have

8. Seymour to Marcy, St. Petersburg, March 31, 1854, DDRDS.

9. *Ibid.*, April 13, 1854.

10. Sartiges believed that Russia's ostentatious frigate orders in New York were primarily given to disquiet Europe. Russia could, however, fairly easily acquire ships in the Northwest Pacific and use them against allied commerce. This genuine possibility called for special vigilance in the Pacific. Sartiges to Drouyn de Lhuys, Washington, January 8 and February 26, 1854, CPEU, CX; and Montholon to Drouyn de Lhuys, New York, June 8, 1854, Correspondance Commerciale, New York, 16.

an ominous bearing on America's economic future.[11] Secretary of State Marcy was above all upset by the immediate economic effects of the Crimean War. However much certain American business interests profited from increased sales, the war disrupted world trade in general. Even worse, it not only tightened the credits Europeans normally extended to American business, it prompted many European creditors to demand immediate specie payments. The resulting complications created serious financial problems.[12]

Yielding to American business pressures and perhaps as a friendly gesture toward Russia, the Pierce administration decided to offer its good offices for an amicable mediation of the conflict.[13] Marcy talked about it with the French minister in June, 1854, hoping that this extraordinary initiative might help speed an early end of the war. Drouyn de Lhuys had anticipated such an offer and advised his minister "to elude it politely." While passing through Paris early in 1853, Pierre Soulé, the controversial American diplomat in Spain, had mentioned to him that Russia was exploring the possibility of America's diplomatic intervention in the oriental question, not so much to facilitate a diplomatic arrangement as to embarrass Franco-American relations.[14] Drouyn de Lhuys took advantage of this opportunity to tell official Washington that it had no right to become an arbiter of the political equilibrium in a hemisphere of which it was not a part and in which it had no vital interests. Since there was no doubt in his mind that the allies were fighting to protect Turkey against Russian aggression, the French foreign minister felt that the United States should actually lend its moral support to the entente cordiale. Fortunately the war was soon nearing

11. Seymour to Marcy, St. Petersburg, June 2, 1854, DDRDS.

12. Sartiges to Drouyn de Lhuys, Washington, June 26, 1854, CPEU, CXI.

13. A. G. Jomini, *Diplomatic Study on the Crimean War (1852 to 1856)* (London, 1882), II, 80.

14. Drouyn de Lhuys to Sartiges, Paris, July 20, 1854, CPEU, CXI.

its end. The fall of Sevastopol in September, 1855, demonstrated to many Americans that Russia was not as invulnerable as they had imagined.[15] Taking a narrow view, they became therefore more readily convinced that their government's neutrality policy had been sound. The wider ramifications of the Crimean War as they might affect future Franco-American relations turned out to be of much greater concern at the beginning of the war than at its end. And the long-range global consequences of the war were hardly seen by any contemporaries.

To understand these broader aspects, it is essential to examine French evaluations of Russia and the United States in the nineteenth century. As far back as 1826 French leaders discovered the surprisingly friendly bonds between these two countries.[16] Somehow they began to wonder whether the Americans would ungratefully turn their back on France and rely mainly on cooperation with the Russians. What made such a prospect undesirable was the fact that the Russians were eagerly seeking to draw on the resources of the United States in their struggle against the western maritime powers. It was no secret that during President Jackson's administration Russia and the United States had come to a tacit agreement on the rights of neutrals which conveyed the impression of a much closer understanding than really existed. When in the mid-nineteenth century Frenchmen speculated about the future of France and Europe they seldom considered merely the impact of Russia or merely that of the United States; they usually saw the shadow of both these giants darkening that future. As bizarre as the attraction between the most despotic autocracy and the freest republic appeared, Frenchmen discovered many common elements in the Russian and American civilizations. For that matter, aside from the observable affinity between political extremes, leading Russians and Americans alike

15. Boilleau to Walewski, Washington, October 2, 1855, CPEU, CXIII.
16. Baron de Damas to Marneuil, Paris, August 30, 1826, CPEU, XXXII.

thought that the democratic republic and the absolute monarchy constituted the only two forms of government destined to survive the test of time.[17] Such informed Frenchmen as the critic Emile Montégut, the publicists Agénor de Gasparin and Charles de Mazade, and Adolphe Thiers were more impressed by Russo-American similarities than differences.[18] Their generalizations were widely shared by many other upper-class Europeans. They saw two materialistically oriented nations in possession of tremendous resources and continent-sized countries. They saw in both countries semi-civilized populations having socially leveling instincts and lacking in shame or an appreciation of honor. They saw two societies in which serfdom and slavery degraded and exploited men and which showed little respect for the law and even less genuine regard for the individual. They regarded both as a menace, a menace to their neighbors and to the universe. Ruthlessly advancing, these superpowers of the future, so it seemed to them, threatened literally, though perhaps unintentionally, to overwhelm all other powers and, in the process, to destroy Western civilization.

So great became the obsession with this somber outlook that in the summer of 1853 the influential *Revue des deux mondes* lamented the hesistancy and division of Europe in the face of the unchecked American and Russian expansion. The time, it pleaded, had come "for Europe to regain its freedom of action and the instinct of its true interests" or to face the alternative of more cruel disappointments.[19] Following the lead of Fran-

17. George Ticknor to John, King of Saxony, Boston, May 7, 1855, George Ticknor Papers, "Letters" (Massachusetts Historical Society MS). See also Julius Fröbel, *Amerika, Europa und die politischen Gesichtspunkte der Gegenwart* (Berlin, 1859), pp. 11–12, 54–55.

18. Emile Montégut, *Libres Opinions—Morales et Historiques* (Paris, 1888), 230–33. See also Agénor Etienne de Gasparin, *Après la Paix—Considérations sur le Libéralisme et la Guerre d'Orient* (Paris, 1856), p. 155; Charles de Mazade, "Chronique de la Quinzaine," *RDDM* (August 14, 1854), p. 843; and Adolphe Thiers, "Discours sur le régime commercial de la France," *Assemblée Nationale*, séance de 27 juin 1851.

19. "Chronique," *RDDM* (June 30, 1853), pp. 199–200.

çois Guizot, Napoleon III and his foreign minister, Drouyn de Lhuys, continued to look upon Russia as the chief enemy of France. To save European civilization, they deemed it necessary to drive the "Tatars" from Europe and to use emancipated Poland and unified Germany as a buffer between East and West.[20] Although some French monarchists and other Europeans would have liked to humble the United States, distance, tradition, and trade counseled against such a foolhardy undertaking.

In his extraordinarily keen analysis of America's place in the contemporary system of European power politics, Julius Fröbel observed in 1859 that as Russia was neither European nor Asian, and therefore not a part of the occident, the United States, too, was a stranger to the occidental states.[21] Fröbel saw the Europeans as disdainfully looking down on the civilization of these two outsiders, expecting their internal weaknesses and shortcomings to hasten their collapse. If this expectation had any sound basis, then the fear of the giant powers was both unwarranted and exaggerated. Flattered by the feeling of their superiority, the Western powers deceived themselves also, according to Fröbel, when they interpreted the outcome of the Crimean War as a great victory. In effect, they forced the Russians to withdraw to their own domain and to concentrate on their internal development, an essential requisite if Russia ever decided to play a more challenging international political role in the future. And if their entente cordiale was directed not only against Russia but against the United States as well, Fröbel pointed out that in the unlikely case of an entente war against the United States, a Russo-American alliance, so dreaded by France and Great Britain, would be a certainty. But he doubted that the entente cordiale could be an effective instrument against the United States, not only because of Britain's growing economic stake

20. Louis-Paul Deschanel, *Histoire de la Politique Extérieure de la France, 806–1936* (Paris, 1936) , p. 239.
21. Fröbel, *Amerika*, pp. 33–34.

in the United States but also because of Anglo-French conflicts of interests in the Western hemisphere. And in the event
of a war against the United States alone, the author argued
that Britain would have to be on America's side, because
"every French gain and every American defeat would amount
to a loss for Britain."[22] Having exhausted the mathematical
combinations of power constellations and looking into the
more distant future, Fröbel finally commented on the effects
of an alliance on the part of France, Russia, and the United
States against England. Its very idea, he estimated, would be
sufficient for England to seek America's friendship. Should
such an alliance nevertheless come about, Europe would find
itself being centralized under French leadership or absorbed
by Russia.[23] In either case, mighty "Europe" would ultimately
challenge the New World, a prospect to which the United
States could obviously not be a party.

7. *France and the American Civil War*

France and Great Britain had their chance to fell one
of the giants when the American Union was torn asunder during the Civil War.[1] One is of course tempted to ask, Why did
they not take advantage of this opportunity? And, more specifically, If the United States really endangered Europe's future,
why didn't Napoleon III act to safeguard its independence
and leading position? Ever since the middle 1850's many
Americans and Europeans were struck by the growing mili-
tancy in the United States, which seemed to foreshadow a

22. *Ibid.,* p. 37.
23. *Ibid.,* pp. 210–12.
1. For supplementary information about France and the American Civil
War, see Blumenthal, *Reappraisal,* pp. 119–65.

showdown fight between the North and the South. The dissolution of the federal Union was certain to produce far-reaching international consequences, whatever the reasons that had
brought it about. In the long run, it would not matter much
whether Southerners fought to preserve their way of life and
their peculiar institution or whether they wanted to free
themselves from what they regarded as a semicolonial status
in which the North placed them in violation of the Constitution. In case of a Southern victory, it would have been similarly academic whether the Union had fought not only for its
preservation in accordance with its interpretation of the Constitution or whether its manufacturing and business leaders
had wished to free themselves from the retarding influences of
politically powerful plantation oligarchs.

Although Northerners and Southerners and those Europeans who were observing the American scene anticipated the
possibility of secession and perhaps the likelihood of war, they
did not seriously prepare themselves for these eventualities. The military unpreparedness of both the North and the
South was of course remarkable. Since in case of secession or
war the North could rest its defense in the international arena
on grounds of legitimacy, there was little else for it to do
prior to these potential developments but to maintain mutually acceptable working relationships with Europe. Regardless
of the frictions and resentments that marred the relations between the United States and the major European powers, the
United States could reasonably bank on its transcending value
to each one of them. Its maritime and material resources, its
business and financial opportunities, its unrestricted export of
vitally needed raw materials, its stand-by function as an emergency food supplier during poor-crop years, and its contribution to European housing problems through absorbing millions of immigrants—all these factors made the American republic too significant for Old World governments to toss its
many advantages lightly aside. Furthermore, England, France,

and Russia treated the United States as a potentially balancing element in their calculations of political power. And finally, the extraordinary regard for the model republic manifested by the masses of Europe, who longed for their own political emancipation, was as reassuring to the federal government as it was a source of genuine concern to the monarchs of Europe. A war against the American republic, and particularly one on the side of slavery, would have been extremely unpopular in France and England. Indeed, its disruptive domestic effects might well have been beyond calculation. Napoleon III was fully alert to the dangerous momentum that these repercussions might produce in France. Despite their entente cordiale, moreover, if either France or Great Britain became sidetracked by a war against the United States, they knew that they might expose themselves to dangerous complications in Europe and elsewhere.

But if European military intervention in support of the future Confederate States was out of the question or deemed superfluous, what justified the Southern leaders' expectation of European cooperation in case secession from the Union became a reality?[2] In the first place, they believed that secession could and would be peaceful. Should war nevertheless ensue, they figured that in view of their superior military prowess it would be of such a short duration that no foreign military assistance would be required. Convinced of their invincibility, they counted heavily, however, on the prompt diplomatic recognition of their independence. They took it absolutely for granted that the dependence of France and Great Britain on Southern cotton would leave these two countries no choice but to recognize the Confederacy or to run the risk of seeing their textile plants shut down for lack of essential cotton supplies. Remembering that before the impending crisis influential British interest groups had frequently asserted that their

2. Henry Blumenthal, "Confederate Diplomacy: Popular Notions and International Realities," *Journal of Southern History*, XXXII (1966), 151–71.

government could not afford to tolerate the second alternative, the secessionists concluded that recognition would be extended as a matter of course. In addition to these pivotal considerations, they were also convinced that other factors, such as the economic rivalry between Britain and the United States and the South's cultural affinity to Western Europe plus its distinct national character, would sway Europe toward immediate recognition.

Underlying this expectation was the belief that the monarchical governments of France and England particularly would favor the division of the ever-expanding, encroaching, and overbearing republic across the Atlantic. That these basic assumptions prior to secession proved to be fatal miscalculations does not change the fact that they appeared to be sound to those who made them. The major maritime powers might not dare make war upon the United States; but as some Southerners noted in the 1850's, Frenchmen and Englishmen exulted at the prospect of the Union's dissolution as the eventual consequence of the militant antislavery movement. In anticipation of this event, some French merchants wished to establish commercial relations with the South so as to be able to appropriate the business heretofore transacted by merchants in Boston and New York.[3] In 1859, to facilitate such a change, an honorary member of the Chamber of Commerce of Norfolk, Virginia, addressed a memorandum to Napoleon III recommending the establishment of direct trans-Atlantic shipping services between Saint-Nazaire and Norfolk.[4] Events moved

3. William Elliott to his wife, Paris, September 20 and October 6, 1855, Elliott Family Papers (University of North Carolina MS).

4. Edouard Lacouture, *Mémoire à Sa Majesté l'Empereur Napoléon III: La Vérité sur la Guerre d'Amérique* (Paris, 1862), pp. 3–4. Southerners had long been playing with the idea of creating a port that would rival New York, so that they could receive goods from Europe directly. In 1853 the French consul in New Orleans encouraged his government to consider the many benefits France would derive from such a direct facility. But such a project involved more initiative and capital than Americans or Frenchmen were willing to risk in the 1850's. Roger to French

too fast for French experts to take action on this proposal prior to secession, however. Also looking ahead, in 1852 a Southern gentleman suggested to Robert M. T. Hunter, who in time became the Confederate secretary of state: "It strikes me, that it would be a good stroke of policy . . . if we could form a treaty with England, giving her certain privileges in the cotton trade and vast navigation in return for which she could stand by the South and crush the Free Soilers between Canada and the United States."[5] Late in 1860 false rumors circulated in the North that an understanding already existed between Southern leaders and Napoleon, which amounted to an offensive and defensive alliance.[6] Though quite unrealistic in its conception, the suggestion of an offensive operation with the help of a foreign ally had at least constituted a recognition of the advisability of some advanced planning, so badly neglected by the Confederates when they actually broke away from the Union.

As far back as March, 1858, Eugène de Sartiges wrote to his foreign minister that in his judgment secession could not be effected without civil war. The French consul at Richmond, Virginia, and other informed diplomats shared this view late in 1860.[7] These foreigners failed to see how the federal government could possibly permit the rupture of the Union without making a valiant effort to preserve it at all costs. Unlike the emotionally involved Southerners, Europeans made penetrating and detached inquiries into the likely foreign political

foreign minister, New Orleans, June 1, 1853, Correspondance Commerciale, New Orleans, 12.

5. Charles Henry Ambler (ed.) , "Correspondence of Robert M. T. Hunter, 1826–1876" in American Historical Association, *Annual Report, 1916* (Washington, D. C., 1918) , II, 145.

6. Ticknor doubted the existence of such an understanding, but he believed "it may come with time." Ticknor, *Life, Letters, and Journals,* II, 430–32.

7. Sartiges to Walewski, Washington, March 2, 1858, CPEU, CXVIII. See also Alfred Paul to Thouvenel, Richmond, December 22, 1860, "Reports of Alfred Paul, 1860–61" (Virginia State Library) , No. 22992.

impact of the contemplated Southern Confederacy. Had the advocates of secession, for instance, been familiar with the geopolitical analysis of the European publicist Julius Fröbel, published in 1859, many of their delusions about the European powers might have been dispelled.[8] Fröbel rejected the simplistic notion of prejudiced Europeans that the rupture of the American republic would remove the twofold challenge it posed to Europe as a major economic competitor and as the successful symbol of republicanism. Should the South triumph over the North and the federal Union be divided, according to Fröbel, it was by no means a foregone conclusion that Europe's interests would be furthered. One could reasonably predict that both former regions of the United States would feel compelled to secure their common frontier militarily and that they would furthermore compete with each other in an effort to accelerate their economic productivity. Soon, this analyst argued, Europe would find itself confronted by two American republics whose combined productivity and might would constitute a greater challenge than it faced before the split. It also stood to reason that the momentum of their internal expansion would eventually lead to their external expansion; the North moving northward, and the South southward. It is of course impossible to determine how much the leaders of Europe were influenced by these analytical comments. But since foresight is one of the essential marks of statesmanship, it is noteworthy that neither the French nor the British governments actively sought the division of the Union. Had they thought it to their advantage, they would hardly have hesitated to avail themselves of the many opportunities to pursue such a course before and after the outbreak of hostilities. According to an old Chinese proverb, wars are decided before they begin. In view of the total perspective of the diplomacy of the American Civil War, these thoughts about it prior to its eruption are extraordinarily intriguing.

8. Fröbel, *Amerika*, pp. 37–46.

Whatever resentments Napoleon III harbored against the American republic, many of whose citizens had vilified him personally and mercilessly criticized his imperial policies,[9] he still took no decisive action to help bring about the victory of the Confederacy. Tempted to cut down the American giant and to humble those republicans who would have liked to see his throne in flames, the emperor nevertheless helped save the Union through his relative inaction. He did not go out of his way to demonstrate his friendly attitude toward the United States by unequivocally informing the Confederates that to gain their independence they must rely on themselves. The North, of course, had no right to expect him to go that far. After all, where would such an undiplomatic statement have left him in case of a Confederate victory? It was quite a different matter for France and Great Britain to indicate that the military outcome of the war would decide the question of recognition for them. This procedure had not only the virtue of impartiality, quite in accordance with their declarations of neutrality, but also of postponing their ultimate decision. In the meantime they did not violate their neutrality by recognizing the belligerent status of the Confederacy once Lincoln had proclaimed the blockade of Southern ports.

Thinking in the first instance about the disruptive effect of the war on their respective economies, the governments of the two European powers had come to an early verbal understanding to coordinate their Civil War policies.[10] Accordingly, the French emperor limited his freedom of action when he persistently refused to intervene, unless joined by Great Britain.

9. Gazley, *German Unification,* pp. 232–320; see also Elizabeth Brett White, *American Opinion of France from Lafayette to Poincaré* (New York, 1927).

10. William L. Dayton, the United States minister to France, was concerned about this understanding because "the *entente cordiale* with England is so much more important to France than her relations to the United States, that she would not hesitate, if necessary, to sacrifice us to retain it." Dayton to Seward, Paris, July 13, 1861, DDFDS.

Persuaded by his foreign ministers, Thouvenel and Drouyn de Lhuys, to exercise this prudence as a reinsurance against any international embarrassments growing out of independent action, it followed logically that Napoleon III was willing to accept Britain's leadership in this issue. In spite of the emperor's activities in Mexico, America clearly occupied a subordinate place in French foreign policy. It was Great Britain, not France, that in the last analysis charted Europe's course with respect to the Civil War in America and consequently was in a position to decide whether there should be two North American republics or one.

As might be expected, this decision was as much influenced by Britain's relations with France as by those with the United States. If the British government had determined to offer its good offices to the two American belligerents, to raise the blockade, or to recognize the Confederacy, the French government could have fully supported these British initiatives, because at given times they actually coincided with the dispositions of the French government. Napoleon's mediation effort in the fall of 1862, on the other hand, was rejected by the British because, ostensibly, they judged it to be premature. Actually, the interests of France and Great Britain in the American Civil War were related to their respective interests in the Western hemisphere. And, in turn, the stronger power with more extensive interests was destined to prevail in policy decisions respecting this war. More than that, its considerable stakes in the New World provided Britain with the motivation for protecting them alone, if necessary. Its defense of Canada and the West Indies influenced British policy as much as the profitable Anglo-American trade and heavy investments in the United States.[11] It was not surprising, moreover, that at a time when Anglo-Saxon ascendency caused Frenchmen to be apprehensive, long-range cultural and strategic factors also tipped the British scale in favor of the United

11. Blumenthal, "Confederate Diplomacy," pp. 166–68.

States. With the exception of the significant Franco-American
trade and holdings in the West Indies, the French stake in the
hemisphere simply did not justify an outright and, if necessary, independent challenge of the United States. When Napoleon III decided to enhance his influence on the American
continent by establishing a Catholic Latin monarchy in Mexico, he learned in the process that he had offended the Mexi-
cans, antagonized the Americans, and aroused the suspicions
of his entente partner. Great Britain had, of course, no intention of helping the French emperor build an empire in the
Western hemisphere. Though in some respects French and
British interests in the New World overlapped, they were altogether too divergent to have permitted an over-all coordination of policies. Anglo-French cooperation on such issues as
the recognition of the Confederacy's belligerency, the *Trent*
affair, and other maritime problems was largely of a technical
nature. Coordination between the British and the French of
their Civil War policies actually served more as a check on
France and Britain than on the United States.

The Civil War in America presented Napoleon with so
many difficulties that he found it impossible to cope with
them to the satisfaction of anyone, probably including himself. He and his wife, Empress Eugénie, sympathized personally with the Confederate cause and seemed for a long time
convinced that the rupture of the Union would be permanent.
But many matters of state compelled him in the meantime to
respect the integrity of the United States. In addition to Anglo-French conflicts of interests, the French emperor also had
to keep his eye on the attitudes of Russia, Prussia, and Austria
concerning the conflict in America and to consider their bearing on continental European policies. In this analysis Napoleon III could not ignore Russia's relations with the United
States. A Russo-American combination might in the future
become a genuine threat to the independence of the various
continental European states. On the other hand, an under-

standing between France, Russia, and the United States, with
France assuming the role of moderating middleman, would
not only establish French supremacy in Western Europe, it
would also cut England down to size. If, as Fröbel did not
doubt, Napoleon was aware of these larger questions of diplomatic strategy, he needed the cooperation and good will of the
Northern states even more than those of the South.[12] He could
ill afford, moreover, to risk losing the American market, an almost certain long-range consequence of any unilateral French
intervention. Surrounded by advisers, some of whom counseled a prudently neutral course, while others recommended
intervention favoring the Confederacy, Napoleon also had to
take cognizance of the similarly divided opinions of the
French people.

Among those Frenchmen who hoped that their government
would not do anything to hurt the cause of the federal Union
were republicans and monarchists, conservatives and liberals,
ordinary workingmen and the elite of the French intelligent-
sia. The traditional bonds between the two nations and deep-
rooted antislavery sentiments headed the list of arguments
prompting these people to side with the North. Their spokesmen reminded their compatriots that it was self-interest that
had motivated France in its contributions to the independence and grandeur of the United States. Nothing had
changed in this respect.[13] France still needed the United States
as a counterweight to British sea power and as an attractive
market for its goods. France, they proclaimed confidently, had
nothing to fear from a friendly, though mighty, United
States. Its industrious people, wrote Agénor de Gasparin,
"know how to make a noble use of their fortune" and is likely

12. Julius Fröbel, *Theorie der Politik, als Ergebnis einer erneuerten
Prüfung demokratischer Lehrmeinungen* (Vienna, 1864) , II, 338.
13. A. E. de Gasparin, *L'Amérique devant l'Europe* (Paris, 1879) , pp.
398–405.

to contribute generously to the welfare of mankind.[14] To many Frenchmen America represented the avant-garde of human progress. They admired America's religious and individual freedom, its philanthropic practices, its ingenious scientific applications, and its industrial and commercial resourcefulness. Instead of war and intervention, they advised their government to capitalize on America's future by promoting the most active collaboration between Frenchmen and Americans in trade, finance, and technology.[15]

These Frenchmen abhorred the existence of slavery, especially in an otherwise enlightened modern society, and they were willing to make sacrifices for the sake of its abolition.[16] Since the Confederates unhesitatingly admitted that "slavery is the cornerstone of the Southern edifice," French workers, like those of England, decided they would rather tighten their belts than lend support to the American slave owners. Somehow they could not understand why Lincoln issued the Emancipation Proclamation so late and as a war measure of limited scope. In any case, they denied that the Southern slave society possessed the elements of a nation entitled to recognition by the civilized community. Voluntary abolition of slavery in exchange for Northern compensation, suggested Le Temps, would be the only reasonable basis for a compromise solution.[17] Taking an extremely broad view of races in general, however, Gasparin advanced the theory that the Latin races,

14. A. E. de Gasparin, The Uprising of a Great People, trans. Mary L. Booth (New York, 1862), pp. 55–56, 71.

15. Emile Carrey, Grandeur et Avenir des États-Unis (Paris, 1863), pp. 9–10. See also Gabriel Hanotaux, Études diplomatiques: La Politique de l'Équilibre, 1907–1911 (Paris, 1914), p. 227.

16. Gilbert Chinard, L'Amérique d'Abraham Lincoln et la France (Washington, D.C., 1945), p. 26. See also Samuel Bernstein, Essays in Political and Intellectual History (New York, 1955), pp. 128–33; and Serge Gavronsky, "American Slavery and the French Liberals–An Interpretation of the Role of Slavery in French Politics During the Second Empire," Journal of Negro History, LI (1966), 45–46.

17. Le Temps, July 10 and 14, 1863.

who tended toward excessive centralization at the expense of the individual, should welcome the counterbalancing tendency of the Americans, who stressed individual responsibility. Of particular significance was Gasparin's conclusion that the solidarity of the Anglo-Saxons would not permit Britain to see the United States weakened and divided. Britain, he contended, needed America as much to balance the world's races as France needed it to balance British sea power. Concerned about the growing alienation between France and the United States, one French newspaper, *L'Opinion Nationale,* in its issue of July 19, 1864, raised the question to whom France could turn, if not the United States, "in case English aristocracy thought it useful to join a European alliance against her." And, as a final sampling of French public opinion favoring the Union's cause, the persuasive and pragmatic arguments of Édouard Laboulaye, a prominent French jurist and historian, have left their imprint on history.[18] What would Frenchmen say and do, asked Laboulaye, if a province or two of France decided to secede? Would they not fight to preserve the integrity of France? Can there be any doubt how Frenchmen would react if in such a contingency foreign powers projected themselves, however well intentioned, into such a domestic calamity? Have the advocates of recognition, he questioned pertinently, given any thought to the obvious need on the part of an independent South to rely on British ships and credits and that Britain rather than France would benefit from these developments?

Frenchmen who were enthusiastically rooting for the victory of the Confederacy, among them the bulk of the Catholic clergy and the traditional foes of republicanism, naturally presented a different set of arguments.[19] To them, the slavery

---

18. Edouard Laboulaye, *Upon Whom Rests the Guilt of the War?* (New York, 1863) .

19. Among others, see E. Sain de Boislecomte *De la crise américaine et celles des nationalités en Europe* (Paris, 1862) , p. 61; Emile Nouette-De-

issue was primarily a domestic matter and one in which the hypocritical treatment of Negroes by the North would in all fairness have to be as much considered as the system of enforced servitude in the South. These Frenchmen wanted their government to take the initiative in recognizing the Confederacy's independent national existence, so convincingly demonstrated by its capacity to prosecute a difficult war. To them, the permanent dissolution of the United States would be a blessing to the peace of the world and diminish the chances of a more terrible international war against them in the future. For they looked upon the American republic as a disturber of the existing social and institutional order of the world and as an undesirably aggressive economic and geopolitical menace in the future. They also paid attention to broader racial questions when they stressed the historically closer kinship between the populations of France and the South, paralleling the greater affinity between Anglo-Saxon Yankees and the British. Looking backward, they recalled that it was the North that opposed the war against Great Britain in 1812 and that Northern papers were particularly unfriendly during the Crimean War. What had the United States ever done for France, they asked, to merit recognition at this time when Northern money, munitions, and weapons were helping the forces of Juarez fight France in Mexico? Prolongation of the bloody Civil War, they cautioned in 1862, threatened to compromise the peace of the world and to spread the seeds of revolution. Were not these potential dangers alone sufficient ground for the emperor to intervene?

On the whole, the French press was about equally divided in its leanings. Since its occasionally mercenary nature facilitated the purchase of editorial opinions, it could not be regarded as a reliable barometer of public opinion.[20] To com-

---

lorme, *Les États-Unis et l'Europe* (Paris, 1863), p. 18; and Lacouture, *Mémoire*, pp. 7–14.

20. Charles P. Cullop, "Edwin de Leon, Jefferson Davis Propagandist,"

plicate the French government's task, its representatives in the United States were by and large prejudiced against the federal republic and seemed always prepared to say a few unkind words about Secretary of State William H. Seward. It must have been refreshing to Édouard Thouvenel and Eugène Rouher, two members of the cabinet holding divergent views, to read the private and official correspondence they received from the French consul in Boston, Jean Étienne Souchard. Unlike the French minister in the United States, Édouard-Henri Mercier, in the fall of 1861 Souchard thought it prudent not ro rush into recognizing the South or lifting the blockade.[21] He soberly judged the financial ability of the North to prosecute the war without going into bankruptcy, and by February, 1864, he informed Rouher that the South had lost and could at best postpone the inevitable outcome. By comparison, Mercier recommended as early as on March 29, 1861, recognition of the Confederacy. Time and again he reiterated his biased opinion that the rupture was final and that the old Union could never be re-established. Through his closeness to Southern senators he had been taken into their confidence during the critical weeks after Lincoln's election. Mercier sympathized with their early schemes, not only with that of an independent Confederacy of Southern States, but with the idea of a confederacy of all the states of the Union, except New England, which, together with Canada, was to become a part of the British Empire. His relationship with Seward was distant and at times strained, though always frank and courteous. Charles Sumner, the Chairman of the Senate Foreign Relations Committee, once snapped his finger at Mercier when he told him how mistaken the French minister was in his estimate that a permanent division of the country was

---

Civil War History, VIII (1962) , 398.

21. Souchard to Thouvenel, Boston, September 17, 1861, Correspondance Commerciale, Boston, 7; and French consul to Rouher, Boston, January 20, 1862, and February 27, 1864, Papiers Eugène Rouher (Archives Nationales) , 45 AP, carton 3.

inevitable.[22] Mercier probably thought he was being helpful
and constructive when on his unauthorized visit to Richmond
late in April, 1862, he inquired whether an economic union
of the Confederate and United States were feasible. Not having been instructed by his government to make this inquiry,
which, by the way, violated the strict neutrality of France, the
envoy felt doubly embarrassed when Judah Benjamin, the
Confederate secretary of state, dismissed the idea out of hand.
Mercier probably returned from the Confederate capital with
a slightly more realistic understanding of the situation, for in
his report to Thouvenel, dated May 6, 1862, he admitted that
the South's free-trade offer, in exchange for an offensive Fran-
co-Confederate alliance, would not really be profitable.[23]
France not only lacked the ships to take advantage of this
offer, it also would have to do business with an impoverished
customer. Finally he realized that "the North contributes to
our industrial prosperity." Thouvenel did not need this
reminder to insist on his continued advocacy of strict neutrality. His successor, Édouard Drouyn de Lhuys, though originally inclined towards mediation, later saw the wisdom of this
course also.[24] Mercier's promotion, toward the end of 1864, to
the ministerial post at Madrid occurred too late in the Civil
War to have an effect on diplomatic relations between Paris
and Washington. An ardent believer in monarchical institutions and more comfortable in the polished and intellectual
atmosphere of upper-class European society than in the mid-
dle-class society of the common man's republic, Mercier had

22. E. T. Welles (ed.), *The Diary of Gideon Welles* (Boston; 1911), I,
494–95.
23. Mercier to Thouvenel, Washington, April 28 and May 6, 1862,
CPEU, CXXVII.
24. Thouvenel to Mercier, Paris, May 15, 1862, CPEU, CXXVII; see also
Warren F. Spencer, "Édouard Drouyn de Lhuys and the Foreign Policy of
the Second Empire" (Unpublished Ph.D. dissertation, University of
Pennsylvania, 1955); and Martin B. Duberman, *Charles Francis Adams,
1807–1866* (Boston, 1961), p. 296.

never been an ideal choice for the post in Washington.[25] If he was not anti-Union, he certainly was mentally prepared to accept disunion. To make matters worse, according to the observations of a seasoned French publicist, the other members of the French Legation circulated among themselves instead of trying to feel the political pulse of the American people.[26] When the Confederacy collapsed, their main regret was that France had made a mistake when it failed to recognize the Confederacy, even at the risk of war, shortly after the establishment of the Confederate government.

Dr. Thomas W. Evans, the American dentist at the Imperial Court, was undoubtedly correct when he observed that the emperor "was never unwilling to hear the other side."[27] Yet Mercier shared and confirmed the emperor's mixed feelings about the United States, and Napoleon's decisions concerning the Civil War and the Mexican question were more a reflection of his own views than those of "the other side." Both Napoleon and Mercier shared a certain contempt for republican institutions, an admiration for Southern society, and a not-so-secret desire for the triumph of the cotton empire. Both feared that the steadily increasing economic and political power of the United States might in time replace Europe as the center of the world, and both were therefore tempted to decelerate this evil trend by being mentally ready to accept secession as a *fait accompli*. Napoleon felt bitter about the Young Americans, who never permitted him to forget the manner in which the president of the Second Republic had become the emperor of the Second Empire. If he felt personally uncomfortable at being called a usurper, he was resolutely determined to repel the attempts—in no manner sanctioned by the American government—to undermine his im-

25. Seward to Dayton, Washington, January 4, 1864, FIDS, 16.
26. Charles A. de Chambrun, *Impressions of Lincoln and the Civil War —A Foreigner's Account* (New York, 1952) , pp. 29–31.
27. Henry Rainey, *Dr. Thomas Evans—America's Dentist to European Royalty* (Philadelphia, 1956) , p. 26.

perial throne. From his point of view, it was already deplorable that republicanism in Europe derived much of its inspiration and some of its support from America. In view of Lincoln's contention that the preservation of the Union was a test of the viability of democratic institutions, the Civil War afforded Napoleon an excellent opportunity to break the momentum of the rising power of the United States as well as that of republicanism. But instead of accomplishing these goals directly by extending to the Confederacy all the diplomatic, material, and even military assistance it needed to secure its independence, the emperor chose the indirect tactic of setting up a puppet empire in Mexico. Initially, this move boosted the morale of the Southern people and alarmed the North because it was potentially capable of forcing closer cooperation between France and the Confederacy, but, ironically, it did much to ruin whatever chances existed for Franco-Southern cooperation. Britain's unfavorable reaction to Napoleon's ambitious scheme had the effect of deterring the emperor from cooperating with the Confederacy via the back door of Mexico, if indeed he planned to go that far. In the end, the prudently firm policy of the Lincoln administration and the developing French fiasco in Mexico gradually taught the French government to be much more cautious in its American policies than it had been at the outset. By 1864 it was resigned to maintaining its neutrality in the American Civil War in exchange for the neutrality of the United States in the conflict between France and Mexico.

Moving from the general framework to the specifics within which French policies operated, one finds again a bewildering dualism and frequent fluctuations. Aside from the convenient shield of neutrality, the French government evidently improvised its policy on the Civil War in a haphazard fashion. When the Secession Ordinances signaled the dissolution of the American republic, the emperor deplored this turn of events in his conversation with Charles J. Faulkner, the Virginian who then represented the United States in France. But a year later Napoleon III told Lord Cowley, the British ambassador in Paris: "England will never find a more favourable occasion to abase the pride of Americans or to establish her influence in the new world."[28] When Lincoln proclaimed the blockade of the Confederacy in April, 1861, France and Great Britain promptly and quite legitimately recognized the belligerency of the Confederate States, very much to the annoyance of Lincoln's administration. Although this technicality did not constitute recognition of these states or a preliminary to it, it nevertheless seemed to justify the Confederacy's high hopes in that direction. Early in May, the French government instructed Mercier not to leave the American government in the dark concerning its eagerness to be of assistance on behalf of peace and union.[29] But within a month the emperor confided to Lord Cowley his innermost personal feelings by proposing joint Anglo-French recognition of the South. When the British ambassador doubted the wisdom of such precipitate action, Napoleon dropped the seventh veil of his mind and declared that "he could not forget the overbearing insolence of the United States Government in its days of prosperity and hoped that they [sic] might receive a lesson."[30] Sensing this hostile disposition of the French sovereign, Secretary of State Seward officially issued the historic warning, "Let her avoid giving any countenance to treason against this Government."[31] Foreign intervention, he cautioned, would never be forgiven by the American people.

Although President Lincoln had to assume the final responsibility for American foreign policy and indeed played his full part in its formulation, he left its implementation and execu-

28. V. Wellesley and R. Sencourt, *Conversations with Napoleon III* (London, 1934), p. 192.
29. Thouvenel to Mercier, Paris, May 11, 1861, FNTDS, 18.
30. Wellesley and Sencourt, *Conversations*, p. 198.
31. Seward to Mercier, Washington, May 23, 1861, FNFDS.

tion to his skillful secretary of state.[32] As a key figure on the
contemporary international scene, Seward occupied a position
that compelled the attention of the leaders of the French government. The combination of Seward's bluntness, resourcefulness, and firmness puzzled and at times frightened them as
much as the British. This was precisely the impression the secretary wanted to convey to them. When the news of his April
1 recommendation to the president was leaked, the very
thought of an international war as a diversionary maneuver
to prevent the outbreak of civil war seemed to border on sheer
madness. But it was Seward's dramatic way of telling Europeans not to trifle with the United States, now or in the future, or they would face complications of the utmost gravity,
both of an economic and military nature. For the next four
years, and particularly during the crucially important first two
years of his tenure as secretary of state, Seward tried to scare
France and Britain enough to cause them at least to have second thoughts before deciding to intervene in the conflict in
one way or another.

Since these two European powers evidently had agreed to
coordinate their Civil War policies, Seward tried everything
in his power to drive a wedge between them. He refused to
receive them jointly in the State Department and he was usually more emphatic in his conversations with Mercier than in
those with Lord Lyons. He left neither of them in doubt,
however, about the Lincoln administration's resolution to
preserve the Union, whatever the sacrifice. On the positive
side, he naturally radiated his confidence in the unquestiona-
ble ability of the North to restore the federal Union fully intact. Europe's interests and obligations, he never tired of
reminding its envoys, clearly coincided with those of the North,
unless they wished to see the American continent again become a theater of operations for rival European powers, upsetting the balance of power so vital to their own security.

32. Chambrun, *Impressions of Lincoln*, p. 47.

Seward did not hesitate to declare categorically that secession constituted insurrection and that the federal government would not tolerate any interference in this domestic affair, including even the intimation of good offices. Any violation of their strict neutrality, he warned, would bring forth stern retaliation. Recognition of the Confederacy could never end the war. And in case of military intervention, he threatened fire, revolution, and war. If the United States had to go down, it would go down fighting to the last, dragging its enemies down with it! Whether Seward could have carried out his blustering threats was really less relevant than that he made them. As a consummate international poker player, he deliberately raised the cost of intervention so high as to discourage any test of his threats. Using this strategy without moral scruples, he had under the circumstances little to lose and much to gain, even in spite of some of the embarrassing military reverses the North had suffered.

If Seward could be tough and appeared to be reckless, the manner in which he disposed of the *Trent* affair late in 1861 demonstrated the surprising flexibility and sober perspective of his mind. Asked to release the two Southern commissioners, Mason and Slidell, who had been removed, apparently illegally, from a British ship, the Lincoln administration faced a major international crisis fraught with the danger of an Anglo-American war. The international community overwhelmingly agreed that in this incident the American captain had been guilty of violating the rights of neutrals. Without first verifying it, England and France had quickly jumped to the erroneous conclusion that the federal government had authorized Captain Wilkes' action. Also, such smaller powers as Austria and Prussia, who dreaded the prospect of an Anglo-American war, which might encourage Napoleon to pursue his objectives in Europe while England was tied down in America,[33] condemned the seizure of the commissioners as a

33. Ralph Lutz, *Die Beziehungen zwischen Deutschland und den Verei-*

breach of international law. But the apprehensions of these nations turned out to be unfounded. Thouvenel informed Mercier on December 3, 1861, that "after careful reflection the Emperor's Government could not remain wholly silent."[34] It was disturbed because the United States had violated the principles of neutrality it had heretofore championed. William L. Dayton, the American minister to France, learned from Baron Rothschild on December 5 that France would most certainly stay out of an Anglo-American war. On the next day Thouvenel confirmed this information in the course of a conversation with Dayton but added significantly that in this instance the moral force of France would be against the United States.[35] The notion of some overconfident American citizens that France would be on their country's side and against Britain, its traditional enemy, had of course no realistic foundation.[36] Had the French government taken such a position, the federal government might well have considered submitting the *Trent* affair to arbitration, as Lincoln would have preferred, instead of honoring Britain's demand for the release of Mason and Slidell, as Seward was resigned to doing.[37] If arbitration had been decided upon, France would have been the only major power acceptable to both sides as arbitrator. Having already rendered its verdict, France had for all practical purposes removed itself as a referee, and by doing so it helped persuade the Lincoln administration to adopt Seward's alternative. The avoidance of an Anglo-American war brought universal relief. France earned Britain's gratitude for its support in this crisis and, according to the French consul in Boston, Jean Étienne

---

nigten Staaten während des Sezessionskrieges (Heidelberg, 1911), p. 67; see also *Berliner Nationalzeitung*, December 3 and 31, 1861; and Sister M. Claire Lynch, *The Diplomatic Mission of John Lothrop Motley to Austria, 1861–67* (Washington, D.C., 1944), pp. 75 ff.

34. CPEU, CXXV.

35. Dayton to Seward, Paris, December 5 and 6, 1861, DDFDS.

36. *Ibid.*, December 24, 1861.

37. For a recent analysis of this affair, see Lynn M. Case, "La France et l'affaire du 'Trent,'" *Revue Historique* (1961), pp. 57–86.

Souchard, its popularity rose in proportion to the decline of that of Britain.[38] In the perspective of history, the editorial comment of *Le Temps* about the peaceful liquidation of this episode was particularly noteworthy. Praising the wisdom of America's decision to swallow its pride a little, the editors of this newspaper said that as a result of it the United States had gained in stature. "The international prestige of Washington," they commented, "has been fully restored."[39]

On the day before Christmas, 1861, the emperor and his wife granted a lengthy audience to an outstanding American prelate, Archbishop John Hughes of New York. The highly respected Catholic dignitary took advantage of this occasion to implore the emperor to use his prestigious influence on behalf of Anglo-American peace. But the archbishop had not come to Paris to pursue this particular mission. He had in fact been sent by Lincoln and Seward to promote a better understanding of the situation in the United States among French Catholics. As devout Catholics, Their Majesties, who had taken a keen interest in the ugly prejudices of the Know-Nothing movement, were pleased to learn about the progress of the Catholic Church in the Northern part of the United States. Archbishop Hughes pointed out to them how much he and the federal government deplored the widely circulated exaggerations about the persecution of American Catholics, when in reality the future of Catholicism in the United States looked much brighter in the North than in the South. Remembering that Empress Eugénie was of Spanish descent and worried about rumors ascribing to the United States designs on Cuba, the American prelate did not miss this opportunity to impress upon his listeners that the Confederates were much more likely to incorporate Catholic Cuba than the Protestant

38. Flahaut to Thouvenel, London, January 11, 1862, CP Angleterre (AMAE), Vol. DCCXXI; and French consul to Rouher, Boston, January 20, 1862, Papiers Eugène Rouher (Archives Nationales).

39. *Le Temps,* January 11, 1862.

Yankees. Hughes proved himself to be an effective good-will ambassador. In his talks with the cardinals of the French Empire and the bishops of many districts he tried his best to win friends for the Northern cause and to reduce the Catholic pressures the Lincoln administration feared might push Napoleon into the arms of the Confederacy.[40]

In spite of the known reservoir of good will the Confederacy possessed among the ranks of the French clergy, Jefferson Davis waited until the spring of 1864 before he sent Bishop Patrick N. Lynch of Charleston to Europe, entrusting him with the confidential mission of pressing for recognition as best he could.[41] The poor bishop arrived in France three years too late to try to secure the backing that might at best have been extended to a victorious Confederacy. Napoleon's religious loyalties did not shape his Civil War policy. In regard to the slavery question, we know from an inside source that the emperor believed it was only an apparent, not an underlying, cause of the war. In his judgment, the clash had been brought to a head by the conflict of interests between the Northern and Southern states.[42] French and British citizens were infinitely more disturbed by the South's peculiar institution than their respective governments. In contrast to the widespread opposition to it on the part of the French public, the French government treated slavery as a matter of local concern. As far as the emperor was concerned, this socioeconomic issue would not and should not determine his Civil War policy, even though he loathed the idea of a state whose cornerstone was slavery.[43] And like Great Britain, France decided that the legal questions arising out of the originally quite ineffective blockade should not be stretched to the

40. Blumenthal, *Reappraisal*, pp. 131–32.

41. See *The Catholic Banner*, Charleston, S.C., December 4, 1960.

42. L. F. Alfred Maury, "Souvenirs d'un homme de lettres" (Unpublished manuscript, Institut de France, MS 2650), IV, 223–25.

43. Thomas W. Evans, *Memoirs: The Second French Empire* (New York, 1905), p. 138.

breaking point because the precedents established in this war might be of advantage in future wars. French and British admirals therefore rationalized that the blockade proclaimed by the North was "not ineffective enough" to justify official protests against it. Considerations involving religion, slavery, and international law did not provide adequate motivations for French intervention in the Civil War.

Economic pressures, on the other hand, seemed to demand an early end of the war. Economic dislocations brought about by the disruption of normal trade, vitally important to communities engaged in the production of such French specialties as silks, laces, hats, and china, caused serious hardships to manufacturers and workers alike. Above all else, the developing depression in the cotton industry, it was feared, might reach paralyzing proportions and affect the entire economy. The longer the war lasted, the more unbearable became the realization that almost a million Frenchmen depended for their livelihood on the uninterrupted supply of Southern raw cotton. The political ramifications of this state of affairs were certain to be weighed by the French government in its domestic and foreign policies. For the spread of unemployment and the discontent of large numbers of people introduced one element of instability almost as disturbing and unpredictable as the possible consequences resulting from the lifting of the blockade or the recognition of the Confederacy. Many petitions and reports reaching Paris spelled out the distress in the provinces and called for remedial action. Michel Chevalier, the influential French economist, thought so highly of Richard Cobden's approach to the deteriorating cotton crisis that he asked Rouher in a letter, dated July 23, 1862, to explore it personally with Cobden.[44] The British free-trader recommended a maritime convention with the United States by which certain specified ports would not be blockaded in order

44. Michel Chevalier to Rouher, Paris, July 23, 1862, Papiers Eugène Rouher (Archives Nationales) , 45 AP, Carton 3.

to permit the resumption of cotton shipments to Europe. Cobden looked upon this suggestion as a corollary of the American-sponsored proposition granting full protection to private property on the high seas. James M. Mason, the Confederate commissioner in London, had pledged his full cooperation to Cobden, who felt that the North would have to yield to firm Anglo-French representation on this matter. By then, however, Northern control of New Orleans opened port facilities to French ships, and the Southern strategy of burning cotton in order to force the great maritime powers to lift the blockade altogether became an overriding issue. Trying to goad France into a conflict with the United States, the Confederate government offered it generous inducements. If French ships would bring European supplies to Confederate ports, they would have all the cotton they needed. But France, which found war too high a price to pay for cotton, intensified its search for other sources of supply, besides making greater use of such alternatives as linen, hemp, silk, and wool. If the shortage of cotton had become so acute and the economic effects of the American Civil War on the French economy so disastrous as to force the French government into intervention, as many personalities in the entourage of the emperor claimed, why, then, didn't it take measures necessary for the protection of its vital interests? An analysis of basic facts supplies the answer to this essential question. Significantly, French manufacturers had bought so much cotton between 1859 and 1861 that they had an oversupply of this raw material on hand. Their warehouses and stores were glutted with cotton goods. And with the exception of the year 1862, when the imports of cotton reached a low point, after 1861 manufacturers managed to purchase enough cotton to meet their needs. But if there was no serious interruption of the flow of American cotton to France what accounted for the depression in the French textile industry? Basically, the obsolescence of French textile machines and old-fashioned methods of production prevented the French from competing with the modernized and more efficient British textile industry. The Cobden Treaty of 1860, by which British cotton goods could after October, 1861, enter France at moderate tariff rates would admittedly have created a textile depression in France had the American Civil War not taken place.[45] Well informed about this actual state of affairs, Secretary of State Seward had all along discounted French complaints about the blockade. In spite of the war in America and the economic dislocations it created, Frenchmen succeeded in redressing the temporary decline in Franco-American trade by increasing their business transactions with Great Britain. This over-all picture, of course, offered no consolation to those Frenchmen whose individual plight could in part be attributed to the war. The silk industry of Lyons, the lace producers of Mirecourt, the hat makers of Bordeaux, and the china manufacturers of Limoges were among those French industries and communities who felt the impact of the sharp decline in Franco-American trade more severely than those less dependent on the American market. It was sheer political expediency, on the part of the French government, however, to put the blame on the United States for conditions that could be traced to shortcomings in the French economy.

Thus, economic considerations did not really justify French intervention, though they were the most plausible pretext the French government could advance in its hints and soundings relating to recognition. Until 1864 John Slidell, the Confederate commissioner in Paris, did not give up hope of its eventual extension. This hope had some factual foundation. The emperor was accessible to Slidell and Empress Eugénie's equally friendly treatment of Mrs. Slidell kept the commissioner in close touch with the source of power in France.

45. Claude Fohlen, "La Guerre de Sécession et le Commerce Franco-Américaine," *Revue d'histoire moderne et contemporaine,* VIII (1961), 259–70; see also Blumenthal, *Reappraisal,* pp. 153–56.

Napoleon's disposition appeared to him to be most promising, although Dr. Evans, the emperor's American dentist who was also close to the throne, received the opposite impression. In any case, Slidell did not succeed in developing more than a distant relationship with Foreign Minister Thouvenel, whom he tried vainly to convince that recognition would end the war. Thouvenel's analysis was legalistic and logical. He acknowledged the federal government's right to crush the insurrection, but he doubted that it possessed the power to suppress it and to re-establish the old Union. He counseled against premature recognition, lest it backfire and force France into an undesirable and unnecessary war. "Mexico, the American question, and the Roman developments," he protested, "that is truly too much!"[46] Recognition prior to a clear-cut military decision entailed risks he insisted France must avoid taking. Once the Confederacy won the war, not just battles, recognition would follow as a matter of course and be universal. Rigidly adhering to the alliance with Britain, he opposed any French intervention without British participation in it. When Napoleon III notified Thouvenel on October 15, 1862, that he had decided to replace him as foreign minister, the United States had reason to be gravely concerned,[47] for this was the time that might have gone down in history as the crucial turning point in the war.

After the impressive Southern victory in the Second Battle of Bull Run (August 29–30, 1862), Napoleon launched a major mediation effort, evidently hoping against hope that both belligerents would accept mediation in spite of their firm declarations to the contrary. He asked the governments

46. L. Thouvenel, *Le secret de l'empereur—correspondance confidentielle et inédite échangée entre M. Thouvenel, le Duc de Gramont et le Général Comte de Flahaut, 1860–1863* (Paris, 1889), II, 414 ff.; see also Dayton to Seward, Paris, September 13 and October 2, 1862, DDFDS.

47. Richard Korolewicz-Carlton, "Napoléon III, Thouvenel et la guerre de sécession" (Unpublished Ph.D. dissertation, Université de Paris, 1951), pp. 187–88.

in London and St. Petersburg to join him in a move to bring representatives of the two American governments to the conference table. Once that was accomplished, the belligerents were to be left completely free to discuss terms that would end their ruinous conflict. As in the past, Great Britain's response would determine the success or failure of Napoleon's endeavor. The wavering attitude of several members of the British Cabinet seemed to foreshadow success and to belie the existence of a secret understanding between Lord Russell and Secretary Seward, of which Benjamin Disraeli claimed to have knowledge. Would the British government continue to wait and see and do nothing that might possibly weaken the efforts of those Northerners who were striving for peace? Would it no longer be deterred by the Liberals, headed by John Bright, who strongly opposed giving aid and comfort to the Southern slavocracy? Would it abandon all the international arguments that had heretofore restrained it from any intervention? Or would it this time give its assent to a move likely to lead to the permanent independence of the Confederate States of America? Lord Palmerston scheduled a special cabinet meeting for October 23 to discuss, and perhaps decide, these questions. Confidence filled the air in Paris and Richmond and uneasiness prevailed in Washington until Britain and Russia rejected Napoleon's overtures. The British decision to stay out of the Civil War was undoubtedly influenced by a change for the better in the military fortunes of the North and by Lord Russell's conviction that no combination of powers should in any way impose a pacification that only the parties directly involved could effectively accomplish. That Palmerston and other members of the Cabinet[48]—for a moment even Lord Russell—were at all contemplating a reversal of their American

48. See Elihu Washburne's dispatch No. 470, dated Paris, 21, 1871, DDFDS. That "the want of sympathy of the United States during the Crimean War" was one of the more important reasons for Britain's policy with respect to the American Civil War seems somewhat specious. See Hamilton Fish Papers, "Diary," V, September 17, 1875 (LC).

policy admittedly weakens all retrospective theses in justification of Britain's actual nonintervention. But it also lends
strength to the conclusion that Britain's crucially important
rejection of Napoleon's initiative does after all confirm the
merit of these theses and suggests additional ones. Britain's inaction had the effect of favoring the North, although it was
not intended to do so. In view of the potential threat posed by
the existence of America's ironclad navy, this inaction was designed to further Britain's own interests by exhausting both
belligerents, to the ultimate benefit of Britain's trade and
merchant marine. For this reason, Lord Clarendon attempted
to persuade the French that nonintervention meant prolong-
ing the war and, consequently, impairing American power for
a long time to come.[49] This essentially negative and ruthlessly
calculating attitude contradicted the validity of all those political arguments that supposedly made the United States attractive to France and Great Britain. The great powers were
obviously not immune to shortsightedness.

Russia had its own reasons for turning Napoleon's overture
down. If and when the opportunity presented itself for successful mediation, it wanted to be the sole mediator. But more
important, just as France and Great Britain could not forget
America's unsympathetic attitude during the Crimean War,
Russia remembered it in a positive sense and liked to think of
Russo-American relations in terms of a long-range association
capable of counteracting the unfriendly maneuvers of the *entente* powers. As Prince Gortchakov had told the French ambassador in St. Petersburg, "In case of Europen complications,
America is an ally of Russia without the neccessity of an alliance."[50] Though Gortchakov overstated the extent of Russo-
American cooperation in the future, Secretary of State Seward

49. Robert M. McLane, *Reminiscences, 1827–1897* (printed privately,
1903; rare books, LC) , pp. 148–49.
50. Fournier to Thouvenel, St. Petersburg, July 29, 1862, CP Russie
(AMAE) , Vol. CCXXVIII.

defined it more appropriately, but somewhat ambiguously: "Russia has our friendship in every case in preference to any other European power simply because she always wishes us well, and leaves us to conduct our affairs as we think best."[51] Soon thereafter the Polish uprising in 1863 subjected Russo-American relations to an important test. To the satisfaction of St. Petersburg, the United States declined participation in a conference on the Polish question to which it had been invited by France, Great Britain, and Austria. Opposed to Europe's intervention in America, the Lincoln-Seward administration could not very well have agreed to intervene in a European crisis. The Polish question illustrated another pertinent link in the interconnection between contemporary European and American problems. As a Southern commentator observed in an effort to console his disappointed compatriots, France could hardly recognize the Confederacy without first recognizing Poland, whose claims to French support realistically superseded those of the Confederacy.[52] Faced with the prospect that the recognition of either might involve it in a European as well as an American war, France decided to recognize neither.

By June, 1863, Slidell admitted that Mexico and Poland were the two major stumbling blocks impeding French participation in Confederate affairs. Nevertheless the emperor continued to search for a diplomatic way out of the American impasse.[53] He agreed, moreover, to render covert assistance to

51. Seward to Bayard Taylor, Washington, December 23, 1862, RIDS.
52. Henry St. Paul, *Our Home and Foreign Policy* (Mobile, Ala., 1863), p. 21. In 1863, though the Russian fleet seemed to be safer in American waters than in the Baltic, its reception in the United States seemed to Henry Sanford, a distinguished American diplomat in Europe, potentially harmful. Sanford suggested that if Napoleon III decided to make war with Russia, he might "hit at Russia through us." Sanford to Seward, Paris, October 27, 1863, William H. Seward Papers (Rochester University).
53. Drouyn de Lhuys authorized Mercier to leave a copy of his dispatch, dated Paris, January, 9, 1863, with Secretary of State Seward. In it

the Confederacy by permitting it to construct ships in French shipyards[54] and by affording its commerce raiders the facilities of French ports.[55] So as to leave no doubt in Napoleon's mind, Secretary of State Seward instructed Dayton on July 8, 1863: "If the emperor shall by an official act violate the sovereignty which you represent, your functions will be suspended." Time and circumstances worked against Napoleon III as far as America was concerned. European complications in Greece, Italy, Poland, and the Austro-Prussian war against Denmark, the unexpected difficulties in Mexico, and the telling effects of the North's grand strategy of attrition gradually brought the emperor face to face with the ugly realities.[56] Alone he would not decisively act on behalf of the Confederacy. Britain, Russia, Prussia, and Austria had their own respective reasons for refusing to underwrite Napoleon's American Civil War policy.

In reality, the emperor had no thought-out policy; rather he drifted from day to day, assuring both sides of his sympathy.[57] Dayton's appraisal of French policy, at least ever since November, 1862, turned out to be very perceptive. It seemed to him "to have no fixed purpose, but grows out of circumstances; it is the result of current events." Napoleon's half-hearted en-

---

he raised the question: "If the Federal Government declines the friendly intervention of the maritime powers of Europe, could it not honorably think of direct conversations with the authorities of the South?" CPEU, CXXIX. See also *Le Temps*, November 16, 1862.

54. Drouyn de Lhuys helped to frustrate these Confederate schemes. See Warren F. Spencer, "Drouyn de Lhuys et les navires Confédérés en France—L'affaire des navires d'Arman (1863–1865)," *Revue d'histoire diplomatique* (1963), pp. 314–41.

55. Gideon Welles to William H. Seward, Navy Department, September 21, 1863. Correspondence relative to observance of International Law by vessels of the U.S. navy (National Archives), VI, Box I, 1861–65.

56. Late in August, 1864, Dr. Thomas Evans went as Napoleon's "trusted messenger" to the United States to study the situation firsthand. See Rainey, *Dr. Thomas Evans*, pp. 27–28.

57. Renouvin, *Histoire des relations internationales*, V, 345. See also Dayton to Seward, Paris, November 21, 1862, DDFDS.

couragements of the Confederacy, which, by holding out the hope of recognition and assistance, certainly did not contribute to a shortening of the war, earned him in the end the South's scornful contempt and the North's unforgiving resentment. Somehow Napoleon deluded himself when he steadfastly refused to see that recognition of the Confederacy might actually enlarge the war by bringing other foreign powers into the picture, and that mediation, no matter how well intentioned, would be rejected by both belligerents.

Napoleon III had all too whimsically steered away from the Franco-American course imaginatively charted by Napoleon I. All the traditional justifications for a close cooperation between France and the United States the emperor seemed to be willing to cast aside without serious scruples. Beyond that, the relatively few French investments and possessions in the New World made it a continent of secondary importance to France, certainly not worth the gamble Napoleon found so tempting. And finally, with the natural priority Europe occupied in any realistic analysis of French policy—and at a time of growing emphasis on French interests in Africa and Asia—Napoleon was heading toward actions in America prompted more by emotional and personal sentiments than by statesmanlike determination of national interest. That his two foreign ministers succeeded in restraining him from committing what they considered a potential blunder reflected on the dual personality of the emperor. The wishful dreamer was quite capable, however reluctantly, of bowing in this instance to the realities of the situation.

The triumph and tragedy of the federal Union in April, 1865, evoked in the emperor feelings of regret and indignation. His genuine sorrow on the occasion of Lincoln's assassination was accompanied by his belated realization of his political misjudgments and his desire to improve his relations with the United States. By a strange coincidence Napoleon III felt as remorseful about his recent policy vis-à-vis the United

States as Napoleon I had been half a century ago. The speedy dismemberment of the American forces amazed the emperor as much as the rest of Europe and dispelled the gnawing fear of the potential danger of American militarism.[58] The popular reaction in France to the outcome of the war and to Lincoln's tragic death enlightened the emperor about the depth and extent of the fraternal feelings so many French citizens professed for their American brethren. The triumph of republicanism and democratic institutions in America was so impressive and indisputable that the spokesmen for thousands of French students assured John Bigelow, the able American envoy in France at the time of Lincoln's death: "We are the fellow citizens of John Brown, Abraham Lincoln, and Mr. Seward. We, the young, to whom the future belongs, shall have the courage to erect a true democracy and to learn from the American people the lessons of liberty."[59]

8. Napoleon's Mexican Debacle

The expulsion of France from Canada at the end of the Seven Years' War and Napoleon's sale of the Louisiana territory four decades later removed France as a major political power in the Western hemisphere. By the middle of the nineteenth century France's strategic foothold in the West Indies[1] was hardly more than a reminder of the possibilities of an em-

58. The speedy creation of a militia when the war broke out and its equally speedy dissolution when it ended impressed French believers in disarmament as an example Europe would be wise to adopt. See Montalembert, *La Victoire du Nord aux États-Unis,* p. 110; *and Le Temps,* May 5, 1865.

59. J. J. Jusserand, *En Amérique, Jadis et Maintenant* (Paris, 1918), p. 315; see also Chinard, *L'Amérique,* pp. 27–29.

1. Adolphe Roberts, *The French in the West Indies* (New York, 1942), pp. 262–69.

pire in the New World that earlier generations of Frenchmen had neither the vision nor the means to develop. Their wars against European powers had so sapped their strength that after 1803 it seemed wiser to Napoleon I to do business with the United States than to assume the risks involved in building a French empire across the Atlantic. And despite the too rapid growth of the American republic before 1860, it seemed wiser on the whole to later French statesmen to respect the interlocking principles of the Monroe Doctrine than to provoke America's eventual intervention in European affairs. In other words, up to that time France was resigned, however reluctantly, to accept American leadership in the Western hemisphere.

Carried away by the romantic notions he had had as Louis Napoleon, the prisoner of Ham, Napoleon III embarked upon his Mexican adventure with great expectations. He hoped that Mexico might take the place in the French empire that India occupied in the British. His puppet regime was meant to be a deliberate challenge of the Protestant and republican United States. Encouraged by his wife and other advisers and misinformed by his diplomatic agents in Mexico and by Mexican monarchists in Paris, the emperor hoped to contribute to the grandeur of France by promoting a Catholic and Latin monarchy in the New World. When one attempts to analyze the well-known historical facts surrounding the initial phases of the Maximilian affair, one is above all struck by the amateurish approach to this risky enterprise and the unhesitating disposition on the part of the French government to discard a major traditional policy. Napoleon's appalling ignorance about Mexico, his wishful thinking with respect to the outcome of the Civil War in America, and his failure to weigh the possible international consequences of his Mexican gamble irreparably damaged his reputation as a statesman.[2]

2. The emperor's interest in the exploitation of Mexico's mines was encouraged by his half-brother de Morny, a great speculator and gambler.

From the unpublished memoirs of L. F. Alfred Maury,[3] one of the librarians and members of the Institut de France who saw Napoleon III quite frequently, we learn that the emperor had the habit of seeking information in support of his vaguely conceived opinions with respect to Mexico and other foreign countries, instead of undertaking serious studies and analyses before arriving at his conclusions. Just as he and Empress Eugénie were convinced that the Confederate States of America would establish their independence and work closely with him, he assumed that the establishment of the French puppet regime in Mexico would be accomplished by little more than a "military parade." When the emperor once asked Maury to show him the routes by which French troops could reach Mexico City from Vera Cruz, the librarian was shocked by the fact that Napoleon had never studied the detailed map that was available in the Institut. Napoleon's lack of knowledge regarding Mexico was confirmed by Jean-Baptiste Boussingault, another distinguished member of the Institut, who regretted that the French government sought his expert advice on Mexico only when it was much too late to save France from incredible embarrassments. For unfortunately Napoleon's unfamiliarity with Mexico's geography was matched by his unrealistic estimates of the Mexican people's reaction to an alien monarch.

Judged by the truism that a great power must act like one, Napoleon's predictable miscalculations reflected not only on the quality of his judgment, but also on that of the people who had elevated him to his imperial rank. That Britain would not have passively acquiesced in the successful establishment of a French empire in a region in which it had vital interests to protect can hardly be dismissed as hindsight. And

McLane, *Reminiscences,* pp. 148–49. See also E. W. Richards, "Louis Napoleon and Central America," *Journal of Modern History,* XXXIV (1962) , 178–84.

3. Maury, "Souvenirs," IV, 223–25.

could Napoleon entirely disregard the argument of the brilliant journalist Prévost-Paradol that the Confederate States of America, once established with the help of France, "would soon astonish the world with their ingratitude" by bringing Cuba and at least part of Mexico under their control? France would then be obliged, argued Paradol, to rescue its protégé, Emperor Maximilian. Moreover, what was Napoleon's justification for assuming that a successful Austrian monarch in Mexico would have willingly continued to accept French overlordship?[4] But even if, for argument's sake, the contentions implied in these observations could be challenged, was it not a foregone conclusion that the United States would not tolerate this French violation of the Monroe Doctrine as long as it was in its power to do something about it? Secretary of State Seward had repeatedly warned France that any attempt to go beyond its legitimate collection of debts—particularly the arbitrary establishment of a French-inspired monarchical government in Mexico—would lead to fatal animosities between France and the United States.[5] Seward could not only count on the support of Congress, which on April 4, 1864, unanimously passed a joint resolution to that effect,[6] but also on the backing of Latin American republics who feared the ultimate effects of French imperialism in the hemisphere as far as

4. Empress Eugénie later contended that the choice of the Austrian archduke was designed ultimately "to obtain ultimately from Francis Joseph the cession of Venice to Italy." See Nancy Nichols Barker, "France, Austria, and the Mexican Venture, 1861–1864," *French Historical Studies*, III (1963), 226–27.

5. Blumenthal, *Reappraisal*, p. 169.

6. Glyndon G. Van Deusen, *William Henry Seward* (New York, 1967), p. 368. The Republican platform of 1864 stated unequivocally: "The people of the United States can never regard with indifference the attempt of any European power to overthrow by force or to supplant by fraud the institutions of any Republican Government on the western continent and that they will view with extreme jealousy, as menacing to the peace and independence of their own country, the efforts of any such power to obtain footholds for Monarchical Government sustained by foreign military force, in near proximity to the United States." Kirk H. Porter and Bruce Johnson, *National Platforms, 1840–1956* (Urbana, Ill., 1956), pp. 34–36.

they themselves were concerned. Napoleon III had to consider still another aspect of his Mexican policy that deprived him of being a completely free agent in the determination of his course of action. According to all indications, a war against the United States resulting from French military intervention on the side of the Confederacy or from the decision of the victorious United States to drive Napoleon's soldiers from Mexico might well have endangered the emperor's throne. Reflecting a frequently expressed sentiment, *Le Temps* stressed the opinion that the only honorable and sensible policy for France was the maintenance of peace with the United States.[7]

The end of the Civil War in America caused Napoleon such severe political headaches that the withdrawal of his forces from Mexico became merely a question of time and face-saving maneuvering. Those Frenchmen who had rationalized the emperor's policy as an operation that would benefit Mexico now exposed themselves to unusually militant criticism. French parliamentarians and journalists took the lead in condemning a policy that "confounded reason" and amounted to a "gigantic blunder," pressing for an end of this senseless and costly involvement that was fraught with incalculable dangers. Not the least of their anxieties concerned Count Bismarck's likely exploitation of the French dilemma in Mexico.[8] Since the Prussian statesman endeavored to minimize French intervention in the impending conflict between Prussia and Austria, he looked upon the dissipation of French power in imperial enterprises as a fortunate break. Realistically, though, Bismarck drew a line between dissipation and humiliation, lest the French emperor seek to regain in Europe the prestige he was losing in Mexico.

As important as the European ramifications of Napoleon's Mexican extravaganza were, ever since 1865 the spotlight was on Washington's handling of this Franco-American crisis. As

7. February 28, 1865; see also *Le Temps*, August 15, 1863.
8. See Blumenthal, *Reappraisal*, pp. 176–77.

long as the Civil War lasted, the Lincoln-Seward administration pursued the prudent course of warning France that its political interference in the Western hemisphere was inadmissible. At the same time, the Northern government treaded softly so as not to provoke French military intervention in the Civil War. "Why should we gasconade about Mexico," wrote Seward in the spring of 1864, "when we are in a struggle for our own life?" At that time it was in the interest of the United States to observe its neutrality in the Franco-Mexican conflict, as long as France was apparently willing to continue its neutral policy in the War Between the States. The full restoration of the Union also restored Seward's relative freedom of action concerning the French challenge. In 1865, Lincoln and Seward, who had had enough of war, felt confident that a satisfactory diplomatic solution could be found to settle this irritating controversy. Inexperienced as he was in foreign affairs, President Andrew Johnson also had confidence in Seward's ability to arrange a peaceful settlement.[9] But these dispositions did not preclude bellicose statements and ominous hints during the ensuing war of nerves. Nor did they foreclose the possibility of President Johnson's suddenly becoming interested in a foreign quarrel as a diversion from his domestic troubles.

The attitude of his Southern "friends" in the final stages of their war must have shocked Napoleon into the realization that his original assumptions regarding American affairs had been so erroneous as to compel an agonizing reappraisal. Contrary to his expectations, the North won the war, Maximilian failed to obtain the support of the Mexican people, and in their desperation the emperor's disenchanted Southern "friends" proposed to the North joint military action to drive the foreigners out of Mexico.[10] With the military machine of the United States in high gear, some American generals, in-

9. Chambrun, *Impressions of Lincoln*, pp. 85–86, 121–22.
10. *Ibid.*, pp. 53–55.

cluding General Ulysses S. Grant, showed their impatience
with any policy likely to delay the expulsion of the French
forces from Mexico. Indeed, Grant opposed the very existence
of Maximilian's throne as detrimental to the democratic institutions of the United States, as well as to its peace and safety.
Maximilian's necessary reliance on armed forces for the security of his empire, Grant argued, would leave the United States
no choice but to maintain a military establishment for purposes of adequate defense. As General Grant saw it, such an
establishment would subvert the traditional institutions of
the United States, besides being wasteful.[11] Napoleon III had
evidently never thought that as a by-product of his Mexican
scheme, France—and all of Europe—might be confronted with
the highly undesirable prospect of a permanent American military force. Europeans had heretofore felt more secure exactly
because of the absence of such a force.

From April, 1865, until the spring of 1866 talk of a Franco-
American war was in the air and the suspense surrounding it
seems to have been studiously cultivated. Americans who bit-
terly resented Napoleon's duplicity during the Civil War
would have loved nothing better than to teach him a memora-
ble lesson. They were confident that their army could accomplish this feat in short order and that the latest American
ironclads could put the French fleet out of action. Their "toy-
gun batteries and flimsy side armor" supposedly made French
ships an easy target.[12] Rumors were also circulating to the effect that American volunteers flocking to the republican
forces of Juarez would obviate a head-on clash with the
French in Mexico, a step Americans would take only with the
greatest reluctance.[13] On the diplomatic front, Seward grad-

11. *Le Temps,* December 31, 1865.

12. *The Nation,* March 1, 1866, p. 265. Some French officers were also
looking forward to "une belle et bonne guerre" with the United States.
Taxile Delord, *Histoire du Second Empire* (Paris, 1869), IV, 273.

13. *Le Temps,* April 13, 1865. See also Georges Clémenceau's report in
F. Baldensperger, "L'initiation américaine de Georges Clémenceau," *Revue*

ually stepped up his pressures as the year came to a close. Until then he had wisely observed John Bigelow's counsel not to offend the French nation unduly in the manner of President Jackson.[14] But in November, 1865, the United States nominated a minister to the Republic of Mexico and sent General John M. Schofield, a known advocate of military intervention in Mexico, to Paris with the mission of creating an "either-withdraw-or-face-war" atmosphere. And Seward himself saw no harm in telling foreign diplomats in Washington that the Mexican question was generating public pressures in the United States, which might compel the government to intervene in Mexico.

It was to the credit of Napoleon III that he was, after all, magnanimous enough to admit, first to himself and then to the world, that his Mexican adventure had been a mistake he was prepared to liquidate. The manner in which he extricated himself from this dilemma was as skillful and professional as the original decision that pushed him into it had been ill-conceived. In view of the developments on the European continent, a war against the United States was the last thing French leaders wanted to worry about. But having maneuvered themselves into a situation that was potentially explosive, they wished first of all to protect themselves against the eventuality of such a war. Toward that end, they proposed a defensive alliance to Britain (November 30, 1865) by which the two countries would mutually assist each other should the United States attack either one of them. Having concluded that France stood more to gain from such an alliance than Britain and that it might actually provoke American aggression, Lord Clarendon promptly turned the proposal down.[15]

---

de littérature comparée, VIII (1928), 127–54.

14. Van Deusen, William Henry Seward, p. 490.

15. See H. R. C. Wellesley, Secrets of the Second Empire: Private Letters from the Paris Embassy (New York, 1929), p. 290; and Bourne, Britain and the Balance of Power in North America, p. 301.

In the meantime, Napoleon's government indicated to Washington that it wished to find a satisfactory answer to the controversy temporarily disturbing their relations. In October, 1865, Drouyn de Lhuys made the unacceptable suggestion of a *quid pro quo* arrangement amounting to the evacuation of French troops from Mexico and the simultaneous recognition of Maximilian by the United States. Another approach was more constructive. Fond of secret and personalized diplomacy enabling him to circumvent official channels, the French emperor entrusted to General James Watson Webb, with whom he had been in private correspondence for a good many years, a verbal message to President Johnson.[16] On the morning of November 10, 1865, General Webb and the emperor breakfasted at Saint-Cloud for about two hours and in the course of their conversation Napoleon promised to withdraw his temporary "police force" from Mexico within the next two years. If President Johnson would agree to this informal offer, the emperor was prepared to announce it officially in April, 1866. Although this withdrawal was clearly dictated by the circumstances confronting the emperor, he and Secretary of State Seward engaged in last-minute tactical maneuvers of a psychological nature. General Webb, who by chance had been entrusted with the transmission of the emperor's decision, saw Seward immediately upon his return, on December 6, 1865. Either to magnify his own successful role in this international problem or to impress upon the French government once again the urgency of an early removal of its troops, Seward, in his notes to the French government, beginning with the one of December 6, became increasingly insistent. Only after the *Moniteur* announced on April 6, 1866, that the withdrawal of the French troops from Mexico would be completed by November, 1867, did Seward change his tone. From then on he conducted himself in a manner most conducive to the smooth liquidation of this episode.

16. See Blumenthal, *Reappraisal*, pp. 178–80.

Just as the French foreign ministry had previously tried to
salvage as much as it could by vainly proposing the withdrawal of French troops in exchange for American recognition
of Maximilian, it tried once again, at the very end, to save its
honor vis-à-vis Maximilian. The evacuation of French troops,
it maintained, in no way abrogated French recognition of
Maximilian's legitimacy. But Washington was quite willing
to leave this question to the judgment of the Mexican people.
There was much to be said for the method used to bring the
embarrassing controversy to a close. There was neither an
official confrontation or negotiation between representatives
of France and the United States nor a formal and binding
agreement mutually arrived at. To minimize the psychological effects of what would in any case be a difficult decision for
the French, the United States did not make humiliating demands. France could "voluntarily" announce the withdrawal
and the time it would require to carry it out.[17]

In their session of July 10, 1867, French legislators listened
to Eugène Rouher, Napoleon's powerful minister of state and
finances, exclaim, "Dieu ne l'a pas voulu!"[18] Denying that
France had set out to conquer Mexico or that it had been
guided by selfish and petty motives, Rouher instead deplored
France's failure in this most promising civilizing mission. As
a politician, he evidently deemed it advisable to soothe the
embittered feelings of many accusing critics rather than to ra-
tionalize the imperialistic enterprise. The emperor, too,
wished to soften the effects of his disastrous American policies
by acting as if the last six years had been only a bad dream.
Ignoring all he had done during these years that had been so
extremely difficult for the United States, he now asserted that
he "was not disposed to repudiate the great design of Napoleon

17. Jean-Baptiste Barbier, *Outrances sur le Second Empire* (Paris,
1956), pp. 112–13.
18. *Le Temps,* July 12, 1867.

I regarding the United States."[19] But the damage had been done and its consequences were soon manifested.

9. *The United States and the Franco-Prussian War*

The Mexican adventure had weakened Napoleon III at home and abroad, and coinciding as it did with his two-faced dealings during the Civil War, it earned him a harvest of ill will throughout the United States. This became evident during the Franco-Prussian War.[1] A conflict between France and Germany had been anticipated for some years, but when it broke out during the summer of 1870 it caught President Grant by complete surprise. He had not even been aware of its impending approach. As was to be expected, the president issued a neutrality proclamation, thus honoring on August 22 the verbal assurances given to the belligerents a month earlier.

Strangely, though, whereas France asked Britain to look after its interests in Germany, Bismarck entrusted to the United States the protection of German citizens and affairs in France. Unlike Napoleon III, who had for many years antagonized and irritated the United States, Bismarck had cultivated close ties with the American republic.[2] In addition to the advantages to be derived from increased German-American trade and the fact that "Germany had in the United States her second largest state after Prussia," Bismarck hoped, in an emergency, to draw on the naval resources of the United States. His instruction of July 12, 1870, to Secretary of State

19. Drouyn de Lhuys to Montholon, Paris, January 9, 1866, CPEU, CXXXVI.

1. For supplementary information about the United States and the Franco-Prussian War, see Blumenthal, *Reappraisal*, pp. 183–206.

2. See Henry Blumenthal, "George Bancroft in Berlin, 1867–1874," *New England Quarterly*, XXXVII (1964), 224–41.

von Thile to explore the possibility of acquiring from America "the means of maritime defense" left no doubt about speculations to that effect. The German statesman had gone even further in including the United States in his policy plans. In case of a war between Prussia-Germany and another European power he counted on friendly America to assert the rights of neutrals. Furthermore, if in a Franco-Prussian war the United States could not be benevolently neutral toward Prussia, he did not want it to render any material assistance to France either. With the exception of minor infractions, benefiting at times one belligerent or the other, the American government did indeed maintain a strict neutrality.

As far as the attitude of the American public was concerned, it was anything but neutral. Generally speaking, though Republicans and Protestants leaned toward Germany and Democrats and Catholics were inclined to sympathize with France, the over-all sentiment was strongly in favor of Germany. It should be noted, however, that on both sides extraneous political factors were brought to bear on political leaders. The presence of large numbers of German-Americans permitted them in some states to exercise political pressures Republican politicians felt they could ill afford to ignore. Irish Democrats, too, were motivated by more than sympathy in their support of the French, for they hoped to see France help the Irish in their struggle for independence should England go to the assistance of Germany. That the capture of Napoleon and the fall of the Second Empire brought about a noticeable change in American public opinion clearly indicated that Americans had primarily taken issue with the objectionable policies of the emperor. The list of grievances against Napoleon III dated back to the never-forgotten nor forgiven coup d'état and included not only his anti-American policies but also his assumed role as the worldly defender of Catholicism and the persecutions growing out of his antirepublicanism.[3]

3. Gazley, *German Unification*, pp. 320–424.

Many American Protestants wished to see France humbled because they saw in the defeat of Catholic France a blow to the ever-expanding power of the "infallible" pope. They did not hesitate to express their religious and racial prejudices quite openly. Such representative intellectuals as George Ticknor and James Russell Lowell confessed their admiration for the Teutons. They and others judged French civilization as being rotten to the core and afflicted by a perverted sense of truth, honesty, and morality. Many Americans considered French leadership in Europe a hindrance to the progress of civilization and would have applauded Lowell's comment that "anything that knocks the nonsense of Johnny Crapaud will be a blessing to the world."[4] They wished to see the French soundly thrashed because their European neighbors would never be safe until "the taint of Louis XIV is drawn out of their blood."[5] Their low estimate of the "arrogant, aggressive, and unscrupulous French" contrasted sharply with their image of the Germans as "a more honest, cultivated and, above all, a faithful and true race of men."[6] If the then-celebrated historian George Bancroft could have had his way, an entente, if not an alliance, between Germany and the United States would have been the cardinal factor in the shaping of the long-range foreign policy of the United States. But such a replacement of America's traditional orientation toward France and Great Britain was an alternative the political leaders of the United States were not prepared to consider.

With respect to the immediate issue of German unification, Germany found heartening support in the United States. As to the responsibility for the outbreak of the war, however, opinions were divided. Those Americans who sided with Ger-

4. Charles Elliot Norton (ed.), *Letters of James Russell Lowell* (New York, 1894), II, 62–63.

5. *Ibid.*, p. 71.

6. See, for instance, George Ticknor to John, King of Saxony, Boston, August 3, 1870. George Ticknor Papers, "Letters." (Massachusetts Historical Society MS).

many accused Napoleon III, the "elected dictator," of provoking a war of succession when he insisted on the pledge that no Hohenzollern prince should ever occupy the throne of Spain. They suspected the emperor's motives precisely because in their judgment the withdrawal of the Hohenzollern candidacy should have satisfied the sensibilities of France and its sovereign.[7] Was not Napoleon's insolent demand, they asked, designed to bring about a situation enabling him to humble the rising power of Prussia and to extend the frontiers of France as far as the Rhine? In a similar vein, others argued that Bismarck may have used the Hohenzollern candidacy issue as a clever ruse to elevate Prussia-Germany to a leading position on the continent. The *Atlanta Constitution*,[8] for instance, noted that if, in addition to Portugal, another Prussian prince occupied the Spanish throne, "France would be surrounded, except on her sea coast, by powers in alliance with or under control of Prussia." Such a state of affairs, the newspaper contended, might jeopardize the safety of France and peace of Europe because it would gravely upset the balance of power on the Continent. France could not tolerate any European leadership by the ambitious military masters of Prussia. Had it not been for the Hohenzollern incident, some of Napoleon's American admirers said, the emperor would never have been in favor of war against Prussia, for he was too clever for that. A prominent Philadelphian, for instance, accepted at face value the statement of his French friend, Prévost-Paradol, that before he was appointed minister to the United States the emperor "gave him positive assurances that there would be no war with Germany."[9] This assurance was, of course, irrecon-

7. *The Nation,* July 21, 1870, pp. 33–36. See also Gazley, *German Unification,* pp. 324–26.
8. Editorial comment on "The European War," July 19, 1870.
9. Edward Swift Balch Papers, "Journal, 1859–1906," I, 5 (University of Virginia MS).

cilable with the compliment Rouher,[10] a power close to the throne, extended to the emperor for having prepared for this war "for four years." Whether Rouher stated the truth—and thus unwittingly impugned Napoleon's veracity—or whether he merely meant to flatter his master or reassure the French public, the quick advances of the Prussians demonstrated conclusively that the emperor and his advisers had made major military and political miscalculations. The leaders of the French army had evidently overestimated its ability and underestimated the military efficiency and resourcefulness of the Prussians.

Since a protracted drought in 1870 threatened the crops in Europe, Americans read no special meaning into the extraordinarily heavy French purchases of flour and grain early in June of that year. Neither was much heed given to rumors that the weakness of the Paris Bourse could be traced to the fact that "persons high in the Emperor's confidence were large sellers."[11] When the Duke de Gramont demanded the withdrawal of the Hohenzollern candidacy, however, and delivered a virtual threat of war against Prussia, the international money markets in Europe reacted sharply. Americans could still not see how the European war, if it should break out, could materially affect them. In Frankfurt, then the principal financial center of Germany, excited Germans liquidated their American bonds because they were the most readily salable property they possessed. Naturally, the price of these bonds fell several points in Frankfurt and London where they had been sent posthaste. Since these bonds were transacted at a higher price in the American market than in Frankfurt or London, large amounts of them were sent to New York where they had to be paid for in coin. The detrimental effect of the

10. "Right and Wrong in France," *The Nation*, August 18, 1870, pp. 103–4.
11. "European War and American Finance," *The Nation*, August 11, 1870, pp. 84–85.

war on the United States also made itself felt in other ways. The British economy suffered a great deal from the sudden interruption of regular trade. As a result, Anglo-American business accounts, often settled by new purchasing orders, now had to be paid for in cash. British bankers, moreover, asked their American clients to make their due payments in coin rather than in bills. In the first three weeks after the declaration of war more than eighteen million dollars in coin were shipped from America to Europe. This drain was equal to the total amount shipped during the entire six months prior to the war. It was not surprising therefore that Americans and Europeans alike learned the lesson of their interdependence more quickly in the commercial and financial than in the political world.

The news of the capture of Napoleon was obviously a blow to the French people. In the United States, this dramatic turn of events caused a certain satisfaction, while the misfortune of the French people was received with genuine sadness. Echoing the views of at least a minority of Americans the *Atlanta Constitution*[12] soberly acknowledged in the hour of Napoleon's tragic plight that, whatever faults he possessed and errors he had committed, his reign had "some salient features of marvelous brilliancy." On the whole, ambivalence continued to characterize American attitudes toward France and Germany, reconciling the consciences of individual citizens holding a variety of different viewpoints but disappointing the two warring nations. Americans hailed the proclamation of the French republic as a welcome step that would put an end to the "odious despotism" of the empire, and yet they doubted that the French people possessed the degree of enlightenment and moral discipline necessary to meet the responsibilities of a democratic republic.[13] Henry S. Sanford, one of America's

12. Editorial comment on "The War," September 6, 1870.
13. See *Washington Chronicle*, September 6, 1870; and *The Nation*, October 27, 1870.

better-known nineteenth-century diplomats, also quite realistically questioned the wisdom of the hasty assumption of power by the republicans in France, instead of letting the imperial dynasty first assume full responsibility for the disastrous consequences of the war.[14] But the proclamation of the Third Republic was a *fait accompli* and shifted American sentiment toward greater solidarity with the new sister republic. Once the Second Empire had been swept away and German unification could take its natural course, the further prosecution of the war seemed no longer justified. And yet, though some Americans deplored the continuation of the war and "the steady advance and unbroken victories of the swag-bellied Germans,"[15] other citizens of the country of immigrants admired the military victories of the Prussian army.[16] A growing number of Americans deplored the dilemma in which the French found themselves, but hardly any let their imagination go as far as a few French dreamers who envisioned an American expeditionary force to rescue France. The principle of nonintervention in strictly European affairs and the consequences of America's own recent tragic war eliminated any possibility of an American Lafayette heading such a force. The disillusioned editor of *Le Patriote* therefore warned his countrymen: "France must rely on itself . . . God is too high in heaven, and the United States is too far away."[17] France could not even count on huge amounts of arms being rushed from Eng-

14. Henry S. Sanford to Hamilton Fish, Brussels, September 15, 1870, Hamilton Fish Papers (LC), Vol. LXXII.

15. Walter G. MacRae to his brother John, Wilmington, N.C., September 27, 1870, Hugh MacRae Letters (Duke University MS).

16. J. B. Ravold, *Français et Allemands aux États-Unis d'Amérique pendant l'année terrible* (Nancy, 1883), p. 22.

17. September 12, 1870; see also issue of September 8, 1870. American volunteers were few, as Mary C. Putnam's comment indicates: "I should have been prouder of my country had it extended a helping hand to a cause which is identical with its own." "Paris 1870: Letters of Mary C. Putnam," *AHR*, XXII (1917), 836–41.

land and America to armies to be miraculously raised for the liberation of France.

The suggestion of leading American newspapers that **President Grant** should offer his good offices to mediate the conflict merited further exploration.[18] Successful mediation would have meant an end of the war with the approval of both belligerents. It would also have enhanced the prestige of the United States and given satisfaction to many of its fairminded citizens. More than that, America had a stake in an early peace. A couple of years before the outbreak of hostilities George Bancroft, the United States minister to Prussia, had been among the few Americans who anticipated the costly economic effects of a long Franco-Prussian war.[19] It would interrupt the continuous flow of German-American immigration, trade, and investment of truly significant proportions. Even the relatively short duration of the war confirmed the accuracy of these expected consequences. Very much to the concern of America's financial community, the war also detrimentally affected the sales of United States government bonds and the values of federal obligations in Europe.

When Foreign Minister Jules Favre officially asked the Grant administration on September 8 to join other powers in mediation efforts, the president and his secretary of state, Hamilton Fish, were initially favorably disposed to it. But Bismarck's rejection of all overtures to that effect, emphatically seconded by the Germanophile Bancroft, led Grant henceforth to abstain from any diplomatic intervention, unless requested by both belligerents. Various subsequent French appeals fell on deaf ears in Washington where the president and Hamilton Fish found it "difficult to comprehend how France could repudiate the responsibility for the war."[20] To some extent influenced by Bancroft, and remembering the

18. *Journal Officiel de la République Française,* September 13, 1870.
19. Blumenthal, "George Bancroft," pp. 232–33.
20. Berthemy to Favre, Washington, October 23, 1870, CPEU CXLVII.

nerve-racking complications the French had unhesitatingly created for the United States during the 1860's, and their historically troublesome policies on the European continent, Grant made no secret of his personal inclination toward the German viewpoint. He and his advisers felt that Germany was entitled to frontiers best designed to guarantee its security, as long as the country of Lafayette would not be unduly humiliated in the process. Since under existing circumstances nothing short of America's military intervention would have impressed the astoundingly successful military masters of Prussia-Germany, Grant saw no active role for himself in this conflict. The French envoy in Washington summed the situation up quite accurately when he sent the disappointing message to his government that "it must not count on any assistance whatsoever from the Federal Government."[21] Although he was familiar with the officially stated justifications for America's inaction, he knew very well that deference to German-American voters also prevented President Grant from taking any steps that might be objectionable to Prussia.

For that matter, the European powers who were directly affected by shifts in the political balance of power in their part of the world were as reluctant to mediate or intervene in this conflict as the United States. When soon after the French capitulation at Sedan Adolphe Thiers knocked at the doors of several European chancelleries, he felt so let down by them that he concealed his irritation with difficulty. Neither Russia nor Great Britain held out hope for their diplomatic intervention.[22] England, in particular, disappointed Thiers when it

21. See Berthemy's cable of October 23, 1870. Papiers Jules Favre (AMAE) , II, 67–68.

22. See Adolphe Thiers' report to Jules Favre, dated September 14, 1870, in Papiers Jules Favre (AMAE) , I; Richard Millman, *British Foreign Policy and the Coming of the Franco-Prussian War* (Oxford, England, 1965) , pp. 214–17; and Edmond Magnier's article, "L'Europe et la France," in *Le Figaro*, September 13, 1870. In his circular to the diplomatic representatives of France abroad Jules Favre deplored that instead of mediation the European cabinets limited themselves to sterile testi-

refused to participate in any mediation as distinguished from the mere technicality of being willing to help bring the two belligerents to the conference table. Beyond that, England was militarily too unprepared and politically too aloof from continental affairs to become more deeply involved in them. If anything, the rise of a Central European power capable of checking France and Russia appeared to be an advantageous development from Britain's point of view. And Russia, which decided to abstain from any intervention whatsoever, had not forgotten Napoleon's participation in the Crimean War, his sympathetic attitude toward the Poles in 1863, and his radical social policy. If any further European complications should develop, Russia wanted to be free to meet them.[23]

In the absence of high-level mediation machinery, Jules Favre took advantage of the next-best opportunity opened up by the private mission of General Ambrose Everett Burnside.[24] The discussions of this American general with the French foreign minister and General Trochu in Paris and with Count Bismarck in Versailles during the first two weeks of October provided at least a desirable forum for the exchange and clarification of important political questions. Bismarck was reminded in the course of these meetings that Jules Favre was willing to meet with him at any time or to receive any com-

monials of cordiality. This meant the continuation of a "barbarous and disastrous war which is an outrage to civilization." *Figaro*, October 20, 1870. To end the war, Louis Blanc proposed the creation of an arbitration tribunal in which the influences of two monarchical powers should be counterbalanced by two republican governments, namely, those of the United States and Switzerland. *Le Temps*, November 11, 1870.

23. Consult Robert F. Byrnes, "Some Russian Views of France in Nineteenth Century," in Acomb and Brown, *French Society*, p. 213. At this time Russia fostered the closest ties with the United States. In anticipation of a general conference at which the future of Europe would be the main issue, Russia's minister in Washington let Senator Charles Sumner know that his government would like to see the United States participate in it. Berthemy to Jules Favre, Washington, November 21, 1870, CPEU, CXLVII.

24. For more details, see Blumenthal, *Reappraisal*, pp. 197–200.

munication from him signaling the end of the senseless destruction and suffering. Burnside also informed the Prussian statesman about Jules Favre's desire for a lasting and honorable peace and the French people's determination to fight to the last if Prussia should attempt to impose humiliating terms. Any violation of the territorial integrity of France was unacceptable. Since Bismarck was unwilling to make concessions at this time, Burnside failed in his mission. Despite this outcome, however, Favre appreciated his effort and did not consider it a total failure. At least he felt somewhat more comfortable knowing that Bismarck did not intend to restore Napoleon III to his throne.[25] Burnside's mission and the visits of the Russian Prince de Wittgenstein to Paris and to the Prussian military headquarters also aroused Britain's curiosity and finally stirred it enough to explore the feasibility of a diplomatic solution to ending the war.[26] Britain's soundings did not receive the response the French people were praying for, however. Instead, as so often happens in history, the woes of one nation opened up opportunities for others. Both Russia and the United States chose this period of crisis in Europe to pursue their own respective interests, Russia by trying to bring about a revision of the Treaty of 1856 and the United States by stepping up the negotiations concerning the *Alabama* claims.

The heroic sacrifice of the besieged population of Paris during the final stages of the war vindicated in the eyes of many Americans the disgrace of Sedan. They would probably have been outraged had they known of the espionage activities of a few members of the American colony in Paris, particularly those of German descent.[27] In the long run, however, this un-

25. About the Burnside mission, see Jules Favre's reports of October 3, 1870, in Papiers Jules Favre (AMAE), I; see also *Le Temps*, October 14, 1870.

26. See "10ᵉ rapport par pigeon," Tours, October 19, 1870, in Papiers Jules Favre (AMAE), I, 160; and "32ᵉ rapport," Bordeaux, January 8, 1871, in Papiers Jules Favre (AMAE), III, 203–6.

27. See telegrams dated November 10, 11, and 13, 1870, in Papiers Jules Favre (AMAE), II, 67–68, 77–78, and 88.

fortunate conduct was more than counterbalanced by the humanitarian services rendered by the American Ambulance during the war and by charitable organizations immediately following it.[28] Similarly, President Grant offended the French when, in accordance with protocol, he sent a congratulatory message to the emperor of the German Reich. Many prominent American citizens, on the other hand, felt a deep sorrow for the French and disapproved of Prussia's decision to take Alsace and Lorraine from France. 'It is time,' protested William James, "that the principle of territorial conquest were abolished."[29]

On balance, though, France had lost more than a war. The defeat at Sedan not only sealed the fate of the Second Empire, it seemed to have removed France from the rank of the truly great Western powers. The nation that worshipped glory found itself at least reduced to a dubious rank in the family of nations. As the *New York Tribune* commented on the occasion of the emperor's death, "the end showed how utterly hollow and unsubstantial was the Imperial structure."[30] Unfortunately the sickening excesses of the Commune did not encourage Americans to have faith in the capacity of the French people to lay a solid foundation for republican institutions that would both meet the needs of modern times and restore to France its longed-for international respect.[31]

28. See, for instance, "Franco-Prussian War Victims, 1870–1871," (Tulane University MS), M 71; and *Lettre-Journal de Paris, Gazette des Absents,* February 15, 1871.

29. Gazley, *German Unification,* pp. 403–4.

30. See Noailles to Rémusat, Washington, January 14, 1873, CPEU, CLI.

31. Elihu Washburne was appalled by the murder of the Archbishop of Paris, whom he had tried to save. "The frightful excesses of the Commune," he wrote, "have brought reproach upon the sacred name of the Republic, and the good name of Republicanism suffers." Washburne to Fish, Paris, May 31 and June 2, 1871, DDFDS. See also White, *American Opinion,* p. 209.

II

Franco-American
Diplomatic Relations
1871–1900

1. France, Russia, and the United States

The deterioration of Franco-American diplomatic relations during the Second Empire contrasted sharply with the friendly ties between Russia and the United States. The latter were manifested quite conspicuously during the 1860's, a period of major upheavals, in Russia's rejection of Napoleon's mediation proposal during the Civil War, the hands-off policy of the United States with respect to the Polish uprising in 1863, and the sale of Alaska. This strange friendship was also evidenced in 1863 by the extended stay of Russian naval units in New York and San Francisco and the enthusiastic reception in 1866 of an American good-will mission to Russia.[1] The knowledge that the Russian fleet, which summered in the Baltic, could, at little expense, winter in safe American waters attracted international attention.

On September 9, 1866, *Le Temps* criticized the French people and its leaders for being too much attached to traditional policies and for failing to see that sooner or later the distribution of power in the world would be "terribly altered." The editors of the newspaper did not fear that Russia and the United States would declare war against the rest of the world, but they did feel obliged to admit that "the day these two nations became more aggressive, western Europe will find it difficult to extricate itself from its dilemma." *Le Temps* traced the recent closeness between Russia and the United States chiefly to "the coincidence of common grievances against France and Great Britain," such as the interventions in the Crimea and Mexico. Whatever the reasons for the existence of

1. See Thomas A. Bailey, "The Russian Fleet Myth Reexamined," *Mississippi Valley Historical Review*, XXXVIII (1951), 81–90; and Debidour, *Histoire diplomatique*, II, 323.

this Russo-American entente, the French government took cognizance of it in the formulation of its own policies. On September 17, 1866, the *Moniteur* published the *La Valette Circular,* which outlined Napoleon's vision of a Europe of cooperating states strong enough to maintain its geopolitical position between Russia and the United States.[2] The *Circular* was explicit on this point: "An irresistible force, regrettable as it may be, is impelling peoples to unite into great agglomerations by causing secondary states to disappear. . . . Although the growth of the two great empires (of the United States and Russia) may not be for us a matter of concern, it is to the provident interest of the European center not to be split up into so many different states without strength or public spirit." As important as France's contribution was to Europe's future within the international framework, by aiming at an international balance of power, Bismarck's successful maneuvers compelled the French government to assign top priority to the contemporary problem of maintaining a balance on the continent.

In view of the tenuousness of the Anglo-French entente, still favored by the Duke de Persigny, the Duke de Morny, the half-brother of Napoleon III, headed another school of thought, which advocated a rapprochment with Russia.[3] Recognizing that the outcome of the Austro-Prussian War foreshadowed potential dangers to the security of Russia and France, Napoleon III hoped that common interests would facilitate common policies. Belatedly the emperor realized that France would have much to gain from cooperation with both England and Russia.[4] By the time of the Franco-Prussian

2. See Lynn M. Case, *French Opinion on War and Diplomacy During the Second Empire* (Philadelphia, 1954) , pp. 221–26.

3. Deschanel, *Histoire de la Politique Extérieure,* p. 243.

4. A. J. P. Taylor, *The Struggle for Mastery in Europe, 1848–1918* (Oxford, England, 1954) , p. 200. See also John A. Scott, Republican Ideas and the Liberal Tradition in France, *1870–1914* (*New York,* 1966) , pp. 47–49; and John Rothney, *Bonapartism After Sedan* (*Ithaca, N.Y.,* 1968) .

War, however, this objective had eluded him. But the disastrous collapse of the Second Empire made it more imperative than ever to rely on Russia as the only power on the continent capable of coping with Germany and of helping France to recover its share of influence in the European concert.[5] Some Frenchmen entertained even more ambitious visions. In its issue of February 21, 1871, *L'Ami de la France,* a newspaper reflecting Jules Favre's views, put forth the idea that the peace of the world and the stability and grandeur of France would be ideally served by a triple entente embracing France, Russia, and the United States. Since the trend of the future pointed unquestionably toward a hegemony of superpowers, it seemed wiser for France to work with them than to worry about them.

Proponents of this strictly European approach to international questions ignored any realistic consideration of America's unwillingness to be drawn into the vortex of European power politics. With the exception of their interest in a continental balance, Americans did not actively pursue specific goals in the Old World. The United States certainly had no policy with respect to the Eastern question. During one of the perennial Eastern crises in the 1870's the chargé d'affaires of the French Legation in Washington observed that Americans would be inclined to sympathize with the Christians against the Moslems but that their overriding interest in any European war would be the prospect of increased exports of foodstuffs and war supplies.[6]

When in 1877 Russia and Turkey were again engaged in a war, the United States maintained its traditional neutrality.[7] But typically, just before the outbreak of hostilities, Foreign

5. See Washburne to Fish, Paris, June 1, 1876, DDFDS; and *La Vérité,* November 20, 1870.

6. Vaugelas to Decazes, Washington, October 22 and 24, 1876, CPEU, CLIV.

7. Chester L. Barrows, *William M. Evarts—Lawyer, Diplomat, Statesman* (Chapel Hill, N.C., 1941) , p. 402.

Minister Charles Decazes inquired in Washington whether the
rumor was true that Russia and the United States had concluded a convention by which they would make common
cause, should England suddenly give Turkey naval support.[8]
The mysteriously long stay of the Russian fleet in Norfolk
and San Francisco in the early months of 1877 lent support to
such rumors.[9] Maxime Outrey, the French minister to the
United States, was certain that no such secret convention
existed, although he thought the Russians might have sounded
out the United States on its feasibility. He added, moreover,
that America would not only be opposed to any military involvement in Europe but that in a showdown it would also
stand by its British cousins rather than by any continental
power.[10] And in a comment indicative of the constant fluctuations in international relationships, Outrey said that furthermore he sensed that the improved atmosphere in Anglo-
American relations ever since the *Alabama* settlement had
resulted in a slightly diminished intimacy between Washington and St. Petersburg.[11]

Russia watched these developments and America's growing
interest in the Chinese market with restrained apprehension,
though still confident that no serious clash of interests was in
the making.[12] But the relative vagueness of the Russo-American relationship made it somewhat easier for France to conclude its alliance with Russia in 1894.

8. Decazes to Outrey, Paris, May 5, 1877 (confidential), CPEU, CLIV.
9. Vaugelas to Decazes, Washington, January 24, 1877; and Outrey to
Decazes, Washington, April 12, 1877, CPEU, CLIV.
10. *Ibid.*, May 12, 1877.
11. *Ibid.*, May 26, 1877.
12. Edward H. Zabriskie, *American-Russian Rivalry in the Far East—A
Study in Diplomacy and Power Politics, 1895–1914* (Philadelphia, 1946),
pp. 46–49.

2. The Third Republic and the Western Hemisphere

In the years following the War of 1870, the stability of the Third French Republic remained doubtful. A sigh of relief greeted the relatively early suppression of the Commune, even though the immediate situation still reflected the volcanic nature of French politics, which had earned France such a poor reputation.[1] Some doubts existed whether President Thiers would strengthen the republic or follow precedent by moving toward a one-man "guided republic." Actually, much of the credit for the early survival of the Third Republic belongs to Adolphe Thiers and Léon Gambetta,[2] the one a conservative and the other a leader of the radical Left, who made the republic respectable. For in France the term "republican," which historically was associated with "revolutionary" upheavals, frightened many moderate citizens. In his message to the French Chamber of Deputies on November 13, 1872, Thiers warned that the republic "is the legal government of this country; to wish for anything else would be tantamount to revolution, the most formidable of revolutions."[3] In spite of the fact that the monarchists looked with disdain on the Third Republic, they were too divided to muster enough support for another change in the form of government. The unusually strong leadership Thiers provided until his opponents succeeded in November, 1873, in electing Marshal MacMa-

1. *The Nation,* June 8, 1871, pp. 397–98 and January 25, 1872, pp. 52–54.
2. Gambetta was an enthusiastic admirer of American Institutions. As foreign minister, he intimated to the American minister that he would receive him "at any time and at any hour." Morton to Frelinghuysen, Paris, January 12, 1883, DDFDS.
3. J. P. T. Bury, *France, 1814–1940* (London, 1962), pp. 144, 153.

hon, a political nonentity, to succeed him was only one of the many factors that kept the republic alive. The French peasantry gradually came around to the viewpoint that the republic had more to offer them than the old Notables. And though there was a revival of Bonapartism in the late 1870's and General Boulanger's spectacular rise in the late 1880's looked ominous, the relative stability of the Third Republic had become one of the amazing facts of French life by 1890.[4] At this time the republic received invaluable support from Pope Leo XIII, who asked all good French Catholics to accommodate themselves to the existing form of government.[5]

It was quite extraordinary that the Third Republic, established at an extremely critical moment in French history, withstood the trials and tribulations to which it was subjected during the early years of its existence. From 1871 to 1875, the supporters of monarchical institutions tried hard, with the help of the large number of conservatives in the constituent assembly, to return to dynastic rule. But as a result of the general elections of 1876, 340 republican deputies were in a position to check the maneuvers of the 153 monarchists in Parliament. Ironically, though, the liberal republicans, who for the next generation exercised a dominant influence in France, felt it necessary to cooperate with clerical and royalist adherents in their effort to check the radical republicans. The extremists of the Left threatened the survival of the Third Republic as much as those of the Right.

By the time of Thiers' death France had not only paid off the indemnity the Prussians had imposed upon it, but the people of France were well on their way toward achieving genuine and enduring liberty. In 1881 the United States min-

4. *Ibid.*, pp. 149, 179–82; and Wright, *France in Modern Times,* pp. 195, 412. By 1881 the republican form of government seemed to divide Frenchmen the least. George Merrill, "The French Republic," *Harper's New Monthly Magazine,* LXII (March 1881) , 582.

5. Henry Haynie, "The French Republic Not a Failure," *National Magazine,* VI (August 1897) , 444.

ister to France, Levi P. Morton, observed with a certain pride, "Ninety years of perplexing experience has developed democratic ideas [in France] into a tower of strength."[6] This exaggerated view appealed to all who believed that the future belonged to democracy and, therefore, to peace and the unification of democratic peoples on both sides of the Atlantic.[7] But even though Frenchmen admired the material progress of the United States and the moral fiber it displayed when it spared the lives of the "conquered chiefs of the Southern rebellion," there were still those among them who feared the tyranny of the majority as much as that of a single tyrant.[8] Another reservation was somewhat related to this genuine fear. It had not escaped the attention of keen French observers that though Americans almost worshipped brilliance, on the whole they rewarded mediocrity in politics. Men like Henry Clay, John C. Calhoun, Daniel Webster, and Henry W. Seward, who towered above many of their contemporaries, were suspected of possibly being too independent to be controlled as presidents. The large number of mediocre presidents may have contributed to the stability of republican institutions in the United States,[9] but such a prospect did not appeal to Frenchmen. French republicanism was largely shaped by domestic forces and conditions. American example and influence affected it little. The anticlericalism of French republicanism

6. Morton to Blaine, Paris, Septmber 1, 1881, DDFDS. See also Washburne to Fish, Paris, March 8, 1872, DDFDS; and A. D. White to J. A. Briggs, Paris, August 2, 1878, Claude W. Unger Collection (Pennsylvania Historical Society MS).

7. One of the more extreme views in this respect was expressed by Victor Hugo, who favored "l'alliance de l'Europe avec elle-même, et de l'Europe avec Amérique." See Henry Dupont, L'Amérique dans l'oeuvre de Victor Hugo (New York, 1952), p. 22; on Hugo's views regarding the unification of the United States of America and of the United States of Europe, see also New York Tribune, May 2, 1876.

8. Max O'Rell, A Frenchman in America (New York, 1891), p. 86; American Citizens, Paris, "Mr. Whitelaw Reid in France, 1889–1892—Farewell Dinner" (Paris, 1892), pp. 46–49.

9. Bartholdi to Decazes, Washington, June 20, 1876, CPEU, CLIV.

was a typically French phenomenon.[10] Interestingly, French republicans took pride in the observation that public opinion, once crystallized, found more speedy application in France than in the United States.

Once the Third Republic began to assert itself in the family of nations, its colonial and economic policies collided occasionally with those of the United States, in spite of fairly successful attempts on the part of the sister republics to benefit each other. The Western hemisphere constituted one of the sensitive areas in which the two countries did not always see eye-to-eye. At the center of their controversies usually stood the Monroe Doctrine, which to French statesmen of the late nineteenth century, appeared to be an indefensibly anachronistic barrier between the two continents.[11] When in 1881 President Grévy recommended a concerted effort on the part of France, Great Britain, and the United States to bring the conflict between Chile and Peru to an end, Secretary of State James G. Blaine questioned both the expediency of such joint intervention in the affairs of American states and the wisdom of any United States intervention in South America.[12] To do so effectively, he contended, would require an expensive army and navy for the benefit of foreign countries. Because the American people were not willing to assume such a burden, the United States government was particularly anxious to keep European guns out of the hemisphere, even for the collection of debts.

The American government gladly assisted France in the reestablishment of its relations with Mexico, but it did not want to see France penetrate the hemisphere.[13] Repeated ru-

10. David Thomson, *Democracy in France since 1870* (London, 1964); p. 139.

11. Morton to Bayard, Paris, April 2, 1885, DDFDS.

12. Blaine to Morton, Washington, September 5, 1881, FIDS. See also Outrey to Gambetta, Washington, January, 31, 1882, CPEU, CLIX.

13. France was grateful for this assistance. See Broglie to Noailles, Versailles, September 10, 1873, FNTDS; and Waddington to Outrey, Paris, March 14, 1878, CPEU, CLV.

mors of French designs on Venezuela and Haiti, though officially denied by the Quai d'Orsay, aroused American suspicions.[14] When in 1895 French soldiers were sent to take over a sizable area of land in Brazil to which France laid claim, the United States officially warned it to stay out of the country.[15] At about the same time, a controversy over French claims against Santo Domingo customs houses was diplomatically settled only after a French naval squadron sent there was being "watched" by an American ship charged with this specific mission. In the final decades of the nineteenth century France established a strong foothold in Argentina where, in cultural respects, its influence was unsurpassed. Its imports into Argentina in 1894 were nearly four times those of the United States. And by 1892 French, British, and German investments in Argentina had assumed such proportions that the Argentine foreign minister began to look toward the United States to help free his country from Europe.[16]

One of the more ambitious and potentially far-reaching schemes Frenchmen were actively pursuing involved the construction of an isthmian canal in Panama. France had from the start resented the bilateral Clayton-Bulwer Treaty (1850) by which the Anglo-Americans had agreed neither to fortify

14. See Blaine to Morton, Washington, December 16, 1881, FIDS; Outrey to Gambetta, Washington, January 16, 1882, CPEU, CLIX; Morton to Frelinghuysen, Paris, March 19, 1885, DDFDS; Bayard to McLane, Washington, December 21, 1888, FIDS; L. L. Montague, *Haiti and the United States, 1714–1938* (New York, 1966), pp. 175–76; and David M. Pletcher, *The Awkward Years—American Foreign Relations under Garfield and Arthur* (Columbia, Mo., 1962), 129–30.

15. Walter Lafeber, *The New Empire: An Interpretation of American Expansionism, 1860–1898* (Ithaca, N.Y., 1967), pp. 246–47. It is noteworthy that early in the twentieth century Brazil shifted its policy from Europe to the United States, a fact the governments of France and Great Britain discovered only belatedly. E. Bradford Burns, *The Unwritten Alliance—Rio Branco and Brazilian-American Relations* (New York, 1966), pp. 197–98.

16. Thomas F. McGann, *Argentina, the United States, and the Inter-American System, 1880–1914* (Cambridge, Mass., 1957), pp. 172–75.

nor to exercise exclusive control over an isthmian canal. In the late 1870's a group of Frenchmen hoping to revive the imperial greatness of France obtained a concession from Colombia for a canal through the Isthmus of Panama, and in February, 1881, a French company actually began to dig the canal. Convinced that the United States alone must control such a waterway, for strategic as well as commercial reasons, James G. Blaine, the energetic American secretary of state, set out immediately to free the United States from the restrictions of the Clayton-Bulwer Treaty, an objective that was not reached until the turn of the century.[17] In the meantime this private French enterprise threatened to become a major bone of contention between France and the United States. Until the financial failure of de Lesseps' interoceanic canal project, Americans found it also difficult to believe that in spite of its denials, the French company was not acting as an agent for the French government. The Senate and the American press voiced strong objections to this intolerable European intrusion.[18] From the point of view of the French government, however, even the privately controlled isthmian canal would have enhanced the prestige and commercial opportunities of France. The Panama Canal would have offered the advantage, moreover, of an alternative route to China and Indochina, in case the Suez Canal should for one reason or another be tem-

17. French observers believed that Blaine was capable of being imprudent. Outrey to Gambetta, Washington, November 21 and December 4, 1881, CPEU, CLVIII. See also White, *American Opinion*, 219–23; and Victor Bérard, "Questions extérieures—Panama," *Revue de Paris;* January 15, 1902, pp. 434–38.

18. Secretary of State Thomas F. Bayard reminded the French government that "no part of America is to be considered as a subject for future colonization by any European power. Bayard to McLane, Washington, December 21, 1888, FIDS. The secretary's allusion to the prudence of preparing for war in defense of an American interoceanic canal led to many newspaper attacks against France. G. Edgar-Bonnet, "Ferdinand de Lesseps et les États-Unis," *Revue d'histoire diplomatique* (1956), pp. 297–301; see also Pletcher, *The Awkward Years*, p. 8.

porarily closed.[19] America's defiance of Europe, as far as hemispheric affairs were concerned, merely confirmed the conviction of most Frenchmen that America was determined to maintain its hegemony in that part of the world. On the other hand, major French initiative in the Western hemisphere, from the time of Napoleon I to the end of the nineteenth century, with respect to Santo Domingo, various marriage schemes, Mexico, and now the Panama Canal, somehow ended in failure.

The strongest foothold of France in America centered of course in Canada.[20] The presence of large numbers of French-speaking Canadians created both in France and in Canada a sentimental atmosphere pregnant with illusory visions. France obviously did not want to see Canada become a part of the United States, one of the possibilities that loomed again on the political horizon during the last decade of the nineteenth century.[21] After two centuries of resistance, the merging of the two countries would inevitably have meant the absorption of the French element by American society. Among others, the ultramontane publicist Paul Tardivel mobilized French Canadian opinion against such a cultural and religious disaster.[22] Interestingly enough, he also tried to insulate the French in Canada from the evil effects of the decadent civilization of the Third Republic. With respect to this phenomenon, a French

19. McLane to Bayard, Paris, July 9, 1886, DDFDS.
20. Both at the time of the American Revolutionary War and the Napoleonic wars prominent Frenchmen entertained the vague notion of reconquering Canada. Général Turreau, "Le Canada sous le premier Empire," *Revue de la Révolution*, VII (1886), 97–98.
21. See Patenôtre to Ribot, Washington, November 30, 1892, CPEU, CLXIX. In the middle of the nineteenth century some French-Canadians favored union with the United States. The majority of French Catholics, however, followed the leadership of their priests, who were anxious to preserve the Catholic and French character of their flocks. Hugh L. Keenleyside and Gerald S. Brown, *Canada and the United States—Some Aspects of Their Historical Relations* (New York, 1952), p. 103.
22. See Pierre Savard, *Jules-Paul Tardivel, La France et les États-Unis, 1851–1905* (Quebec, 1967).

consul in Montreal offered the most enlightening explana-
tion when he made the penetrating observation that, by and
large, French Canadians were very French vis-à-vis the English, but vis-à-vis the French they preferred to be just Canadians.[23] In spite of their mystic attachment to France, the
large majority of French Canadians did not identify themselves with the sophisticated civilization of France, which was
basically alien to the inhabitants of Britain's North American
dominion. And they realized of course that it was the British
rather than the French that provided them with a home, offered them opportunities for earning a livelihood, and pro-
tected their existence.[24]

3. The United States and French Colonialism
   in Africa and Asia

In the final decades of the nineteenth century several
African questions were the cause of minor frictions between
France and the United States. Unlike many European states,
the United States had no colonial aspirations in that part of
the world but it wished to keep the doors open for future
trade and development. Ever since 1821, though, it possessed a
"peculiar" foothold on the west coast of Africa. Originally established by the American Colonization Society as a colony of
freed Negroes, Liberia had for all practical purposes become a
de facto colony of the United States.[1] When it gained its in-

23. A. Kleczkowski to Delcassé, Montréal, October 31, 1899, Politique
Étrangère, Canada, Relations avec la France, I (1897–1904) (AMAE).
24. G. P. de T. Glazebrook, *A History of Canadian External Relations*
(Toronto, 1950), pp. 21–22.
1. See Roland P. Falkner, "The United States and Liberia," *American
Journal of International Law*, IV (1910), 534–39.

dependence in 1847, it was promptly recognized by several European states. Its recognition by the United States was delayed until 1862 only because of the opposition of the Southern states. American money and supplies contributed generously to the maintenance of the Liberian republic, whose many American-born leaders were naturally looking to the United States for assistance and protection.[2]

It required only a look at the map to see why any attempt to unite the scattered French possessions in Africa, stretching from Algiers to Senegal, the Ivory Coast, and the mouth of the Congo, would jeopardize the independence of Liberia. When American officials learned in 1879 that France had offered its protection to the Liberian government, they let it be known that they were opposed to any "movement to divert the independent political life of Liberia for the aggrandizement of a great continental power."[3] Since the adjacent British settlement of Sierra Leone had in recent years been encroaching on Liberia, the American government first inquired cautiously whether France intended to annex Liberia or to help it protect itself against any British designs on it. But on its own, the State Department soon related French moves in regard to Liberia to the improvement of railways and highways in Algeria, French attempts to gain a foothold in Tunis, the rapid growth of French influence on the west coast of Africa, and determined French efforts to penetrate Africa's rich interior. American leaders consequently realized that just as France and Great Britain were in search of new markets, so should the United States.[4] The lingering effects of the international economic depression of 1873 and the increased productive capacity made possible by the industrial revolution persuaded

2. D'Alzac to LaValette, Philadelphia, May 15, 1869, Correspondance Commerciale, Philadelphia, 19 (AMAE).
3. W. Hunter to Edward F. Noyes, Washington, July 17, 1897 (confidential), FIDS.
4. F. W. Seward to E. F. Noyes, Washington, August 29, 1879 FIDS.

the United States to join in the competition for trade in the Mediterranean, the interior districts of North Africa, and perhaps the west coast of Africa. America's interest in Liberia, for a long time prompted by a limited desire to afford recently emancipated Afro-Americans a field for emigration and enterprise, thus suddenly widened.

This interest also involved the United States in the colonial rivalries between France and Great Britain.[5] In 1884, in spite of its suavely phrased disclaimers, the French government sought boundary adjustments in Liberia to which the United States objected as strongly as Great Britain. Secretary of State Frederick Frelinghuysen's unusually sharp note to the French Legation left no doubt of his view that America's intimate relationship with Liberia entitled it to be consulted on boundary disputes, a privilege Britain and Liberia had willingly recognized on the occasion of a recent settlement.[6] French violation of that very settlement, establishing the line of demarkation between Sierra Leone and Liberia, would, Frelinghuysen warned, be a threat to "the integrity and tranquillity of Liberia." Two years later, upon learning of treaties French naval officers had made with chiefs of native tribes within Liberian territory, Secretary of State Thomas F. Bayard claimed the "right" to protect Liberia's territorial sovereignty and to aid her "in settling any disputes that may arise."[7] French Foreign Minister Charles-Louis Freycinet evaded America's objections by referring to "the already old ties" between France and the tribal populations of Grand and Petit Beriby, in virtue of a treaty their chief had signed as far back as 1868.[8] Subsequent American remonstrances suffered the same fate. Indeed, the informal rather than legal nature of

5. Noyes to Evarts, Paris, May 13, 1880, DDFDS.
6. Frelinghuysen to Roustan, Washington, August 22, 1884, FNFDS.
7. Bayard to McLane, Washington, January 13, 1884, FNFDS.
8. Freycinet to Vignaud, Paris, August 18, 1886, enclosure in McLane to Bayard, Paris, August 23, 1886, DDFDS.

America's protectorate over Liberia prompted the French to take exception to what they described as impudent interferences contrary to international law.[9] In the end, Liberia ceded to France, through the treaty of December 8, 1892, the sea coast east of the Cavally River for certain territorial and financial compensations. Through this treaty France also recognized, to the satisfaction of the United States, the independence of Liberia within the boundary lines just agreed upon.[10] What originally appeared to have been a contemptuous French disregard of American claims ended in fact with a partial French recognition of America's objective.

In other parts of Africa the United States was less directly involved. Nevertheless, the feverish scramble for colonies, markets, and naval stations in Africa during the final decades of the century made occasional differences between the American government and the colonial powers unavoidable. A conversation in July, 1881, between the secretary of the French Legation, François-Henri-Louis de Geoffroy, and Secretary of State Blaine conveyed the friendly, businesslike atmosphere that prevailed then in Franco-American dealings. To the surprise of the French diplomat, Blaine inquired whether France would not want to sell St. Pierre and Miquelon at a good price—a sounding, incidentally, to which the Quai d'Orsay turned a deaf ear. Quickly shifting the scene from the North Atlantic to the heart of Africa, Blaine then raised questions about English and Portuguese activities in the Congo. Apologetically, he hastened to clarify that of course the United States did not intend to interfere in regions the Old World powers regarded as their sphere of operation. "Why not?" replied Geoffroy. "If you have commercial interests in Africa, I don't see why you should not look after them in the

9. T. Jefferson Coolidge, *Autobiography of T. Jefferson Coolidge 1857–1900* (Boston, 1902) pp. 194–96.

10. T. Jefferson Coolidge to John W. Foster, Paris, December 9, 1892, DDFDS; see also Falkner, "The United States and Liberia," pp. 542–44.

same manner in which we intend to protect ours in the New World."[11]

This spirit reflected the determination with which such leaders of the Third Republic as Léon Gambetta and Jules Ferry set out to expand the French empire, by diplomatic means if possible, by force if necessary.[12] As the price of arrangements agreed upon at the Berlin Congress in 1878, France secured from Britain a "free hand" in Tunis in exchange for French acquiescence in Britain's recent acquisition of Cyprus. Bismarck, who thought Tunis was "not worth even a bad cigar," approved of this deal in the hope that it would divert France from any idea of revenge against Germany.[13] To the bitter disappointment of Italy, which had cast its eyes on Tunis, France thereafter lost little time in establishing its protectorate over Tunis through the Treaty of May 12, 1881. Public-opinion media in France and the United States severely condemned the fact that France had resorted to an unprovoked attack on Tunis to compel this treaty. At home, Théodore-Justin Roustan, the former French consul and Minister Resident in Tunis, became the target of such severe criticism for his part in the recent Tunisian maneuvers that the French government deemed it advisable to get rid of him by appointing him as Minister Plenipotentiary to the United States. Suspecting that his exploits in Tunis had given the American people erroneous impressions about him, Roustan

11. Geoffroy to St. Hilaire, Washington, July 16, 1881; and St. Hilaire to Geoffroy, Paris, September 2, 1881 (confidential), CPEU, CLVIII.

12. Graham H. Stuart, *French Foreign Policy—From Fashoda to Serajevo, 1898–1914* (New York, 1921), p. 12. Such opponents of Ferry's colonial policy as Georges Clémenceau wanted the power of France to be concentrated in Europe rather than diffused in colonial enterprises. Gottschalk and Lach, *The Transformation of Modern Europe,* p. 429.

13. H. I. Priestly, *France Overseas—A Study of Modern Imperialism* (New York, 1938), pp. 166–67; and Achille Viallate, *Economic Imperialism and International Relations during the Last Fifty Years* (New York, 1923), pp. 19–20.

tried to dispel the notion of his being an untrustworthy character. Instead of first presenting his credentials to President Chester A. Arthur, he took a *New York Herald* reporter into his confidence as soon as he landed on American soil. In a long and candid interview he defended the capture of Tunis as a means of preventing Italy from acquiring a good African seaport which France needed for the protection of Algiers.[14]

As a French patriot, Roustan found his American experience rather disquieting. The anticolonial attitude of the United States found its expression in disparaging newspaper articles about French colonialism. Attacks against French "filibustering" in the Congo and Madagascar competed with critical comments about French ventures in Tunis and Tonkin.[15] Roustan attributed this unsympathetic reaction to the British press, which, he believed, made deliberate efforts to alienate the American people from the French. And it succeeded so well because the American press relied then almost exclusively on British sources of information for its comments on world affairs. What irked Roustan particularly was the double standard Americans applied with respect to British and French colonial policies.[16] He noted, for instance, that Americans looked askance at the course of events in Tunis, but they accepted Britain's control of Egypt as a *fait accompli*, although it modified the Mediterranean equilibrium much more profoundly than the French control of Tunis. Moreover, when Americans criticized British colonial policies at all, they did it with much greater circumspection than when they criticized French policies. In time this observation led Roustan to the broader conclusion that in a moment of danger France

14. Editorial on "The New French Minister," *New York Times*, June 19, 1882. See also Paul H. B. Baron d'Estournelles de Constant, *La Politique Française en Tunisie—Le Protectorat et ses Origines, 1854–1891* (Paris, 1891) , p. 317.

15. Roustan to Duclerc, Washington, November 29, 1882, CPEU, CLIX.

16. Roustan to Challemel-Lacour, Washington, May 7, 1883, CPEU, CLX.

might discover how great the illusion of the presumed Franco-American friendship had been.

Those who rationalized that empire-building was a civilizing enterprise[17] ignored the fact that international law was one of its major victims. Although the limited American dealings with Tunis and Madagascar hardly merited much official attention, legal questions concerning them led to drawn-out controversies. The French interpreted the Tunis Protectorate Treaty of May 12, 1881, as, in effect, giving France the right to represent Tunis in its relations with foreign countries. France consequently refused to recognize the most-favored-nation treatment the United States had previously secured through treaties with Tunis. The State Department insisted repeatedly that France possessed no internationally binding legal authority to denounce these ancient pacts. Getting nowhere, Acting Secretary of State William R. Day finally warned the authorities in Paris that the United States "will hold France internationally responsible for any act she may perform in contravention or disrespect of their provisions."[18] Similarly, through the Treaty of December 17, 1885, France established a protectorate over Madagascar, which both the United States and Great Britain recognized. Within another decade, however, France subjugated Madagascar and, once it had accomplished this task, refused to recognize the special treaty rights of Britain and the United States. The French government bluntly advised the two powers that their anterior treaties with Madagascar were "incompatible with the new situation created by the conquest of the Island."[19]

17. Maurice Reclus, *Grandeur de "La Troisième" de Gambetta à Poincaré* (Paris, 1948), p. 173. On the Tunisian question, the following references may be of interest: Olney to Patenôtre, Washington, December 3, 1896, and January 15, 1897, FNTDS; Vignaud to Olney, Paris, February 1, 1897, DDFDS; Jules Cambon to John Sherman, Washington, February 19, 1898, FNTDS.

18. William R. Day, to Paul Lefaivre, Washington, December 2, 1897, FNFDS.

19. Vignaud to Olney, Paris, June 23, 1896. DDFDS. See also Patenôtre

In the energetic pursuit of its colonial goals France relied on legal references when they served its ends and, as in the instances just referred to, dismissed them when they interfered with its ambitions. In the Congo it relied on internationally recognized territorial claims based on discovery and exploration, as well as on a treaty with the natives by which Savorgnan de Brazza had secured a protectorate of all the land north of the Congo. For these very reasons France was initially reluctant to recognize as a sovereign state the privately sponsored International Association of the Congo, occupying territory claimed by France. The French were also not eager to share the exploitation of red rubber with their European competitors in the Congo.[20] To protect whatever commercial gains the American business community might derive from trade with this region, the United States was the first great power to recognize the sovereignty of the Association of the Congo on April 22, 1884.[21] Guided by the same motivation, it accepted, with traditional qualifications, its invitation to the Berlin Conference on the Congo (1884–85). Here was an opportunity for the American government to press for the abolition of slavery contracts and to make it possible for the native races of Africa to develop their own civilization in their own land.[22] To shut the door to any exclusive exploitation of this region, Secretary Frelinghuysen instructed the American delegate to the conference, therefore, to promote the neutralization of the Congo Basin. This proposition, designed to serve the interests

---

to Hanotaux, Washington, June 11, 1894. CPEU, CLXXI; and *The Nation*, December 12, 1895, p. 419.

20. Stephen H. Roberts, *History of French Colonial Policy, 1870–1925* (London, 1929) , p. 340.

21. Thomas F. Power, Jr., *Jules Ferry and the Renaissance of French Imperialism* (New York, 1944) , pp. 97, 106–7; see also Leo Thomas Molloy, *Henry Shelton Sanford, 1823–1891–A Biography* (Derby, Conn., 1952) , p. 27.

22. See Albrecht zu Stolberg-Wernigerode, *Germany and the United States of America During the Era of Bismarck* (Philadelphia, 1937) , p. 207.

of all peoples, was vigorously challenged by the French government, fearing, as it did, possible infringements on its own possessions. Officially, the French delegate at the conference objected to the American proposal not so much on legal as on functional grounds. He questioned whether the neutralization of a territory would not amount to an empty formality, without guaranties by neutral powers. In the end, the conference recognized the sovereignty of the Association, it adopted the principle of freedom of commerce and navigation in the Congo Basin, and it engaged the signatory powers to the General Act to respect a qualified system of neutrality *in the conventional area* of the Congo.[23] Under this system neutrality in this area was to be respected as long as the duties of neutrality were being observed. Even though the United States signed but did not ratify the Berlin Act, it was extraordinary for it to participate so actively in the discussions at the center of which lay the European balance of power in Africa.

A different situation had traditionally prevailed in the Far East. There, the Western powers wanted to present a common front vis-à-vis the Orientals, even though each one of these powers competed with the others for spheres, markets, and influence. In the 1880's French leaders became very active in overseas enterprises.[24] A variety of motivations explained their activities. They wished to keep pace with their European rivals and enhance the power and recover the lost prestige of France, as well as meet the needs of an expanding economy. As much as the French took exception to any American projection into strictly European affairs, they frequently sought and took ad-

23. On the Congo question, see U.S. Senate Ex. Doc. 196, pp. 176–77, 186–92; "Affaires du Congo" Berlin, Sessions of November 19 and December 10, 1884, pp. 73 and 174; Morton to Frelinghuyson, Paris, January 8, 1885, DDFDS; and Jesse S. Reeves, *The International Beginnings of the Congo Free State* (Baltimore, 1894), p. 31.

24. Consult J. F. Cady, *The Roots of French Imperialism in Eastern Asia* (Ithaca, N.Y., 1954), pp. 294–95; and Jules Ferry, *Le Tonkin et la mère patrie* (Paris, 1890), pp. 37–44, 48–52.

vantage of America's participation in Far Eastern affairs. French colonial policy in Indochina was a particularly interesting case in point. Exploits in Africa were simultaneously duplicated in Asia, with Jules Ferry energetically leading the drive for empire. As Ferry saw it, French control of the Tonkin route to China might not only be as effective as Britain's approach via Hong Kong, it would also create access to the proverbial wealth of the Orient. Since the opportunities for expansion in Europe appeared to be vanishing and those in the Western hemisphere were unavailable, Ferry felt that French Indochina might well "mean bread for our children in fifty or one hundred years." This economic motivation should not obscure the fact however, that national pride and prestige drove the French to export their "superior" culture to East Asia.

Following many years of economic and political penetration, France recognized Annam's independence in 1887 through the treaty of Saigon.[25] Although it also assumed the protection of Annam, it did not legally establish a protectorate over it. Only a few years later, differences of opinion over the interpretation of this treaty induced the emperor of Annam to enlist the assistance of China, Annam's suzerain. Compounding the developing confusion, Annam also asked France, under the treaty of 1874, to send reinforcements, only to let French and Chinese forces settle the issue of how far France should be permitted to "protect" Annam.[26] And if this strange procedure were not perplexing enough, the Marquis de Tseng, China's diplomatic representative in Paris, succeeded in making a Chinese puzzle out of the whole situation. Soon after France moved into Annam and Tonkin in 1881, it found itself confronted with more difficulties than it had an-

25. For a brief summary of French policies on Indochina during the Second Empire, see Roberts, *History of French Colonial Policy*, pp. 419–24.
26. *Ibid.*, pp. 425–26.

ticipated.[27] It was easier for Paris to shrug off Tseng's protest against the occupation of Tonkin than to cope with the combined opposition of regular Chinese troops and the Black Flags of Taiping Rebellion fame. Soon the French found themselves in an unenviable position in Indochina where, as the *New York Tribune* phrased it, "mismanagement has been followed by misfortune."[28] The attempt to establish French influence and spread French culture in Asia clearly ran into unexpected native resistance. Oriental peoples, taking pride in their own ancient civilization, resented this new intrusion of Westerners.

Serious trouble began to develop in 1883 when the Chinese challenged French control of Annam and Tonkin. Taking a special interest in this region, the Chinese government suggested to the American minister in Peking that it would be prepared to agree to American arbitration of the Tonkin dispute. The French government's first reaction to this suggestion was vague but sympathetic. On July 17, 1883, Foreign Minister Paul Armand Challemel-Lacour wrote to the United States Legation in Paris, "We certainly should be happy for the good offices of your government." He was not clear, however, about "the questions upon which the efforts of the Government of Washington should be brought to bear." One week later, on July 24, 1883, Challemel-Lacour changed his mind and emphatically assured the chargé d'affaires of the American Legation that "We have no difficulty at all with China."[29] He could not think, he claimed, of any reason why China should be dissatisfied with France. But China did not leave him long in doubt about its grievances. Under the date line, "Chinese Legation, Paris, August 7, 1883," Tseng handed a

27. See John F. Cady, *Thailand, Burma, Laos, and Cambodia* (Englewood Cliffs, N.J., 1966), p. 109; and Priestley, *France Overseas*, pp. 219–20.

28. *New York Daily Tribune*, June 2, 1883. To this newspaper the Tonkin episode illustrated "at once the greed and the recklessness of the French Government."

29. See Brulatour to Frelinghuysen, Paris, July 18 and 24, 1883, DDFDS.

memorandum to the American chargé d'affaires with a request to make its substance known to the French foreign minister.[30] It stated the conditions under which the imperial government of China was willing to come to an understanding with France: "(1) France will not infringe upon the political position of the kingdom of Annam and will not annex any territory beyond the six southern provinces she had annexed or occupied in 1862 and 1867. (2) The bonds of vassalage by which Annam is united to China will remain as in the past. (3) The territory presently occupied by the French troops in Tonkin will be evacuated and certain cities, after agreement, shall be designated to be opened to foreign commerce. . . . (4) The Red River will be opened to the navigation of foreign ships up to Toung Ho Kouan. . . . (5) China pledges herself to use the influence she derives from her situation to facilitate commerce on the Red River. . . . (6) Any new convention between France and Annam is to be made the object of an understanding with China."

Convinced of the friendly and impartial disposition of the United States in this issue, Foreign Minister Challemel-Lacour found it painful to see the United States made the bearer of proposals that the honor and dignity of France did not permit it to entertain. Having resumed his functions as head of the American Legation in Paris, Morton reminded Challemel-Lacour that the government in Washington "had neither suggested nor endorsed the proposals of the Marquis de Tseng." But why, asked Challemel-Lacour, this mysterious roundabout way of communicating the "offensive terms of settlement," when he was in daily touch with the Chinese minister?[31] According to him, Tseng had very recently assured him of China's friendly sentiments and said that "he had no instruction to make any complaint or to present or suggest proposals" with respect to the Tonkin affair. It became obvious

30. *Ibid.*, August 9, 1883.
31. Morton to Frelinghuysen, Paris, August 22, 1883, DDFDS.

that both the Chinese and the French were using the United
States as a convenient channel they wished to fall back on
whenever circumstances warranted it. On July 23 Challemel-
Lacour expressed his desire to the American Minister, Levi P.
Morton, to be informed about China's grievances. Less than a
month later, when France had evidently decided to deal with
China and Annam directly, Challemel-Lacour was no longer
interested in them. He wanted to settle matters directly, with
Annam, however, rather than with China. Through the Treaty
of Hué of August 5, 1883, France managed to establish a
protectorate over Annam and Tonkin, excluding China altogether.

Yet this treaty did not bring peace. Supported by China, the
Black Flags continued to engage the French in warfare. Once
again, the United States stood ready to be the mediator between France and China, a role the French government both
appreciated and suspected. American opposition to continued
warfare, expressed more frankly by the press than by the
government, found a strong echo in France where anticolonialists protested against what they considered to be a highly
objectionable and wasteful adventure. As its friend, the United
States sympathized with China's desire not to see French control of Tonkin extended to its borders. But France, which was
determined to teach the Chinese not to trifle with the French
government,[32] rebuffed Washington's renewed offer of good
offices. This determined stand, backed up by force, finally led
to the preliminary peace between France and China at Tientsin
(May 11, 1884) providing for the evacuation of Chinese
troops from Tonkin, Peking's acceptance of French suzerainty
over Annam, and the extension of exclusive commercial advantages to France.[33] Subsequent treaties, signed in June, confirmed the establishment of French protectorates for Annam,
Tonkin, and Cambodia. On May 13, 1884, Morton sent to

32. Beckles Willson, *America's Ambassadors to France (1777–1927)*
(New York, 1928) , pp. 324–25.

33. Morton to Frelinghuysen, Paris, May 13, 1884, DDFDS. See also
Roberts, *History of French Colonial Policy*, p. 426.

Secretary of State Frelinghuysen an overly optimistic dispatch in which, with reference to the exclusive commercial advantages granted France, he remarked, "It seems to be the general understanding that these advantages are to be shared by all other nations." And assuming the role of defender of French colonialism, Morton permitted himself to be carried away by adding, "The victory of France will thus have been a victory for the whole world and a triumph for the cause of civilization."

The Chinese continued to demonstrate their inexhaustible skill in exasperating their opponents. For another year they forced the French government to send military and naval reinforcements to Tonkin. At the same time they carried on stubborn diplomatic exchanges, causing their American go-between embarrassments in the process. The Chinese not only delayed the withdrawal of their forces from Tonkin, in further violation of the Tientsin peace treaty, which they regarded as not totally binding because of its "preliminary" character, they also ambushed French troops, inflicting outrageous losses.[34] French reprisals and demands for a sizable indemnity promptly reactivated the military and diplomatic fronts. In spite of strong political opposition and scathing criticism at home, Jules Ferry firmly rejected the inspired suggestions of American mediation of this new dispute.[35] Such mediation, the *New York Times* commented, would get France "gracefully out of a position into which she has too rashly ventured, and which may give her serious trouble."[36] And when Paris "persistently rejects proposals for peaceful arbitration," the *Times* editorialized, "she cannot complain if distant observers suspect the Chinese of having the better cause."[37]

34. *Ibid.,* pp. 428–29; Priestley, *France Overseas,* pp. 220–21.
35. Ferry to Patenôtre, Paris, August 10, 1884. *Affaires de Chine et du Tonkin,* p. 28; Li-Hong-Tchang to Li-Fong-Pao, Tien-Tsin, July 31, 1884; *ibid,* pp. 3–4; and Frelinghuysen to Morton, Somerville, N.J., July 3, 1884, FIDS.
36. September 6, 1884, p. 4.
37. September 22, 1884, p. 4.

Soon the Chinese seemed once again to give convincing evidence of their desire for a diplomatic solution of the new crisis when they took the initiative in trying to secure American arbitration of the indemnity demanded by France. Paris had second thoughts about the usefulness of America's friendly intervention, but procedural questions of a very delicate nature now complicated the adoption of such a course. Morton, the United States minister in France, contended that since Ferry had declined the recent American offer of good offices, it was he who should solicit them this time.[38] The French statesman was in principle willing to accept them, provided the United States tendered them in response to Chinese initiative. Otherwise, he decided, France could not very well ask for the good offices or even intimate that it would favorably respond to their offer "because such action would be *misinterpreted by China as a sign of weakness.*" He emphasized, however, that the implementation of the Tientsin Treaty and a greatly reduced indemnity would satisfy his conditions for a settlement of the Tonkin question. In the meantime new developments introduced more procedural alternatives. China suggested Germany as a possible mediator; Britain's diplomatic cooperation was also available. While the French government was weighing the advantages and drawbacks of collective and individual mediation, China proceeded to ascertain from French officials in Tientsin and Peking the conditions under which France would agree to arbitration. Significantly, the terms Ferry outlined to them were harder than those he had previously alluded to in conversations with the American minister in Paris. He toned down the punitive aspect of the indemnity payments, but until the Tientsin Treaty had been fully implemented and a commercial treaty been concluded, he insisted on the temporary occupation of Chinese territory as a guarantee.[39]

38. Morton to Frelinghuysen, Paris, September 12, 1884, DDFDS.
39. Consult the private correspondence of Jules Ferry with Waddington,

It was probably no coincidence that twenty-four hours prior to this Chinese inquiry, the American minister in Peking had failed to make any headway when he proposed to his French colleague an armistice of six months and American arbitration of the disputed issues. On his part, Secretary of State Frelinghuysen unofficially explored whether the French would agree to a solution calling for the execution of the Tientsin Treaty and mediation rather than arbitration of the indemnity question. From the French point of view, this procedure was preferable, even though the suggested solution implied an American bias in favor of China.[40] Still considering a concerted Anglo-American diplomatic intervention in November, 1884, the French government was pleased to find the American secretary of state always ready to cooperate in any constructive manner. Anxious to settle the Chinese difficulty, Ferry was inclined to enlist American aid. In the end, though, secret negotiations, to which Sir Robert Hart, the British envoy to China, made quietly important contributions, culminated in a new Treaty of Tientsin, signed on June 9, 1885. Through this compromise treaty China recognized in a fashion, without clearly defining the extent of French authority, the French protectorate over Annam. It granted France, moreover, undisputed possession of the whole of Tonkin and exclusive commercial advantages in Yunnan as compensation for its sacrifices and its decision to drop the indemnity issue. Finally, France was expected to offer China all facilities for the construction of a railroad line connecting Canton with Hanoi, stretching over nearly one thousand miles.[41]

As the future demonstrated, external peace with China did

Paris, October 8 and 18, 1884, in Papiers Waddington, "Lettres et Notes" (AMAE), t. 4.

40. Vignaud to Frelinghuysen, Paris, October 20, 1884, DDFDS.

41. *Ibid.*, November 5, 1884; Billot to Waddington, Paris, November 8, 1884, in Papiers Wadington, "Lettres et Notes" (AMAE), t. 4; McLane to Bayard, Paris, June 24, 1885, DDFDS. See also Priestley, *France Overseas*, pp. 221–22.

not guarantee to France internal peace in Annam. In Madagascar, Tunisia, and Tonkin drift and vacillation gave way to
firmness and force and, in turn, military action prepared the
ground for diplomatic solutions of political objectives. The
colonial battles were not only fought in Indochina and Africa, but also in France itself. Throughout this period of
heightened colonial activity French anticolonialists subjected
Jules Ferry, "the Tonkinese," and other advocates of colonialism to verbal, and, occasionally, even physical attacks.[42] In this
complex situation, the moderating influence of the United
States rendered multiple services to the French government as
well as to its opposition, in domestic as well as foreign political
affairs. Despite the fact that American diplomats could not ignore the economic interests of the United States in Asia and
Africa, their friendly interventions demonstrated concretely
America's international concern and usefulness. Beyond that,
one of the most influential American magazines in the nineteenth century, the liberal *Nation*,[43] took a long view of these
French ventures. Expressing the regrets of many Americans, it
finally concluded, as many Frenchmen themselves contended,
that France's empire was destined to cost the country militarily,
financially, politically, and morally more than it was bargain-
ing for. Certainly, until 1914 the relatively small investments in the empire and the trade it stimulated did not justify the struggle for its acquisition.[44] The empire offered few
economic gains; its significance was of a strategic, political,
and psychological nature. As the later experience of the
United States also demonstrated, neither the prosperity of

42. Fresnette Pisani-Ferry, *Jules Ferry et le partage du monde* (Paris,
1962), pp. 147–222; see also Roberts, *History of French Colonial Policy*, p.
382.

43. December 12, 1895.

44. Wright, *France in Modern Times*, p. 383; see also Henri Brunschwig, *French Colonialism, 1871–1914: Myths and Realities* (New York,
1960), p. 96.

France nor that of the United States depended on their respective colonial empires.

4. The French Navy and the United States

The accelerated pace of French colonial activity in the last two decades of the century induced some Americans to focus sharply on the influence of sea power in the making of history. Their historical experiences and the geographic realities of their country had of course made them long ago aware of the significance of sea power. How could Americans forget the major contribution of the French fleet under the command of Admiral de Grasse to General Cornwallis' surrender at Yorktown? How could they ever forget the lessons taught them during the era of the French Revolution when belligerents and neutrals alike were exposed to the overpowering impact of superior sea power?[1] The sudden appearance of French or British naval squadrons in Cuban waters, whether in the 1820's or the 1850's, conveyed to the United States the intended warning signal to keep its hands off this island.[2] Interestingly, such intimidating maneuvers not only caused a great deal of resentment, they also provided the Americans with an opportunity to point out the inadequate state of their naval posture. When, during the spoliation crisis of 1835–36, France reportedly sent across the Atlantic a "squadron of observation," the prominent Jacksonian Democrat, Senator

1. Alfred T. Mahan, *The Influence of Sea Power upon the French Revolution and Empire, 1793–1812* (Boston, 1898), II, 195. Mahan shared the view expressed by Barbé-Marbois, Napoleon's finance minister, that fear of Britain's sea power influenced the Emperor's decision to sell Louisiana to the United States.

2. Kenneth Bourne, *Britain and the Balance of Power in North America, 1815–1908* (Berkeley, 1967), p. 37.

Thomas Hart Benton of Missouri, asked, "How comes it that we have no force to oppose to this squadron which comes here . . . to show us that it knows the way to Washington as well as the English?"[3]

The steady growth of the American merchant marine, whose tonnage was by 1860 unsurpassed by any other power, reflected the economic ascendancy of the United States and enhanced its international prestige. Except for its potential privateering capacity, it did not, however, contribute substantially to America's naval power. For years to come, the American navy did not rank very high among the navies of the world. Fortunately, the United States was aided by the maritime rivalry between France and Great Britain and by the technological advances in naval construction and weaponry, especially during the mid-nineteenth century. In the 1840's and the 1860's France rather than Britain boasted of the superiority of its steam and ironclad ships, compelling Britain temporarily to act with greater than usual caution in international affairs. Both during the Oregon crisis and the American Civil War the United States benefited from Britain's fear of potential French challenges. Britain did not want to be caught with a portion of its fleet tied up in America as long as it thought France capable of starting a conflict in British waters, the Mediterranean, or elsewhere.[4]

Although Napoleon III was impressed with the ingenious naval designs of John Ericsson, the Swedish-American naval engineer, he appointed the Frenchman Dupuy de Lôme to bring about a major revolution in naval architecture, utiliz-

3. Thomas H. Benton, *Thirty Years' View* (New York, 1879), I, 593. This squadron was composed of sixty vessels. See also Harold and Margaret Sprout, *The Rise of American Naval Power, 1776–1918* (Princeton, 1946), p. 106.

4. James Phinney Baxter, *The Introduction of the Ironclad Warship* (Cambridge, Mass., 1933), pp. 65–67; see also John S. Galbraith, "France as a Factor in the Oregon Negotiations," *Pacific Northwest Quarterly*, XLIV (1953), 70.

ing the lessons of the Crimean War. De Lôme's introduction of seagoing ironclads, armored ships, and shell guns soon involved Britain and France in a naval race of major proportions. Lord Palmerston, the aged British prime minister, distrusted the French emperor—"the crafty spider of the Tuileries"—so much that he was determined to modernize the British navy, whatever the financial sacrifices. Admiral Robinson's confidential report to the British Admiralty, dated February 11, 1863, asserting that at that time England lacked "an iron clad squadron capable of fighting a duel with a French iron clad squadron on equal terms" was indeed distressing.[5] In essence, the admiral was reiterating the alarming observation of the *London Times* in the spring of 1862 when it commented with respect to the extraordinary naval engagement between the *Monitor* and the *Merrimac* that "England had no navy; all she had . . . was a parcel of old tubs that would not stand up for an hour before the 'Monitors' which were being constructed in the United States."[6]

Contrary to a long-lingering myth, France rather than the United States led in the development of ironclads. In fact, French leadership in naval construction ever since 1854 ultimately also affected the United States, which before 1860 had built only three unarmored iron warships. According to a prominent American shipbuilder familiar with English and French navy yards in 1860, "the steam fleet of the United States is hardly equal to that of third-rate European powers."[7] Sharing this concern, navy-minded Americans urged the construction of "floating batteries and ironclad steamers," to follow the lead of England and France. "Before the end of this year," the *Philadelphia Press* noted early in 1861, "France will have eight and England six such vessels. How many are we to

5. Baxter, *Ironclad Warship*, pp. 317, 330–31.
6. Thomas H. Dudley, "Three Critical Periods in Our Diplomatic Relations with England During the Late War," *The Pennsylvania Magazine of History and Biography*, XVII (1893), 45.
7. Baxter, *Ironclad Warship*, p. 239.

have?"[8] To the amazement of the world, by the end of 1864 the United States possessed a fleet of 671 vessels, most of them steam-propelled and mounting 4,610 guns. Though the majority of these ships were hastily converted merchantmen, by the end of the war 85 wooden, steam-operated naval vessels and 39 ironclads had been built and more were to follow.[9]

Just as Great Britain now felt obliged to pay as much attention to the American as to the French ironclad navy, French observers were quite convinced that immediately following the Civil War the United States wanted "a navy capable of fighting anywhere in the world against a European navy." But while aiming at an early parity with the British and French navies, Americans seemed to be interested in frigates and corvettes with great speed and fire power designed to hunt down merchantmen rather than to fight in Europe. The impressive performance of the American navy during the late war and the projection of its recent momentum into the future apparently justified the expectation of further American naval expansion.[10] As the major maritime powers, France and Great Britain felt obliged to take these estimates into consideration in planning the future of their own navies. It came as a great surprise to them that until 1883 the post-Civil War Congress had neglected the American navy in its appropriations.[11] During those years of remarkable industrial development the United States did not keep pace with the navies of the major powers and could therefore in no respect compete with them militarily. The American navy was not only outnumbered

8. *Ibid.*, p. 220; see also William Covant Church, *Life of John Ericsson* (New York, 1890) , I, 242.

9. Bourne, *Britain and the Balance of Power in North America,* pp. 274–75.

10. P. Dislère, "Notes sur la marine des États-Unis," *Revue maritime et coloniale,* XXII (January, 1868) , 288–89, 293, 301. The French were particularly interested in the revolving turret and in the mechanical devices Americans used in heavy ordnance.

11. Donald W. Mitchell, *History of the Modern American Navy: From 1883 through Pearl Harbor* (New York, 1946) , pp. 3–21.

and in many ways obsolete, even the range and penetrating power of its guns did not match those of France and Great Britain. No wonder that critical comments in the United States regarding French moves in Madagascar prompted the *Moniteur Universelle* to ridicule the American navy and to boast that French warships could easily burn down all American ports.[12] As even the French envoy to the United States protested, this "French insolence" was obviously not well received by a country with an enormous capacity for naval expansion and a naval-officer corps of outstanding reputation. Such a gratuitous insult not only poisoned the diplomatic air, if anything it accomplished the opposite of what Frenchmen contemptuous of the United States could possibly have desired. It served as a catalyst that cleared the way for increased naval construction in the United States. This issue was dramatized by the remarkable report Rear Admiral Daniel Ammen submitted in 1883 to Secretary of the Navy William E. Chandler.[13] In essence, Admiral Ammen contended that in case of war with Great Britain or France the United States would find it more difficult to cope with the French navy than with the British.

The admiral substantiated his unorthodox thesis with cogently reasoned arguments: "Whilst the navy of Great Britain," he wrote, "could not fail to commit great havoc and destruction, our land forces could speedily possess themselves of British America from Nova Scotia to the shores of the Pacific. Upon the high seas a great many of her merchant marine would be destroyed, but most of all would she suffer through a loss of commercial intercourse with us and some of her colonies. . . . Nothing short of national insanity of one or both could bring about a war between them." But, he continued, "a war with France . . . could be maintained indefinitely by her against us at a very inconsiderable cost, and our

12. Roustan to Duclerc, Washington, December 7, 1882, CPEU, CLIX.
13. House Ex. Doc., 48 Cong., 1st sess., No. 1, 3, I (1883), 93–99.

defense would be not only enormously expensive, but quite unsatisfactory. There would be no adjacent territory for us to invade . . . and there would be little or no merchant marine on the high seas for us to destroy. . . . Increased rates of insurance, as compared with neutral flags, would operate to lay up all merchant vessels under the French flag. Our cities, towns, and coasts, imperfectly defended, would be menaced and some of them destroyed, and our attempts at defense would frequently prove abortive and humiliating." By establishing bases on outlying islands of the United States, such as Martha's Vineyard, Admiral Ammen warned furthermore that considerable French land forces "could menace thousands of miles of our coasts." Although popular feeling in France was not hostile to the United States, the admiral referred to recent French activities in Tunis, the Congo, Madagascar, and Tonkin as foreshadowing the possibility "that the same action will sooner or later obtain in Central America." This report, endorsed by other high naval officers, finally recommended the construction of marine rams as an effective defense against French armored vessels.

Admiral Ammen's acknowledgment of the rising power and prestige of France took the British by surprise.[14] In a way, it was the modern version of a warning signal the *New York Times* had issued in the late 1850's when French, British, and American ships had gathered in Nicaraguan waters. At that time, a French naval force of nearly one thousand guns assembled in the Atlantic waters of the New World to "restrain lawless enterprises." Singling France out as the one power in the world that "at this moment . . . could most easily afford to break with the United States, and which possesses the most formidable means of interfering with our prosperity," the *Times* recommended abstention from diplomacy by the cannon.[15] Reaction was different in the 1880's. Alarmed by the

14. Roustan to Jules Ferry, Washington, August 1, 1884, CPEU, CLXI.
15. See issues of December 7 and 8, 1858.

ominous Frenchification of Panama as a possible forerunner
to other acts of defiance of the Monroe Doctrine, and appalled
by the huge sums "civilized" Europe spent on armaments, concerned Americans began to lobby for a strong navy.[16] By the
1890's, the French took note of the steady rise of America's
naval power, ranking in 1892 as the seventh in the world and
on its way toward overtaking the size of the German and
Spanish navies. In view of Germany's ambitions in the Pacific
and America's customary cooperation with the Western powers in Chinese waters, France was not unduly disturbed by the
growing strength of the American navy.[17] Unlike the United
States, which could not safely ignore the possibility of French
intervention in the Western hemisphere, France was comforta-
bly reassured that the United States would not use its naval
forces for hostile operations in European waters.

In the final decades of the century international naval circles engaged in a highly controversial debate on questions of
naval strategy. In the mid-nineteenth century coastal defense
rather than organized fleet action dominated naval thinking in
France and the United States. The experiences of the Franco-
Prussian War, in which a state without a navy to speak of
defeated France in short order, strengthened the traditional notion of European military men that sea power played only a
subordinate role in national defense. The availability of
steam ironclads and torpedo craft and industrialized Britain's
growing dependence on the importing of food and raw materials persuaded Admiral Théophile Aube, who since the early
1880's had headed the Jeune École of French naval strategists,
to think in terms of coastal defense and commerce destruction. Fast cruisers and torpedo boats were accordingly more
likely to protect the national interests of France than a costly

16. See speech of John F. Miller of California in the Senate of the
United States, July 7, 1884, "The Necessity for a Navy." On European armaments, see McLane to Bayard, Paris, September 7, 1888, DDFDS.
17. Patenôtre to Ribot, Washington, April 11, 1892, CPEU, CLXVIII;
and Desprez to Ribot, Washington, November 17, 1891, CPEU, CLXVIII.

fleet of seagoing battleships. These views of the Jeune École also found great support in the United States until Captain Alfred T. Mahan challenged their soundness.

Questioning the effectiveness of commerce destruction and primarily defensive strategy in dealing with an enemy, Mahan stressed the importance of an organized fleet capable of destroying, or at least of decisively crippling, the enemy's fighting capacity.[18] The experiences of the Crimean and Franco-Prussian Wars, he thought, were of too limited a scope to teach major lessons about naval warfare. For this purpose, he preferred to rely on the eventful period from 1660 to 1814. Since his publication in 1890 of the *Influence of Sea Power upon History, 1660–1783* and, three years later, of his *Influence of Sea Power upon the French Revolution and Empire, 1793–1812* his theories of naval strategy had won more than international attention and acclaim. Influenced by Mahan's theories, modern naval leaders, including those of Germany, Japan, England, and France, henceforth saw to it that they had effective fighting units. The eventual supremacy of the French fleet in the Mediterranean, for instance, owed much to Mahan's evidently convincing arguments against mere tactical defense. As long as the United States had no overseas possessions to defend, Mahan's views regarding the American navy were fairly moderate.[19] He related the determination of its strength to "the force that Great Britain or France could probably spare for operations against our coasts," since they were the only potential rivals of the United States.[20] For any

18. E. M. Earle (ed.), *Makers of Modern Strategy* (Princeton, 1944), pp. 446–50; see also William E. Livezey, *Mahan on Sea Power* (Norman, Okla., 1954), p. 57.

19. For French comments on Mahan, consult Léonce Abeille, "Notre puissance maritime et le livre de Mahan," *La Marine Française*, XXV (1912), 1–17, and "La thèse de Mahan," *ibid.*, pp. 102–13; Admiral Raoul Castex, *Théories Stratégiques* (Paris, 1937), I, 39–43; and Auguste Maureau, "La maîtresse de la mer—Les théories du Capitaine Mahan, *RDDM*, XI (October, 1902), 681–708.

20. Alfred T. Mahan, *The Interest of America in Sea Power, Present*

active participation of the United States in world affairs, however, he argued that "nothing short of a numerous and thor-
oughly first class ironclad navy equal either to England or
France" would enable the United States to cope with whatever
exigencies might arise.[21] As far as naval developments were
concerned, the maritime powers could not and did not operate
in an international vacuum. In this area France and the United
States influenced each other considerably, both in theoretical
and practical respects.

5. French-American Economic Relations, 1871–1900

Nothing throws as much light on Franco-American
diplomatic history during the last three decades of the nineteenth century as the economic relations between the two
countries. Indeed, they constituted the most essential link,
probably occupying a more important place than certain aspects of civilization which influenced the over-all developments in France and the United States.

On the whole governed by distinguished mediocrities, both
republics were during the intial phase of this period preoccupied with forgetting the ordeals they had recently experienced.
As the older republic, the United States passed the test of the
strength and endurance of its republican institutions more reas-
suringly than France, where monarchical and clerical opposi-

and Future (Boston, 1898), pp. 16, 182–83. In time, Mahan added Germany to America's rival powers. See W. D. Puleston, Mahan: The Life
and Work of Captain Alfred Thayer Mahan, U.S.N. (New Haven, Conn.,
1946), pp. 270–71.
    21. Livezey, Mahan on Sea Power (1899), p. 208. At the First Hague
Conference (1899) Mahan opposed any reduction of belligerent rights on
the high seas and the principle of compulsory arbitration of international
disputes advocated by the French.

tion asserted its conservatism in such a militant way as to make the stability of the Third Republic problematical. Rich in resources, both nations demonstrated a remarkable capacity for recovery. Their resilience, however, was manifested in different areas, with France emphasizing colonial empire-building as the road leading to greatness and stability and the United States concentrating heavily on its industrial growth. Although this was a period of high protectionism in both countries, the fact that the industrial development of France did not keep pace with modern trends revealed certain weaknesses by the end of the century.[1] In foreign trade, France had fallen behind other countries, relatively speaking. At an important conference of Lyons merchants and bankers, for instance, experts in the field were alarmed by an analytical study showing that between 1886 and 1896 the foreign trade of Germany had increased 46 per cent, that of England 32 per cent, and of the United States 14 per cent, but that the foreign trade of France had fallen off 3 per cent.[2]

In contrast to the enterprising spirit of Americans, Frenchmen were traditionally cautious and conservative in business affairs, which they did not regard as an end in themselves. Americans not only overtook them quantitatively, as far as the production of goods and vital resources was concerned, but also in methods and techniques of mass production, while Frenchmen continued to take pride in the quality production of largely luxury goods.[3] Frenchmen certainly desired to en-

1. In patents and inventions the United States far outdistanced France. E. Levasseur, "The Concentration of Industry and Machinery in the United States," *Annals of the American Academy of Political and Social Science* (February 23, 1897), pp. 178–97. As early as 1867 the French consul in Philadelphia alerted the foreign ministry to the fuel shift by industries in the United States from coal to petroleum, which increased productivity. De La Forest to foreign minister, Philadelphia, July 8, 1867, Correspondance Commerciale, Philadelphia, 19 (AMAE).

2. John C. Covert to William R. Day, Lyons, January 20, 1898. Consular Dispatches, Lyons.

3. See Paul Boutellier, "Les États-Unis—Leur expansion économique et

large the American market for their wares. But, typically, for a long time they did not bother to promote conditions conducive to bringing this about. French ships crossing the Atlantic were slow and, as a rule, went only to New York. They were seldom seen in Boston, Baltimore, Philadelphia, or even New Orleans. It was not until 1880 that an agreement was reached with respect to telegraphic submarine cables between France and the United States, speeding up communication and justifying a reduction of telegraphic costs.[4] Since mail is one of the important vehicles for the dissemination of advertisements, unreasonably high postage rates for mail between the two countries did not help to promote trade. And, like the opponents of Napoleon III, who, during the Second Empire, frequently used the technique of indirectly criticizing the emperor by praising the American republic, Frenchmen were obstructing the conclusion of a Franco-American postal treaty for internal political reasons having nothing to do with the merits of the treaty per se but rather involving conflicts between ultramontane rightists and moderate officials of the Third Republic.[5]

Of more far-reaching consequence was the apparent inability of these two ever-more protectionist countries to negotiate a general trade treaty. They carried on sporadic discussions concerning such a treaty over several decades, in the process

mondiale," *Le Monde Économique* (December 10, 1904) , p. 739; Brooks Adams, *America's Economic Supremacy* (New York, 1900) , p. 39; and D. S. Landes, "French Entrepreneurship and Industrial Growth in the Nineteenth Century," *Journal of Economic History*, IX (1949) , p. 53.

4. See Evarts to Outrey, Washington, November 10, 1879, FNFDS; Outrey to Evarts, Washington, November 15, 1879, FNTDS; Noailles to Rémusat, Washington, February 7, 1873, CPEU, CLI.

5. On the question of the postal treaty, consult Wickham Hoffman to Fish, Paris, December 24, 1872; Washburne to Fish, Paris, January 5 and February 3, 1873, and June 26 and October 3, 1874, DDFDS. After drawn-out negotiations, agreement was reached by 1884 on French and American claims. See French and American Claims Commission, *Final Report of the Agent and Counsel of the United States* [George S. Boutwell] (Washington, D.C., 1884) .

refining procrastinating tactics to the point of exasperation. France pressed time and again for exceptional conditions for the importation of its wines, silks, and fashionable articles into the United States, but it closed its doors to such merchandise as American cotton goods, leather, and paper, and it levied high duties for a variety of other manufactured commodities.[6] When in 1878 a group of interested Frenchmen sent the publicist Léon Chotteau to the United States to advocate the conclusion of a mutually advantageous trade treaty, he encountered, among other vested interests, strong opposition from California wine producers. For that matter, he also failed to convince his own government of the worth of his mission. In 1879 the San Francisco Chamber of Commerce published a pamphlet in which it charged the French with being obstructive and parochial. "Americans," it stated, "need a little of the French conceit to make their own goods fashionable. The French refuse everything that is not French, except raw materials, and a few articles which they do not produce and must have." The charge was concluded with the broader generalization that only the population of Paris was cosmopolitan, "but in taste, in habit, speech, food, diet, and dress, it is intensely French."[7]

Ever since 1857 foreign corporations in France, unlike those in the United States, were greatly handicapped by legal restrictions.[8] American corporations with branches in France were subjected to outright discrimination. Though heavily

6. Frank A. Haight, *A History of French Commercial Policies* (New York, 1941) , pp. 16–17, 43–44. See also *New York Times,* June 24, 1879, p. 4; and Léon Chotteau's speech before the San Francisco Chamber of Commerce on June 13, 1879. Léon Chotteau, "France and the United States—Commercial Intercourse" (San Francisco, 1879) .

7. Chamber of Commerce, San Francisco, *Franco-American Commerce—Statements and Arguments in Behalf of American Industries Against the Proposed Franco-American Commercial Treaty* (San Francisco, 1879) , p. 91; see also Pletcher, *The Awkward Years,* p. 160.

8. Consult Charles G. Loeb, *Legal Status of American Corporations in France* (Paris, 1921) .

taxed, they possessed no legal status in French courts and they were unable to sue. They could not therefore conduct their operations in a safe and businesslike fashion. In 1875 the New York Life Insurance Company finally impressed upon American officials the necessity of putting American corporations in France at least on a footing of equality with other foreign corporations. It took about seven years before Levi P. Morton, the persuasive amateur diplomat, succeeded in breaking down the powerful opposition of French banks and insurance companies. His friendly association with several members of the French Cabinet facilitated the decree of August, 1882, by which American corporations came to enjoy the same privileges as all others.[9] French corporations, however, especially life insurance companies, did their best to obstruct this decree by enlisting the aid of legislators who would help them fight the undesirable American competition. Cumbersome and financially restrictive operating procedures could be almost as discouraging to foreign companies as outright discrimination.[10]

The total amount of American capital invested in Europe was still so small by 1900—rough estimates have set it at fifteen million dollars—that French entrepreneurs had really little to fear from American competition.[11] In need of capital, the United States not only invited it, it also displayed a generous attitude toward foreign investors. Still, in comparison with the British and the Germans, the French were very hesitant to invest in the distant United States. At most only be-

9. See Blaine to Morton, Washington, November 29, 1881, FIDS; Robert McElroy, *Levi Parsons Morton—Banker, Diplomat and Statesman* (New York, 1930) , pp. 138–42: and Clyde W. Phelps, *The Foreign Expansion of American Banks* (New York, 1927) , pp. 176–77.

10. See McLane to Bayard, Paris, March 4, 1886, DDFDS; Bayard to McLane, Washington, March 3, 1886, FIDS; Blaine to Vignaud, Washington, April 6, 1892, FIDS; Porter to Hay, Paris, December 16, 1904, DDFDS.

11. Nathaniel T. Bacon, "American International Indebtedness," *Yale Review*, IX (November 1900) , 275; see also Frank A. Southard, Jr., *American Industry in Europe* (Boston and New York, 1931) , p. xiii.

tween 4 and 5 per cent of their total foreign investments during the second half of the nineteenth century went to America.[12] The international repercussions of the recurring American depressions of 1857, 1873, and 1893 and ruinous investments in American railroads played their part in this hesitancy. The failure of France and the United States at the International Monetary Conferences in Paris in 1878 and 1881 to induce other countries to join them in an international agreement for a bimetallic standard furthermore discouraged those Frenchmen who expected international monetary stability from it. Those capitalists who preferred the adoption of gold as the sole standard and who were afraid of the great amount of paper money in circulation in the United States were even less disposed to invest in such a country.[13]

To understand the decline of French influence in America, one must of course observe that there were few French business houses and representatives in the United States. French trade was largely represented by Americans, Germans, and Swiss. The reluctance of Frenchmen to live in a foreign country extended even to foreign travel, a state of affairs prominent French businessmen tried to remedy at the end of the century by sending their sons to the United States to study American business methods and the English language.[14]

There can be no doubt that, in addition to strictly economic aspects, psychological factors impeded the fullest development of Franco-American trade. It would be a mistake,

12. Rondo E. Cameron, *France and the Economic Development of Europe, 1800–1914* (Princeton, N.J., 1961), pp. 70–71, 85, 88, 486; Herbert Feis, *Europe—The World's Banker, 1870–1914* (New Haven, Conn., 1930), p. 44.

13. See Evarts to Noyes, Washington, March 14, 1878, FIDS; Outrey to St. Hilaire, Washington, February 5, 1881, CPEU CLVII; Paul Leroy-Beaulieu, "Conditions for American Commercial and Financial Supremacy," *The Forum*, XX (December, 1895), 399–400; and the *New York Times*, February 9, 1886, p. 1.

14. "French Chamber of Commerce," *New York Times*, March 23, 1896, p. 5.

however, to assume that only the French introduced "habitual" obstacles. In 1885 the American consul at Marseilles sent a report to the State Department that revealed some detrimental American business habits. According to Frank H. Mason,[15] American merchants and manufacturers seemed to take foreign trade seriously only when business at home was dull and overproduction became a problem. Normally, Frenchmen complained more often than they liked, American exporters filled orders either slowly or with inferior merchandise. Mason deplored this neglect because he sensed a strong sentimental predisposition on the part of French importers to buy from America, the land of ingenious inventions and techniques, one of the best foreign customers of French products, and a land from which they feared no future political complications. "American firms," the consul commented, "which might do a large business with France lose every chance of doing so by presenting their propositions in the English language, which comparatively few French businessmen understand, and by insisting upon their usual home terms in regard to credits and payments. Many houses in the United States refuse to deliver merchandise here (in Marseilles), that is, they will deliver it on shipboard at New York, Baltimore, or New Orleans. . . . Other Americans give their prices and insist upon making their accounts in dollars and American weights while the Frenchman recognizes only Francs and Kilograms." By the end of the nineteenth century nothing had changed in this respect.[16]

The most serious trouble between France and the United States characteristically developed over agricultural questions. By and large, French farmers had done well between 1850 and 1875.[17] But a combination of circumstances suddenly endan-

15. Frank H. Mason to William H. Hunter, Marseilles, March 14, 1885, Consular Dispatches, Marseilles.
16. "France Prefers Home Products," *New York Times,* August 23, 1896, p. 17.
17. Richard Montgomery Packard, "The French Pork Prohibition in

gered their prosperity and prospects in the late 1870's and contributed to the long economic stagnation France experienced almost until the end of the century. The wine industry was severely hurt when after 1878 the phylloxera insect from the United States destroyed grape vines on a disastrous scale. The large-scale importation of American wheat, beef, and pork into France at costs below those of French farmers threatened to be even more runious because it revealed a condition presumably beyond the control of French agriculture. Without state intervention French farmers simply could not compete with their American counterparts, who produced more wheat per acre at lower cost than French growers did, and who could raise in Texas, for instance, a crop of corn after the wheat had been harvested. This, in turn, meant cheaper fodder costs for fattening cattle, hogs, and sheep.[18] To complicate matters further, while cheap American flour and pork products made life a little easier for the families of French workingmen, French packing houses added their voice to that of other vested interests demanding tariff protection. The French government, as did other continental governments, finally decided, through its decree of February 21, 1881, to fight off the American invasion of pork products by prohibiting them altogether on the ground that they were "notoriously infected with trichinae" and presented "the greatest danger to public health."[19] As delighted as French farmers and packers were with this decree, American farmers and their government fought the battle of the pork question for the next decade. The struggle did anything but improve relations between the two countries, and in this particular case it showed the French to be stubborn, narrow-minded, and specious.

Realizing that the prohibition and its justification were

American Diplomacy, 1881–1891" (Unpublished Ph.D. dissertation, Harvard University, 1954), pp. 86–91.

18. "French Agriculture," *New York Times,* November 15, 1880, p. 4.

19. Willson, *America's Ambassadors to France,* p. 316.

merely a pretext for the protection of certain French interests, the United States relied on at least four different approaches in its persistent attempts to bring about the revocation of this decree.[20] It gathered the opinions of reputable French medical experts refuting the health danger of American pork and called them to the attention of the French government. These experts unequivocally asserted that precautions used in cooking were alone sufficient to protect the population. Though it took Congress from 1884 until 1890 to pass a pork inspection law, by doing so it demonstrated its readiness to remove even the slightest doubts about the health hazards of American exports. As so often happens in battles of this kind, one group's gain was another group's loss. Poor people and French importers and shippers had to pay the price for the pork prohibition. The latter induced the Chambers of Commerce of Le Havre, Bordeaux, and Marseilles to petition the government in Paris for the repeal of the decree. And finally, the United States added to these pressures by alluding to retaliatory measures, particularly against French silks and "adulterated" wines sold in the United States.[21] One of the most innocent victims of the Franco-American tariff war during the 1880's was French art. Increased American duties on pictures and other works of art reduced the value of French art exports to the United States

20. Noyes to Blaine, Paris, May 27, and June 23, 1881 DDFDS; Morton to Frelinghuysen, Paris, March 17, 1882, DDFDS; George W. Roosevelt to J. C. Bancroft Davis, Bordeaux, April 17, 1882, Consular Dispatches, Bordeaux. See also Packard, pp. 119 and 144; and John L. Gignilliat, "Pigs, Politics, and Protection: The European Boycott of American Pork, 1879–1891," *Agricultural History*, XXXV (1961) , 7, 10.

21. Some of these "French" wines had been mixed with bonded American alcohol and water. Sometimes the "genuine French wines" did not contain "grapejuice, but were made of water, alcohol, sulphate of gypsum, glycerine, salt of potash, and berries for colouring." Willson, *America's Ambassadors to France*, p. 364; and G. B. Gould to John Hay, Marseilles, May 4, 1881, Consular Dispatches Marseilles. On the question of French wines, see also Léon Say, *Les Finances de la France sous la troisième République* (Paris, 1898) , IV, 261–62.

from $1,800,000 in 1882 to only $600,000 in 1884.[22] As a result of this unfortunate situation, moreover, American art students and exhibitors in France, who were usually most generously treated by French artists and their institutes, ran the risk of being discriminated against.

The credit for the satisfactory disposition of the pork question belongs to Whitelaw Reid, the former editor of the *New York Tribune*, who headed the American Legation in Paris during 1890–91. Originally, it was only with reluctance that the French government agreed to accept the editor, whose paper had for a long time displayed hostile tendencies toward France, as the envoy of a friendly government.[23] Resourceful and understanding, Reid was also blunt and firm in his dealings with French Foreign Minister Alexandre Ribot. Though these two gentlemen were protectionists, they did not believe in carrying economic warfare to a self-defeating extreme. Nevertheless, Reid believed that congressional hints at retaliatory legislation would induce the French government to make concessions. He furthermore recommended to the State Department the repeal of all duties on works of art and flexible tariff rates to make Franco-American trade, including salted meats and lard, attractive to both sides in the dispute.[24] At first Ribot tried to laugh off the whole affair. When Reid talked to him about it, he replied smilingly, "Ah oui! l'affaire des petits cochons!"[25] Reid, however, meant business and it did not take him long to convince the French foreign minister of the seriousness of the situation. He explained to Ribot on July 3, 1890, that neither French farmers nor consumers had bene-

22. *New York Times*, January 9, 1885, p. 1; see also Morton to Frelinghuysen, Paris, December 21, 1883, DDFDS.

23. Spuller to Roustan, Paris, April 12, 1889, CPEU, CLXV; see also Royal Cortissoz, *The Life of Whitelaw Reid* (New York, 1921), II, p. 133.

24. Bingham Duncan, "Protectionism and Pork: Whitelaw Reid as Diplomat, 1889–1891," *Agricultural History*, XXXIII (1959), 190–92.

25. See Whitelaw Reid Papers, "General Correspondence," letter dated March 28, 1890 (LC), Container 94.

fited from the decree of 1881.[26] He followed this argument up with his strong note of July 20 in which he charged, "France is and has been for nine years a persistent aggressor" in its prohibition "of an American product on indefensible charges."[27] As great as the temptation was on the part of France to organize a European *Zollverein* against the United States as Europe's answer to the McKinley tariff, America and its market were too consequential to be challenged in this manner. The high tariff policies of France, Germany, and Russia this time, moreover, made the creation of such a European tariff union unlikely. Following Germany's lead, and somewhat pacified by the reciprocity provisions in the new American tariff law, France finally repealed the pork embargo on December 5, 1891.[28]

By considering the respective mentalities of Frenchmen and Americans one comes closer to understanding the hardening of their positions in the 1890's than by studying the functional technicalities of their business relations. Fear of the American giant dominated the thinking of French policymakers, who tried to hide their anxieties behind a wall of petty obstructions and bureaucratic barriers. No amount of suave diplomatic phrases, however, could overcome the annoyance with which Americans reacted to the contrived rationalizations of clearly discriminatory actions. Whatever objections French spokesmen could make with respect to American tariffs, their provisions applied uniformly to the goods of all nations. The French "maximum-minimum system" of rates, established in 1892, was implemented in a manner favoring European countries to the disadvantage of the United States, to

26. Reid to Blaine, Paris, July 4, 1890, DDFDS. See also Allan B. Spetter, "Harrison and Blaine: Foreign Policy, 1889–93" (Unpublished Ph.D. dissertation, Rutgers University, 1967), p. 152.

27. Reid to Ribot, Paris, July 20, 1890, Whitelaw Reid Papers, "General Correspondence" (LC).

28. "France Wants Reciprocity," *New York Times,* October 12, 1890, p. 1.

which minimum rates were not extended in their entirety. France failed to agree unreservedly that reciprocity must rest on equitable equivalence, and not just on mere rates and schedules, which offered a convenient refuge for vested protectionist interests.[29]

Quite apart from a new prohibition of the importation of American cattle into France in 1895, even after the repeal of the decree of February, 1881, the United States did not regain the pork market in France. Such packers as Armour and Cudahy had been so annoyed that they lost their interest in it for the time being. Consequently, the total volume of American pork exports to France from 1891 through 1896 amounted to only 8 per cent of that during the years just previous to the decree of 1881.[30] In trade questions, French politicians wore American blinders since they were habitually moving along familiar narrow paths. They obviously did not realize that discriminatory rates against American cotton-seed oil and animal products, to name just two under consideration in 1897, would incline southern and western states to demand retaliatory measures against French exports.[31] But they consciously added insult to injury when after an interval of five months they gave the special American commissioner, who had submitted specific recommendations for a reciprocal trade agreement, two days to respond to the French counterproposition. The new law establishing prohibitory maximum rates on certain American products was to take effect immediately thereafter. In his reaction Secretary of State William R. Day expressed the prevailing American viewpoint: "We regret to find in this recent legislation of the French Chambers, and in the time and manner of the recent proposals of this Government, indications of an unfriendly disposition on the part of

29. "Hanotaux on the Tariff," *New York Times*, April 17, 1897, p. 3. See also Sherman to Vignaud, Washington, October 29, 1897, FIDS.
30. Vignaud to Gresham, Paris, February 26 and March 7, 1895, DDFDS. See also Packard, "French Pork Prohibition," pp. 547–49.
31. Sherman to Porter, Washington, December 11, 1897, FIDS.

the French government toward the commercial interests of the United States."[32]

Disregarding the downward trends in the foreign trade of France between 1881 and 1886 and, again, from 1891 to 1895, the total volume of French exports and imports changed relatively little during the last three decades of the nineteenth century.[33] During the same period the total volume of the imports of the United States doubled and that of its exports tripled.[34] With the exception of Great Britain, the leading importer of French goods, Germany, Belgium, and the United States were the main customers of France. In the case of America's foreign commerce, France ranked next to Great Britain and Germany, as the following statistics indicate. The balance of trade, however, was usually in favor of France.

Table I. Total value of imports in the United States, 1870–1914[35]
(in million dollars)

Country	1870	1880	1885	1890	1910	1914
Great Britain	152	210	136	186	271	293
Germany	27	52	63	98	168	198
France	42	69	56	77	132	141

32. Day to Porter, Washington, May 16, 1898, FIDS.

33. Consult Henri Sée, *Histoire économique de la France* (Paris, 1942), I, pp. 288–89; and Cameron, *France and the Economic Development of Europe*, pp. 523–24.

34. U.S. Department of Commerce, *Statistical Abstract of the United States, 1946* (Washington, D.C., 1946), p. 892.

35. The statistics in Tables I and II have been derived from the U.S. Census Bureau, "Foreign Commerce and Navigation of the United States" series; see particularly the volume for the year ending June 30, 1914 (Washington, D.C., 1915), p. 158. These statistics are obviously subject to many qualifications and should be regarded only as approximate indicators.

Table II. Total value of domestic exports of merchandise from the United States, 1870–1914
(in million dollars)

Country	1870	1880	1885	1890	1910	1914
Great Britain	201	450	394	444	505	594
Germany	34	56	60	84	249	344
France	37	98	44	49	117	159

Table III. Percentage of total value of imports and exports of merchandise into and from the United States, 1900 and 1914[36]

Country	Imports		Exports	
	1900	1914	1900	1914
Great Britain	18.8	15.5	38.3	25.3
Germany	11.5	10.3	13.4	14.6
France	8.6	7.5	6.0	6.8

6. France and the Spanish-American War

By the end of the nineteenth century Germany, Japan, and the United States confronted the old European empires with challenges the full scope of which only future generations could grasp. As far as France was concerned, "the American peril" became a matter of growing concern when the intensification of the Spanish-American crisis added imperialistic ambitions to the steadily increasing economic competition of the United States.

This one-sided way of judging America simplified historical developments out of all proportion to reality. To President

36. These percentages have been calculated with the help of the U.S. Census Bureau statistics and the *Statistical Abstract, 1946.*

William McKinley the prolonged conflict in Cuba was a human tragedy fraught with potentially dangerous international complications. Aside from the detrimental impact of the hostilities in Cuba on American sugar and tobacco interests,[1] the president was—and had to be—concerned with the possibility that they might open the door to intervention by a combination of European powers. To meet these immediate issues, rather than to build an American empire out of the Spanish empire, McKinley desired the restoration of peace in Cuba. He did not fabricate the Cuban crisis to exploit it for his imperialistic ambitions. Making plans in 1896 for the eventuality of war against Spain, United States naval intelligence officers developed a grand naval strategy designed to compel Spain to make peace with Cuba rather than to yield Cuba and the Philippines to the United States.[2] As McKinley and the Cubans came to understand it, by the spring of 1898, peace meant Cuban independence.[3] Since the government in Madrid felt that it could not go that far without jeopardizing its own existence, McKinley concluded reluctantly that only a firm stand would enable him to bring the tremendous political pressures under control to which he was exposed during the crucial period of diplomatic explorations in April, 1898.[4] Under these circumstances, both Spain and the United States followed a collision course in which the *Maine* incident, the DeLôme letter, and America's ultimatum merely dramatized the central issues at stake and accelerated the pace of the approaching showdown.

1. Ernest R. May, *Imperial Democracy—The Emergence of America as a Great Power* (New York, 1961), pp. 115–16.
2. See U.S. Navy Department, Lt. Kimball's Report of June 1, 1896: "War with Spain," Record group 313, Entry 43. The preparation of contingent strategy plans is of course customary in all countries and does not by itself constitute proof of aggressive designs.
3. J. A. S. Grenville and G. B. Young, *Politics, Strategy and American Diplomatic Studies in Foreign Policy, 1873–1917* (New Haven, Conn., 1966), pp. 249, 264–65.
4. May, *Imperial Democracy*, p. 147.

The possibility of a Spanish-American war induced the two governments to determine the extent to which various European powers might be inclinded to intervene in it. Spain looked forward to a European concert that would bring its pressure to bear on the United States in an effort to prevent the outbreak of such a war. It counted particularly on French intervention because of the common interests of their two friendly nations, both Latin and Catholic. As a European power with colonial possessions in the Western hemisphere, France was expected to protect its self-interest by a show of solidarity with Spain. Frenchmen had a stake in the future prosperity of Spain, moreover, as holders of nearly $400,000,000 worth of Spanish securities. Among the other continental powers, Germany, which was known to desire some of Spain's possessions in the Pacific, was another potential member of such a European concert.

Fully aware of these possibilities, McKinley's newly appointed ambassador to Spain, Stewart L. Woodford, discussed them with his American colleagues in London, Paris, and Berlin, while on his way to Madrid. On August 10, 1897, he reported to John Sherman, the aging secretary of state, that in their considered judgment recognition of Cuban belligerency by the United States would not "be followed by any protest or unfriendly action on the part of either the French or German Governments."[5] Indeed, the Europeans regarded Cuba within the legitimate sphere of the United States and would therefore go along with any American action that "would be just, human, and in line with the progressive purposes of modern civilization." Two months later, Woodford reiterated this view. In the meantime he had pointed out to the French ambassador in Madrid, the Marquis de Reverseaux, that if France were faced with a similar disturbing situation within

5. Woodford to Sherman, Paris, August 10, 1897, DDFDS. See also Louis Martin Sears, "French Opinion of the Spanish American War," *Hispanic-American Historical Review*, VII (1927), 28–29.

one hundred miles of its coast it would insist upon peace and the proper protection of its interests.[6] General Horace Porter, representing the United States in France,[7] was equally confident that the French government would not openly side with Spain in case the McKinley administration decided to stop the disastrous Cuban war in one way or another. Ambassador Porter shrewdly observed that, contrary to Spanish assumptions, a quick end of the war would actually be welcomed by French investors, who dreaded the financially ruinous consequences of a drawn-out conflict.[8]

Developments in the first few months of 1898 tested the validity of these speculations. The sinking of the *Maine* and the resulting heightening of tensions irresponsibly exploited by the yellow press and American jingoists led Spain and the United States to the brink of war. After a brief waiting period, the McKinley administration took the controlling initiative in subsequent developments. It rejected Spain's offer to investigate jointly whether an internal or external explosion had caused the *Maine* disaster. But as late as March 27 it was still trying to find a peaceful solution for the war between Cuba and Spain. On that day Ambassador Woodford was instructed to persuade Spain to grant an armistice until October 1, 1898, and to revoke the *reconcentrado* order. In the meantime, Spain and Cuba were to settle their differences directly. In case they were unable to arrive at a settlement, the United States was to be asked to mediate or, after October 1, to arbitrate the issues in the conflict.[9] In this explosive situation Spain displayed as conciliatory an attitude as its national

6. Woodford to Sherman, Madrid, October 11, 1897 (secret and confidential), DDSDS.

7. Since 1893 the ministers of the United States to France and Great Britain enjoyed the rank of ambassador.

8. Samuel Tinseley Chambers, "Franco-American Relations, 1897–1914" (Unpublished Ph.D. dissertation, Georgetown University, 1951), pp. 13–14.

9. H. Wayne Morgan, *William McKinley and His America* (Syracuse, N.Y., 1963), p. 368.

dignity permitted. On March 30 it revoked the *reconcentrado* order and offered to arbitrate the issues resulting from the *Maine* incident. It decided, however, that it could not very well accept American arbitration of the Cuban question.[10]

More anxiously than ever, Spain now urged the creation of an anti-American combination of European powers to come to its rescue. Apparently none of the European powers fully grasped the long-range significance of Spain's impending catastrophe, and even less America's interference in the affairs of a European nation. As Ambassador Andrew D. White had keenly analyzed it, the diversity of interests on the part of the several European nations blocked any concerted European action against the United States.[11] Though generally sympathizing with Spain, each power had its own domestic and international reasons for abstaining from effective joint intervention. Considerations of trade and investment in the United States exercised as restraining an influence on Great Britain, Germany, and France as the traditional Russo-American friendship or Europe's preoccupation with its own Asian and African affairs.

Nevertheless, for tactical reasons, Gabriel Hanotaux, the learned French foreign minister, gradually became convinced that the international complexities of the Spanish dilemma called for his prudent involvement. Without it, Spain might long nurse a bitter resentment against France and turn to some other power. He realized also that his own position would be further undermined if he did not at least offer his good offices. A host of French royalists, monarchists, ultramontane Catholics, America-haters, and other opponents of the French government would never forgive him for standing idly by while Spain was heading toward a humiliating defeat. It was desirable therefore for him to contribute to a pacific and face-saving solution of the Cuban question. According to the

10. *Ibid.*, p. 371.
11. Andrew D. White to Sherman, Berlin, February 3, 1898, DDGDS.

Spanish ambassador in Paris, France was willing to participate in a joint *démarche* in Washington provided another
power would lead such a move and all other powers concurred
in it. In view of the friendly relationship between Russia and
the United States, France preferred not to take the initiative
in a suggestion that might possibly embarrass its Russian ally.
Bernhard von Bülow, the secretary of state of the German
Office, drew from this cautious attitude the conclusion that
France evidently intended to do little more than go through
the motions of a diplomatic intervention.[12] Hanotaux himself
confirmed in a statement before the French Chamber that
France could at best try to help make an amicable arrangement between Spain and the United States.[13] He moved cautiously, because in his analysis France would be affected less
by the fate of Spain than by its profitable dealings with the
United States, its vitally important alliance with Russia, and
the policies of Great Britain. Since Russia had only recently
taken possession of Port Arthur, Hanotaux was particularly
alert to the disturbing possibility of an Anglo-American deal
involving China and Spain. It seemed to him not to be too
far-fetched that Great Britain might seek American cooperation in China in exchange for an understanding that Britain
would not interfere in the Cuban situation.[14] Certainly, the
French foreign minister did not want to take steps that would
alienate France from the United States and help bring about
the realization of Joseph Chamberlain's dream of an Anglo-
American alliance.

In past critical situations France preferred to coordinate its
policies vis-à-vis the United States with those of Great Britain. French leaders did not like to act alone in these instances, fearing that otherwise the British might outmaneuver

12. Bülow to Eulenburg, Berlin, March 15, 1898, in *Die Grosse Politik
der europäischen Kabinette, 1871–1914* (Berlin, 1922–26) , XV, No. 4125,
pp. 10–11.
13. "No French Aid for Spain," *New York Times,* March 27, 1898, p. 3.
14. May, *Imperial Democracy,* p. 207.

them. On March 25, still guided by these precedents, Hanotaux sent an encoded telegram to the French Embassy in London, inquiring whether the British Cabinet would go along with an appeal to President McKinley to preserve peace between Spain and the United States.[15] As requested, Léon-Marcel Geoffray, in charge of the embassy, replied immediately. He thought London would not refuse to do so, but the same appeal would have to be made in Madrid and in a manner the United States would not find offensive.[16] Thus reassured, Hanotaux assumed a much more active role during the next few critical days than he had been willing to play in the past. He also felt encouraged in that direction by the information Ambassador Jules Cambon was sending him from Washington. Cambon reported that President McKinley and prominent political leaders, including the Speaker of the House and the chairman of the House Foreign Affairs Committee, as well as religious leaders of all denominations desired a peaceful settlement. Dutifully he advised his government also of the existence of a strong popular sentiment favoring an end of the inhumanities in Cuba. He singled out Theodore Roosevelt, the undersecretary of the navy, as one of the leaders who was opposed to further procrastination and who was pressing for an immediate declaration of war because he did not want to see American soldiers fighting in Cuba during the height of summer being decimated by yellow fever. Since time was running out, Cambon emphasized that "only a *démarche* of all civilized powers would impress the arrogantly bellicose opinion of this country."[17]

The Spanish government used all its powers of persuasion to bring about a collective mediation. Each of the great powers appeared to be willing to give Spain its moral support if

15. Hanotaux to Geoffray, Paris, March 25, 1898, Espagne, NS 20, Cuba et Porto Rico, V (AMAE).

16. Geoffray to Hanotaux, London, March 26, 1898, *ibid.*

17. Jules Cambon to Hanotaux, Washington, March 23, 25, 29, and April 1, 1898, *ibid.*

all the others would do likewise. Only Russia balked at a move it thought might not be appreciated in Washington. It considered Cuba, moreover, an island within the vital sphere of America's influence.[18] Hanotaux would have preferred that Emperor Franz Joseph of Austria, a relative of the queen of Spain, ask the tsar to reconsider his position. In view of the developing emergency, however, the French government took this task upon itself and finally succeeded on March 27 in securing Russia's participation in a joint *démarche*.[19] After this accomplishment a new obstacle appeared. In a private and confidential note, dated March 29, Sir Thomas Sanderson of the British Foreign Office, informed the French Embassy in London that on second thought the acting foreign secretary, Arthur James Balfour, found any joint offer of advice at Madrid and Washington to be premature.[20] Once again France intervened successfully. For in spite of America's growing popularity with the English, many Englishmen disapproved of its apparently unyielding attitude toward Spain.[21] Germany and Italy, too, had last-minute doubts and reservations about an appeal that was likely to prove ineffectual. When on April 7 the envoys of Austria-Hungary, France, Germany, Great Britain, Italy, and Russia presented to the American government a collective note suggesting further negotiations to resolve its differences with Spain peacefully, they could hardly have had any illusion about the futility of their unprecedented undertaking.[22] A similar visit in Madrid to the Spanish minister of

18. Chambers, "Franco-American Relations," p. 57.

19. May, *Imperial Democracy*, pp. 170–71.

20. Sir Thomas Sanderson to Geoffray, London, March 29, 1898 (private and confidential), Espagne, NS 20, Cuba et Porto Rico, V (AMAE).

21. Geoffray to Hanotaux, London, April 22, 1898, Espagne, NS 22, Cuba, VIII (AMAE). For Britain's policy with respect to the *Spanish-American War*, see J. A. S. Grenville, *Lord Salisbury and Foreign Policy—The Close of the Nineteenth Century* (London, 1964), pp. 199–217.

22. F. E. Chadwick, *The Relations of the United States and Spain* (New York, 1909, p. 573. When Ambassador Holleben reported to Berlin that Jules Cambon hopefully saw in this joint diplomatic intervention the

state, two days later, was significantly followed by the suspension of hostilities in Cuba. A follow-up attempt to intervene, which the ambassadors of these six powers in Washington proposed to their respective governments on April 14, was for all practical purposes frustrated by Lord Salisbury and the kaiser.[23] It is nevertheless noteworthy that it was Jules Cambon who wished to include in the text of the second note the clause that "American intervention in Cuba would not be justified."[24] Cambon was convinced that the American government might possibly heed a strongly worded disapproval of any military solution. Another innocuous plea would, in his judgment, not at all deter people who respected bluntness more than diplomacy.

In the meantime other activities were going on behind the scenes. The contribution Pope Leo XIII could make to a peaceful and honorable settlement was being explored. These diplomatic maneuvers, in which Cardinal Rampolla, the papal secretary of state, kept channels open between the Spanish government, the Quai d'Orsay, and—through Archbishop Ireland of St. Paul—the White House, shed much light on the deepening crisis. The Vatican had all along shown concern about the difficulties in which Spain found herself. The question was how the pope could most effectively use his influence to reconcile the clashing interests of two Catholic populations and satisfy the expectations of the United States in the process. Late in March the kaiser suggested that the good offices

---

making of a future European league against America, Kaiser William II commented on the margin of the report: "Das hoffe ich von tiefstem Herzensgrund. Aber als Schiffe verlangt wurden, da streikten die braven Continentalen." Alfred Vagts, *Deutschland und die Vereinigten Staaten in der Weltpolitik* (New York, 1935) , p. 1398.

23. The kaiser was convinced that "the Americans [do] not care a straw about our collective notes." See J. Fred Rippy, "The European Powers and the Spanish-American War," *The James Sprunt Historical Studies*, XIX (1927) , 27.

24. Albert L. P. Dennis, *Adventures in American Diplomacy, 1896–1906* (New York, 1928) , pp. 72–73.

of the pope should be offered as a disinterested clearing-house.[25] On April 2 Leo XIII did in fact indicate to the authorities in Madrid that he would be prepared to request an armistice in Cuba. While the Spanish government discussed the question of whether or not it could afford to accept this offer, Archbishop Ireland was carrying out the secret mission of sounding out President McKinley's likely reaction to a final mediation attempt.

On April 4, having been taken into the archbishop's confidence, Jules Cambon sent a lengthy telegraphic report about these immensely enlightening talks to his foreign minister. When Cambon saw the prelate on April 4 he learned that McKinley was most appreciative of the Holy Father's involvements in the crisis. The president had, moreover, assured the archbishop that personally he remained opposed to war, but should war be declared, he could not present the world with the spectacle of disunion between the president and the Congress of the United States. In view of the fact that he had received a quasi-ultimatum from the chairman of the Senate Foreign Relations Committee, the president hinted at the desirability of outside assistance to reduce the war fever of the Congress. McKinley and Ireland agreed that for the European powers to offer their good offices most usefully, they would have to induce Spain to offer an armistice to the United States rather than to the insurgents, who might not be satisfied with it without a clarification of Cuba's future status.[26] The Spanish government would also have to agree to appropriate amends for the *Maine* incident, should an impartial third party establish Spain's responsibility for it. In return, the United States would promise to accept these concessions as wholly satisfactory. The archbishop promptly recommended

25. May, *Imperial Democracy,* p. 214.
26. Jules Cambon to Hanotaux, Washington, April 4, 1898, Espagne, NS 21, Cuba et Porto Rico, VI (AMAE). See also Geneviève Tabouis, *The Life of Jules Cambon,* trans. C. F. Atkinson (London, 1938), p. 95.

such an arrangement to the Holy See, believing that it would improve McKinley's chances to preserve the peace, bolster Spain's morale, and weaken the cause of the insurgents in case they decided to reject a compromise backed by the major powers.

Subsequent developments demonstrated the important bearing of domestic factors and mere technicalities on foreign-policy decisions. The pope had good reason to believe, for instance, that the Spanish government was disposed to grant an armistice. What was holding it back was the likely reaction of its army. The partial or complete withdrawal of the United States fleet from Cuban waters, it suggested, would facilitate the Spanish army's acceptance of an armistice. Cardinal Rampolla notified the Apostolic Nuntius in Paris, therefore, to urge the French government's energetic seconding of this face-saving move.[27] Jules Cambon's reaction to this suggestion left no doubt that an armistice offer must be simple and unconditional or the United States would reject it.[28] He felt it also necessary to warn that American Protestants would be greatly irritated and it would be impossible for McKinley to be conciliatory should the word be spread that the president sought the cooperation of the pope. As the result of a misunderstanding the Spanish ambassador to the Vatican had unfortunately sent a telegraph message to Madrid stating that the president had solicited the pope's good offices. Actually, McKinley had made it plain that he would receive any proposals the pope wished to submit with the respectful attention they merited.[29] When on April 9 the Spanish government gave instructions for the immediate cessation of hostilities in

27. Cardinal Rampolla to Mgr. Clari, Paris, April 4, 1898, Espagne, NS 21 (AMAE) .

28. Jules Cambon to Hanotaux, Washington, April 5, 1898, Espagne, NS 21, Cuba, VI (AMAE) .

29. Patenôtre to Hanotaux, Madrid, April 5, 1898, ibid.

Cuba, McKinley was "delighted."[30] Spain, of course, expected
a more substantial response. Archbishop Ireland visited Jules
Cambon on the next day and commented joyfully that if the
armistice led to peace, in the eyes of the world the prestige of
the pope and of France would be greatly enhanced.

According to Ambassador Woodford's conviction, the
United States could have obtained a fully satisfactory settlement of the Cuban question by merely giving the Spanish government adequate time to prepare the public for further
concessions. Instead, on April 19 the Congress passed the joint
resolution insisting on Cuban independence and empowering
the president to use all means necessary to accomplish it. The
following day President McKinley sent an ultimatum to that
effect to Madrid. For all practical purposes, the Spanish government was confronted with the choice between an internal
revolution or an external war. Spain was too proud to suffer
the humiliation of accepting this ultimatum, even at the risk
of losing more of its empire than Cuba. McKinley had really
presented Spain with unacceptable alternatives. As Woodford
contended, had the president genuinely desired peace, he
could have preserved it.

Upon the outbreak of hostilities between Spain and the
United States, the French government proclaimed its strict
neutrality. Honoring Spain's request, however, it looked after
Spain's interests in the United States. As a precaution, with
Austria, Hanotaux saw to it that French naval vessels in the
West Indies were promptly reinforced. And although the
French Admiralty objected to sending French ships to join the
rendezvous of fleets in Philippine waters Hanotaux's view pre-
vailed.[31] The political connotation of the decision to send
French ships there became clearer as time went on. Alert

30. Patenôtre to Hanotaux, Madrid, April 9, 1898, *ibid.;* Jules Cambon
to Hanotaux, Washington, April 10, 1898, *ibid.*
31. May, *Imperial Democracy*, pp. 231–32. See also Porter to Sherman,
Paris, April 21, 1898, DDFDS.

American consuls in Bordeaux, Martinique, and St. Pierre and Miquelon were particularly on the lookout for possible French violations of neutrality. On the whole, they confirmed the good faith of the neutral French government.[32] When Hanotaux was informed about the presence in St. Pierre and Miquelon of Spanish coaling vessels, he immediately gave instructions that these islands must not be used "as a base of hostile operations against the United States."[33]

French public opinion with respect to the Spanish-American War exhibited a wide spectrum of viewpoints. Quite aside from the central causes of the war, French opinions were influenced by financial, racial, religious, and ideological factors, all subject to divergent interpretations. Sizable French investments in Spain, for instance, were counterbalanced by probably half the amount in the United States. It was a foregone conclusion, however, that the duration of the war would affect the financial condition of Spain more seriously than that of the United States. On balance, then, French investors in Spain had an even greater interest in shortening, and originally preventing, the war than those who had their capital in the United States. Investors in Spain could therefore support two entirely different courses by either advocating a determined European coalition backing Spain or by remaining completely neutral.[34] And although the Franco-Spanish trade volume was considerable, the total import-export value of Fran-

32. See the dispatch the commercial agent in St. Pierre and Miquelon sent on April 23, 1898, to the assistant secretary of state, Dispatches from U.S. consuls in St. Pierre and Miquelon, 1850–1906. See also George L. Darte to Thomas W. Criddler, Martinique, W. I., May 27, 1898, Consular Dispatches, St. Pierre, Martinique.

33. Porter to Day, Paris, May 26, 1898, DDFDS. The French government did, however, send a large cargo of war supplies to Martinique. The American consul at Marseilles specified that this shipment included 9,070 projectiles of assorted sizes and 16 cannons. Skinner to Moore, Marseilles, July 12, 1898, Consular Dispatches, Marseilles.

34. The assumption was that either course would result in a speedy end of the war.

co-American trade was more than twice as large. French ports, manufacturers, and traders depending on trans-Atlantic commerce had not only reason to fear the effects of a long Spanish-American war, they also had an interest in their country's noninvolvement in the war.[35]

The war illustrated once again the fallacy of automatic racial solidarity in international crises. Racial ties may affect, but do not necessarily shape, policies. By themselves, the Latin bonds of France and Spain did not assure cooperation and mutual respect, as had already been demonstrated by the relations between France and Italy. In view of many family ties, moreover, between Spaniards, Arabs, and Moors, the French did not unequivocally accept the Spaniards as full-fledged members of the Latin race.[36] Religious ties played a much more significant role. French clericals strongly supported the cause of Spain, the most devout Roman Catholic society. They and the army, having recently been under a cloud as a result of the Dreyfus affair, would have welcomed a dramatic diversion from the domestic scene.[37] Also siding with the Spanish were the French royalists, who exercised an influence in French society far out of proportion to their numbers.[38] These ideological opponents of republican governments dreaded the prospect of another republic in Cuba and perhaps even in Spain. The republican government of France, on the other hand, wished to see the reigning dynasty in Spain remain in power, because a "return of the Carlists to power would greatly strengthen the monarchical sentiments in

35. *New York Times*, May 22, 1898, p. 18; see also George Charles Mitchell, "La presse française et la guerre hispano-américaine en 1898" (Unpublished Ph.D. dissertation, Université de Paris, Lettres, 1949), pp. 125–26; and May, *Imperial Democracy*, p. 193.

36. *New York Times*, May 2, 1898.

37. See "European Press Comments," *New York Tribune*, April 25, 1898; and the *Nation*, April 28, 1898, p. 315.

38. Porter to Day, Paris, May 24, 1898 (confidential), DDFDS.

France."[39] And finally, the element of fear was present in the various manifestations of French public opinion. Many Frenchmen feared the United States would end by conquering the French possessions in the Caribbean. *Le Populaire,* a newspaper published in Nantes, warned as far back as December 29, 1896, that the fanatical interpreters of the Monroe Doctrine who put Spain on trial might in the future dispossess any other European power of its holdings in the Western hemisphere. Identifying Americans as "Anglo-Saxons," the French feared that a naval war between Spain and the United States would be merely a rehearsal for a future naval war between England and France.[40] Indeed, on the last day of April, 1898, the American consul in Bordeaux asserted that only the fear of an Anglo-American alliance prevented a Franco-Austro-Italian-Spanish alliance against the United States, a combination he thought a long war might yet bring into existence.

Talk of an Anglo-American alliance, inspired by some British political leaders and journalists, caused lasting suspicions and resentments. If Britain assumed that America's desire to suppress "a hell in Cuba" was motivated by humanitarian considerations rather than by aggressive designs, and consequently maintained a very friendly attitude toward the United States, that was one matter. But if it aimed at an Anglo-Saxon alliance, as many Frenchmen assumed, to check the aspirations of continental powers in Africa and Asia, that was quite another matter.[41] Frenchmen could hardly believe their eyes when they read in their press fabricated stories evidently designed to hasten such an alliance. According to these stories, France attempted to form a coalition against the United States before the outbreak of the Spanish-American War and

39. Albion W. Tourgée to Day, Bordeaux, April 30, 1898, Consular Dispatches, Bordeaux.

40. *New York Times,* November 5, 1898 (editorial comment) ; see also May, *Imperial Democracy,* p. 185.

41. "England's Proof of Friendship," *New York Times,* March 27, 1899; see also Porter to Day, Paris, May 24, 1898, DDFDS.

was extending covert assistance to Spain during the war. Both
the French foreign minister and the American ambassador denied these rumors. But denials of unwarranted allegations
seldom succeed in cancelling the effect of their original publication.[42]

Although French public opinion was on the whole sympathetic toward Spain, certain business circles and true believers
in republican institutions sympathized with the United
States.[43] Speaking for the French government at a Fourth of
July banquet of the American Chamber of Commerce in
Paris, the minister of commerce tried to dispel what he described as "the ridiculous idea" of French hostility toward the
United States.[44] Henri Rochefort, a noted French journalist,
claimed that basically the French people favored Cuba's independence.[45] Some French newspapers regretted now that Spain
had not granted this independence long ago or at least initiated measures to improve conditions in Cuba. Remarkably,
the Socialist press held Spain's "deplorable colonial policy and
tyranny" primarily responsible for the war. It contended that
"Spain's retrograde obstinacy has consumed and rendered her
sterile since the time of Philip II," while dynamic America
was in this war driven by the capitalistic compulsion for new
markets.[46] Newspapers in the Midwest of the capitalistic

42. See Elsie Porter Mende, *An American Soldier and Diplomat—Horace Porter* (New York, 1927), pp. 201–3; Sears, "French Opinion of the
Spanish-American War," p. 38; and *New York Times*, March 30, 1899.

43. Among other expressions of humanitarian solidarity, the French
Red Cross donated five thousand dollars for the relief of the suffering
caused by the war.

44. See "French Views of Peace," *New York Times*, July 31, 1898, p. 1.

45. See "The Attitude of France," *Atlanta Constitution*, April 27, 1898.
On April 14, 1898, Rochefort speculated in the *Intransigeant*: "*If one of
the European powers pretended to prepare even the smallest ship to assist
the Spanish fleet, immediately an offensive and defensive alliance would
be formed between England and the American Republic, that is, against
Russia and at the same time against France who is her avowed ally.*" See
also Chambers, "Franco-American Relations," pp. 106–7.

46. Mitchell, "La presse française et la guerre hispano-américaine," pp.
107–10; Sears, "French Opinion of the Spanish-American War," pp. 29–30.

United States went even further, charging Spain with "resistance to the natural expansion of industrial capitalism."[47] And merely changing the national identification used by the French press, these American newspapers echoed familiar arguments when they expressed the fear that other European powers might take over Spain's possessions in the Western hemisphere. Such a danger to American security they found to be intolerable and furthermore the existence of monarchial institutions in the hemisphere appeared to them anachronistic.

The *New York Times* did its share during the war to enlighten the American public about contemporary European propaganda techniques. Just as certain American papers made their sensational and emotional pitches for business reasons, British and German papers printed authoritatively inspired stories to gain political advantages. In France, the situation was different. The editorial comments of quite a number of French publications were a "purchasable commodity." The judicious distribution in France of Spanish secret service funds bought many of the articles condemning the aggressive policies of the Protestant trans-Atlantic imperialists.[48] Believing that these reports truly reflected French opinion, angry American women in New York, Chicago, and elsewhere resolved neither to buy nor to wear French merchandise.[49] These boycotts were discouraged and in time abandoned

47. George W. Auxier, "Middle Western Newspapers and the Spanish-American War, 1895–1898," *Mississippi Valley Historical Review*, XXVI (1940), 524–25.

48. See *New York Times*, May 3 and 17, 1898; and L. LeFur, *Étude sur la guerre hispano-americaine de 1898* (Paris, 1899), pp. 235–36. In a small measure, the United States too purchased favorable French press coverage. Of the $2500 authorized for this purpose, only $500 was actually spent. See Chambers, "Franco-American Relations," p. 85.

49. See *New York Times*, May 23, 1898. In Chicago, the boycott of French goods was also due to a reaction to the Dreyfus affair. This "most disgraceful episode" shocked many Americans and shook their notion of French civilization to its very foundation. See White, *American Opinion*, p. 252; and Frederick W. Whitridge, "Zola, Dreyfus, and the Republic," *Political Science Quarterly*, XIII (1898), pp. 259–72.

when it was better understood that responsible French papers did not participate in anti-American campaigns. Even more sobering was the realization that, whatever the views of French public opinion concerning the United States, the French government maintained a correct attitude in its actions.

The war transformed Washington into one of the truly important capitals in the world. In the past, few European diplomats liked to be assigned to the United States, a post offering few opportunities for the development of their diplomatic talents and subsequent advancement. Jules Cambon, the alert French ambassador realized immediately that this war was projecting the United States into the mainstream of international politics. Unlike the foreign ministers under whom he served, Cambon was capable of ignoring diplomatic restraint as well as observing it. From the beginning he kept his eye on the consequences of the war, which seemed to him much more important than its real or rationalized causes. As he saw it, the fate of the Philippines was likely to intensify international rivalries. A matter of potentially even greater impact on Europe was the sudden awareness of Americans that henceforth they needed a strong military and naval establishment. The likelihood, moreover, of America's more active involvement in world politics led Cambon to the conclusion that these developments "will profoundly revolutionize" America's domestic politics.[50] An early end of the war, he thought, might at least slow down the drift in that direction.

Anxious to do what he could to help restore peace, Foreign Minister Hanotaux had ever since the outbreak of hostilities unofficially offered his good offices, hoping that his motives would not be misinterpreted.[51] In the first place Hanotaux was concerned about the injurious effects of the war on French commerce and the enormous losses suffered by Frenchmen

50. Jules Cambon to Hanotaux, Washington, May 20, 1898, Espagne, NS 32, Philippines, III (AMAE). See also Tabouis, *Cambon*, pp. 98–100.
51. Porter to Day, Paris, June 7, 1898 (confidential), DDFDS.

holding Spanish bonds. But he also told General Porter that the continuance of the struggle might strain the existing Franco-American friendship and "possibly start a conflict among European nations." In the course of his friendly conversation with the American ambassador on June 7, the French foreign minister advanced two—probably Spanish-inspired—suggestions as a basis for peace: the United States should release the Philippines and any newly elected Cuban government should assume Spanish obligations in the form of Cuban bonds. Careful to avoid any diplomatic entrapment, Porter adroitly emphasized that the United States would not entertain any peace terms other than those officially requested by the Spanish government. The McKinley administration was determined that this stipulation be upheld. When Assistant Secretary of State Day received word on June 13 that Hanotaux could arrange a meeting between the ambassadors of Spain and the United States, he replied by cable: "We can under no circumstances admit European intervention in any form."[52] He authorized General Porter, however, to receive any official Spanish peace proposals for transmission to Washington and to thank Hanotaux for his "disinterested and friendly purposes." Actually, France and Austria were bringing great pressures to bear on Spain to end the war at the earliest possible time. On June 21 Hanotaux asked Porter for an interview during the course of which he passed on the information that Spain wished to open negotiations "looking to a declaration of peace."[53] To avoid any false impressions, Hanotaux assured the United States emphatically that France disapproved of any European intervention in the war.[54] Early in July Théophile Delcassé succeeded Hanotaux as foreign minister, and was also ready to serve as an intermediary in a pri-

52. *Ibid.*, July 8, 1898; see also Dennis, *Adventures in American Diplomacy*, p. 79.
53. Porter to Day, Paris, June 21, 1898 (confidential), DDFDS.
54. *Ibid.*, June 29, 1898.

vate capacity, should both belligerents approach him with such a request.[55]

Although ambassadors do not make policy, the analyses of a man of Jules Cambon's standing proved to be a remarkable revelation. As useful as diplomatic dispatches are as a succinct record of conversations and instructions, they seldom allow an insight into the real motivations and personal views of statesmen. Fortunately, Jules Cambon's private and confidential correspondence with Delcassé discloses his amazingly frank opinions about the United States. Commenting on the Spanish-American War in his lengthy letter of July 5, 1898, he severely criticized those Frenchmen who referred to France and the United States as sister republics.[56] In Cambon's judgment, such flowery rhetoric was as ridiculous as the notion that the institutions of the two countries were as similar in substance as in name. Besides, he protested, Americans were nobody's brother or sister: "They envy the British, mistrust the Germans, and since 1871 they have shown a certain contempt for the 'hysterical' French."

The French ambassador warned, moreover, that the Spanish-American War constitued a turning point in world history. Europeans who heretofore had underestimated the extent of America's ambitions had better understand the revolutionary changes in the making. Influenced by Sir John Seeley's vision of a great British empire, Americans seemed to be carried away by the vision of a "Greater America." Cambon believed the idea of a leading role in world affairs flattered not only the vanity of the American nation, but particularly that of its influential women. The longer the war lasted, the more pessimistic became his outlook, for he did not think the government of the United States would be generous enough to offer peace, or that Spain would be wise enough to ask for it. He envisioned dangers of the most ominous nature to France

55. *Ibid.,* July 21, 1898.
56. In Papiers Delcassé (AMAE) , t. 2.

and Europe should the United States decide to widen the scope of the war by including the Canaries and the Mediterranean in its theater of operations. "Americans," he asserted, "are ignorant, brutal, and quite capable of carelessly destroying the complicated European structure." To combat this hazard and Anglo-American domination of the world, he recommended closer cooperation of the continental powers. After all, "Common apprehensions can create, as in China, common interests and even identical action." These comments are seen in a somewhat different light when one reads about contemporary reports published in the *London Daily Chronicle,* according to which France herself had designs upon the Canary Islands and Ceuta in Spanish Morocco. It was perfectly well understood in Great Britain that any transfer of these strategically imporant Spanish possessions to France would necessitate British intervention.[57]

In another letter, three days later,[58] Cambon reiterated his apprehension that the United States might become the neighbor of France in the Mediterranean. For Europe's sake as well as Spain's he therefore hoped for an early peace. Always analyzing the Spanish-American War from an international point of view, he recommended that all problems touching on differences between France and Great Britain in Africa should be taken up after the conclusion of the war. This strategy, he thought, was likely to deprive Britain of using the United States in its African projects. By the same token, France stood to gain from cooperation with Germany. Looking into the future, Cambon deemed it quite conceivable that France might need the Germans in Mediterranean developments, just as the Germans might ask for French assistance in the Philippines.

Unlike the Quai d'Orsay, the French envoy to the United States did not rule out the eventual necessity of continental

57. "Spain and Europe," *New York Times,* June 2, 1898, p. 1.
58. Jules Cambon to Delcassé, Washington, July 8, 1898, Papiers Delcassé (AMAE), t. 2.

intervention in the war. Some French newspapers took an even stronger position. Early in July, the conservative Parisian paper, *Le Figaro*,[59] carried a series of articles advocating "diplomatic intervention now." Impressed by the military victories of the United States, Europeans asked themselves the alarming question, How far does America intend to go? If its successes encouraged it to become more aggressive, Europeans might as well join forces with Spain because it was fighting Europe's battles. Inasmuch as realistic Spaniards were resigned to pay a fair price for an honorable peace, the *Figaro* suggested Europe had an obligation to help conclude such a peace before all-out war caused irreparable damage. Europe could have prevented this war, ran its argument, through energetic action when American jingoism first raised its head. But having failed to do this, it must now resolutely oppose the "false" Monroe Doctrine with the "true" doctrine of European supremacy. Surely, *Le Figaro* protested, it is up to Europe to put the United States in its place. When President McKinley actually considered the bombardment of the Spanish coast as a war measure, he lent strength to Cambon's warnings and he provoked reactions that were hardly in the interest of the United States. As far back as June, 1896, Lt. William W. Kimball of United States Naval Intelligence had for strategic reasons proposed naval attacks against Spain, primarily from the Mediterranean. In preparing these contingency war plans, he, too, did not consider the political consequences of any attack by the American navy against a European country—even a hit-and-run attack. The threat of an American show of force in Europe and the now more-than-academic prospect of American naval bases in the Mediterranean prompted the *Figaro* to demand, if necessary, "the most extreme measures" to put an end to this war. "Europe can nei-

59. See the articles by Dennis Guibert: "L'Espagne et la Paix," "L'Europe et la Paix," and "La Guerre en Europe," in *Le Figaro*, July 3, 6, and 21, 1898.

ther permit nor tolerate American naval action against the
Spanish coast . . . or the meddling of the United States in
European affairs,"[60] it said. McKinley's reassuring statement
that he was opposed to the acquisition of the Canaries because
he did not want to create the false impression in Europe that
the United States sought operational bases against it nevertheless left a trace of uneasiness.

The military balance sheet and diplomatic pressure compelled Spain to sue for an early peace. On July 20 the Spanish
ambassador in Paris explored with Delcassé the possibility of an armistice as a prelude to peace. In the absence of direct diplomatic contact between Spain and the United States,
France was the logical intermediary for the delicate preliminary peace preparations, a role Britain would have liked to assume. Consulted by Delcassé, Cambon urged quick action, lest
further Yankee exploits stiffen American peace terms. He was
also guided by another consideration. He knew of the president's personal desire for peace and he thought the president would have a freer hand with Congress out of session.
Cambon concluded his telegraphic reply with the sound advice that any peace overtures would be more readily acceptable if they were made in the name of Spain rather than
France.[61] In subsequent communications he elaborated these
views.[62] Spain, he commented, had no choice but to sue for
peace. The longer it waited, the more humiliating would be
the final terms. France, too, had a stake in an immediate
peace. Seriously anticipating America's imminent attack
against continental Spain, Jules Cambon emphasized the
alarming consequences of such an unprecedented undertak-

60. *Le Figaro,* July 21, 1898. See also Charles W. Porter, *The Career of
Théophile Delcassé* (Philadelphia, 1936), p. 121.

61. Jules Cambon to Delcassé, Washington, July 21, 1898 (very confidential) Papiers Delcassé, "États-Unis, Espagne, 16" (AMAE).

62. Jules Cambon to Delcassé, Washington August 5, and 19, 1898, Papiers Delcassé (AMAE), t. 2. See also Alberic Neton, *Delcassé* (1852–1923)
(Paris, 1952), p. 177.

ing.[63] As an aside, he aired the historically interesting view that since England was not really a European power, it probably did not see the American peril in the same light as continental France.

Reading Cambon's correspondence, one gains the impression that he was personally anxious to conduct the preliminary peace overtures. Their successful outcome promised to be a precious feather in his cap, even had he not magnified the difficulties of his task. It would have been easier, he remarked, to deal with Napoleon I or Bismarck than to negotiate with McKinley, for "Napoleon and Bismarck were masters who knew what they wanted." Using almost the same words that had been Dupuy de Lôme's undoing, Cambon characterized President McKinley in a private letter to Delcassé of August 5 as "a weak man who fears he might display his weakness by being compassionate. . . . Ultimately, he bows to the politicians, the press, and public opinion." Despite this rather unflattering—and no longer sustained—appraisal of the American president, the French ambassador was on very friendly and close terms with him.

A flurry of diplomatic activities made it possible for Cambon to sign the armistice protocol on behalf of Spain on August 12. Embodying the eventual peace terms, it stipulated that Spain must renounce Cuba and cede Puerto Rico and one of the Marianas islands to the United States. With respect to the Philippines, the United States would hold "the city, bay and harbor of Manila" until a peace treaty determined the future of the islands. As a gesture France sincerely appre-

---

63. A U.S. invasion of European waters would have confirmed Cambon's worst fears. Without considering the serious foreign political ramifications of his war plan, Lt. Kimball of the United States Naval Intelligence had actually proposed naval operations in Spanish waters. They were to be undertaken "for the purpose of striking at Spanish trade and transport service, of harassing the coasts and perhaps holding the Spanish armored fleet at home, and of keeping in touch with this fleet if it operates in European seas." For specific details, see Appendix A below.

ciated, the peace conference was to take place in Paris. Even though McKinley's terms seemed very hard, the end of the war brought universal relief. Inasmuch as the French government had contributed toward the restoration of peace, it emerged with its prestige enhanced, in a year in which the Dreyfus and Fashoda crises cast dark shadows over France.[64]

More than French prestige was involved in the final stages of the Spanish-American War. British diplomats grasped immediately that the choice of Paris for the peace conference and the friendly diplomatic assistance France was rendering to Spain during this troublous time would make Spain "more or less a dependency of France."[65] Spain's decline as a world power was destined to affect British interests in Africa. Just as Delcassé aimed to strengthen his country's influence in Morocco, the British Foreign Office felt that the proximity to Gibraltar made a Franco-Spanish penetration of Morocco a matter of genuine concern.[66] It was only gradually that Britain became convinced of Delcassé's basically friendly disposition toward it. Indeed, when Hanotaux, who had continued to operate within the traditional framework of Anglo-French rivalry, left the foreign ministry, his successor gradually reversed this traditional direction of French policies. Germany's rise and ambitions hastened Anglo-French cooperation. In the light of this new policy, it seemed logical and advisable to Delcassé to emulate the trend toward Anglo-American amity by making every effort to remove all obstacles to improved Franco-American relations.[67]

When the peace commissioners met for the conference, which began on October 1, Delcassé proved himself to be a brilliant and discreet host who did not project himself into the peace negotiations. Intimately familiar with the problems

64. *Le Figaro,* August 20, 1898; Porter, *Delcassé,* p. 128.
65. G. P. Gooch and H. Temperley (eds.), *British Documents on the Origin of the War, 1898–1914* (London, 1927), II, 253–55.
66. Porter, *Delcassé,* pp. 118–26.
67. "Allemands et Anglais," *Le Figaro,* November 13, 1898.

the proud Spaniards faced at this conference, Delcassé also knew that the American commissioners were tough negotiators, representing a young and rich country seemingly immune from aggression and unconcerned about traditions.[68] Whatever influence the French tried to exercise on the final peace terms was done informally at private dinner parties. With Spain's departure from the Western hemisphere a settled issue, the future of the Philippines constituted the central item on the agenda. Nearly all the major powers had paid attention to this question ever since Commodore Dewey's defeat of the Spanish fleet in Manila Bay. Though originally the strategic plans of the United States called for this military objective as a means of forcing Spain to the peace table at which a political settlement regarding Cuba would be arranged, Dewey's naval victory led the McKinley administration to reconsider and enlarge its international objectives. Although American war aims did not include the acquisition of the Philippine Islands, the promotion of trade relations with the entire Pacific region had been a major objective of American foreign policy, particularly since the time of farsighted Secretary of State William H. Seward.[69] The minds of many American business and political leaders were therefore well conditioned for taking another in a series of steps, not specifically blueprinted, toward expansion in Asia. The recent economic depression, the evident need for new markets, and the international scramble for the Chinese market added convincing contemporary justifications for keeping the Philippines.

Rumors and speculations suggested and tested a variety of likely solutions concerning the Philippines. In the course of a dinner conversation at Jules Cambon's residence, Senator Henry Cabot Lodge, the chairman of the Foreign Relations

68. Tabouis, *Cambon*, pp. 80–85; H. Wayne Morgan (ed.), *Making Peace with Spain–The Diary of Whitelaw Reid, September–December, 1898* (Austin, Texas, 1965), p. 37. See also Jules Cambon to Delcassé, Washington, September 23, 1898, Papiers Delcassé, (AMAE), t. 2.

69. Lafeber, *The New Empire*, pp. 416–17.

Committee, intimated on May 3 that the United States would not overreach itself.[70] At that time the assumption was that the United States would keep a coaling station and sell the Philippines to a European power or to Japan. Several months before the war, however, some influential Americans vaguely thought of the Philippines as an "American Hong Kong," from which American goods could be conveniently shipped to China.[71] Soon American imperialists presented economic, strategic, and religious arguments to justify American acquisition of the islands. Different European governments reacted differently to this possibility. If Germany could not acquire the Philippines herself, it would have preferred the status quo ante or partition of the islands among the major colonial powers.[72] Even more objectionable to Germany than American acquisition of the Philippines would have been a deal transferring them to France.[73] With reference to this speculation, one Berlin paper reminded its readers through an implied threat that "once before a Spanish question had brought on the War of 1870."[74] In this connection, Secretary of State von Bülow's telegram of July 1 to the German ambassador in Washington, Theodor von Holleben, illustrated the complex ramifications of the Philippine question. These ramifications had less to do with the islands than with international politics; for if Germany could do nothing to see that its preferences with respect to this question would not be disregarded, it at least wanted

70. Jules Cambon to Hanotaux, Washington, May 4, 1898, Espagne, NS 32, Philippines, III (AMAE).

71. Consult Thomas McCormick, "Insular Imperialism and the Open Door: The China Market and the Spanish-American War," *Pacific Historical Review*, XXXII (1963), 158.

72. Noailles to Delcassé, Berlin, July 10, 1898, Espagne, NS 34, Philippines, V (AMAE).

73. John Hay wrote to Henry Cabot Lodge on July 27, 1898: "They hate us in France . . . but France has nothing to fear from us. . . . [The Germans] want the Philippines, the Carolines, and Samoa—they want to get into our markets and keep us out of theirs." See Dennis, *Adventures in American Diplomacy*, p. 98.

74. *Das Kleine Journal*, May 27, 1898.

to exploit the situation by driving a wedge between the United States and such major interested parties as France, Great Britain, and Russia. Toward that end von Holleben was instructed to remind the State Department of the disfavor with which French and Russain newspapers were looking on the intrusion of other great powers into East Asia. The German government regarded it furthermore as very unlikely that Britain, while welcoming American presence in that region, would stand by the United States in case of serious complications. For these reasons von Bülow wished the State Department to weigh "the practical advantages of securing Germany's friendly attitude."[75]

With an eye on the Philippine question near the end of the Spanish-American War, the Russian government discussed with France ways and means of preventing England from becoming the mediator in this conflict.[76] Russia feared that in that capacity England might maneuver to acquire the Philippines and by doing so upset the balance of power in the Far East. As far as St. Petersburg was concerned, the friendship between Russia and the United States in the nineteenth century was based even more on their common interest in checking some of Britain's offensive policies than on the absence of conflicting interests between them. With major changes in American foreign policy apparently in the making, Russia still wished to keep the traditional Russo-American friendship intact, provided the Anglo-American rapprochement did not draw Americans into "deceitful business."[77] It certainly included the establishment of an Anglo-American protectorate in the Philippines in this objectionable category. Russia hoped the United States alone would keep the islands and just annex

75. Bülow to Holleben, Berlin, July 1, 1898, in *Grosse Politik*, XV, No. 4151, pp. 44–45.

76. James K. Eyre, Jr., "Russia and the American Acquisition of the Philippines," *Mississippi Valley Historical Review*, XXVIII (1942), 549–51.

77. Zabriskie, *American-Russian Rivalry in the Far East*, pp. 46–49.

them without using them as a base for further expansion in Asia.[78]

Britain's attitude throughout the Spanish-American conflict also guided it with regard to the Philippine question.[79] It made no difference to Britain whether Spain or the United States owned the Philippines. In this respect Britain's neutrality disappointed Spain, but it also indicated that Britain was not trying to embroil the United States in the Far East. Freedom of commerce was its prime interest when the war broke out, and the protection of its China trade was its main concern now. The Philippines represented a side issue and even Lord Salisbury, who was much less sympathetic toward the United States than Balfour and Chamberlain, did not oppose America's foothold in the Pacific as being in conflict with British policies in that region. Knowing that the United States favored an open door in China, the British government was not afraid of the eventual use the Americans would make of the islands as a springboard for the development of trade with China. But Lord Salisbury was determined to prevent any of Britain's European rivals from acquiring any of Spain's possessions as a result of the war. On August 2, John Hay, then American ambassador to the Court of St. James's, advised the president of Britain's firm belief that America's abandonment of the Philippines would cause grave European complications. It would rather purchase the islands than see them in the hands of its European rivals. This unalterable British position exercised a decisive influence on McKinley's final disposition of the Philippine issue.

The French did not put as much trust in the United States as their Russian ally. During the Spanish-American War the French government sent large consignments of war material to Cochin China. Since the French press clamored for a naval

78. See the communication the French ambassador in Vienna sent to Hanotaux April 27, 1898, Russie, Politique Etrangère, NS 16, 1 (AMAE).

79. Consult R. G. Neale, *Britain and American Imperialism, 1898–1900* (Brisbane, Australia, 1965), pp. 80–91, 109–11.

station in the Philippines, the shipment of vast quantities of powder and projectiles to the Far East may have been "in pursuance of some general plan to that end."[80] In any case, the notion that American occupation of Manila was only provisional accurately reflected official French thought.[81] Until the final decision, Frenchmen attempted to dissuade the United States from taking the Philippines. Jean Jules Jusserand, one of France's well-known diplomats, explained to a prominent American visitor, for instance, how disadvantageous it would be for the United States to acquire possessions thousands of miles away from its shores and almost certainly to entangle it "in the whirl of European rivalries."[82] In his opinion, the most sensible decision would be "to leave the Philippines to their present owners." While the Spaniards reacted with despairing resignation," according to Peace Commissioner Whitelaw Reid, to McKinley's decision to annex all the islands, Frenchmen made last-minute attempts to soften the American stand. One of the most powerful French statesmen, Alexandre Ribot, invited the Reids to a private dinner party during the course of which he intimated that the United States would alienate world public opinion if it dealt too harshly with Spain.[83] That the United States did not heed such advice came as no surprise to the French ambassador in Washington. On September 23, 1898, Cambon wrote to Delcassé that though England was encouraging the United States to take the entire Philippines, the American sugar trust was the chief proponent of annexation. "These sugar interests," Cambon contended,

80. Robert P. Skinner to J. B. Moore, Marseilles, July 6, 1898, Consular Dispatches, Marseilles.

81. It turned out to be merely a careless oversight, however, that the French Yellow Book about the French contribution to the Armistice protocol had left out the clause relating to the subsequent decision by the Joint Commission as to "the control, disposition and government of the Philippines." Morgan, *Reid Diary*, p. 132.

82. Jean Jules Jusserand, *What Me Befell—Reminiscences of J. J. Jusserand* (Boston, 1933) , p. 165.

83. Cortissoz, *Reid*, II, 249.

"want Hawaii, Cuba, Puerto Rico, and the Philippines because they want to monopolize the production of sugar in the
world and destroy its fabrication in Europe." Significantly he
added, "This is the beginning of the economic war the
United States will soon undertake against the Old World, a
war that will lead to unexpected rapprochements."[84]

The treaty concluding the Spanish-American War compelled Spain to relinquish her sovereignty over Cuba and to
cede the Philippines, Puerto Rico, and Guam to the United
States. Despite the twenty million dollars Spain received as a
sort of compensation for the loss of the Philippine Islands, the
treaty constituted a severe blow to her power and prestige. It
removed Spain entirely from the Western hemisphere, which
its enterprising ancestors had helped to colonize and civilize,
and it accelerated its decline as a world power. How much of
a political and military liability and how inconsequential to
the prosperity of the United States the newly acquired American colonial empire would prove to be was understood by
only a minority of contemporary Americans. To the majority
of the American people and to the world at large, its victory
in this imperialistic war elevated the United States to the
rank of the major world powers.

The establishment of an American empire caused a lively
debate in France. Those relatively few Frenchmen who were
at all qualified to comment upon the causes and effects of the
Spanish-American War in various publications presented a
much wider range of arguments than Cambon. That economic
motives were the driving force of American imperialism was
taken for granted. But instead of emphasizing the limited influence of the sugar trust, Octave Noël, for example, traced
the "American peril" to an artificially accelerated production
system in search of ever-vaster opportunities for economic ex-

84. Jules Cambon to Delcassé, Washington, September 23, 1898, Papiers
Delcassé, (AMAE), t. 2.

pansion.[85] With an agricultural production surpassing that of the entire world and an industrial capacity on its way toward overtaking that of Europe, the United States was destined to establish its economic supremacy in Europe. Demoralizing as this prospect was to Europeans, Noël's perceptive analysis pointed to a much more consequential aspect of this new trend. As Noël observed in 1899, the irresistible force of the machine, which Americans had exploited to the utmost, had badly upset the normal—much slower— pace of economic development. The speed and determination with which Americans imposed their will on modern civilization did not seem to hold out much promise for moral and human values in this world. The greatest danger the American brand of imperialism posed was not merely ruthless economic competition but the dehumanization of life and the attendant decline of Western civilization. Other French writers stressed the impact of the Spanish-American War on institutional questions. They noted that the "model" republic" did not hesitate to conduct an imperialistic war,[86] thus shattering the nineteenth-century belief that if "the people" controlled their government war would become obsolete as an instrument of policy. The democratic republic per se evidently offered no guarantees for peace.[87] One writer even went so far as to predict that a military victory bought at the expense of unfaithfulness to the principles of the founders of the republic spelled the ultimate doom of American democracy itself.[88] This war was a

85. See Octave Noël "Le Péril Américain," *Le Correspondant,* CXCIV (March 25, 1899) , 1083–1104, and CXCV (April 10, 1899) , 116–44.

86. Sears, "French Opinion," p. 41.

87. It might in fact have gone to war to save itself. Rousiers reported that some Americans felt the war necessary to avoid a civil war between the Eastern business interests and the agrarian discontents in the West. "The war helped to cement the nation." Paul de Rousiers, "L'Impérialisme Américain," *Revue de Paris* (March 15, 1899) , p. 428.

88. See *Review of Reviews,* XIX (March 1899) , 336; for a recent discussion of similar views, see Robert L. Beisner, *Twelve Against Empire: The Anti-Imperialists, 1898–1900* (New York, 1968) .

turning point in American as well as in world history, he said, among other reasons, because the "mighty" United States henceforth forfeited the right to be regarded as a great moral example in world affairs.

In his discussion of American imperialism Noël concluded that the mission of France must be to uphold the noble and ideal principles of civilization it had inherited from the Greeks and the Romans. Beyond that it must use its Far Eastern possessions to prepare for the fight against the mercantile invasions of the Anglo-Saxon race. Characteristically, many French critics lumped American and English policies together, thus associating the United States with "the evils of British imperialism." They accused the Anglo-Saxons of striving for world conquest, if not in a physical sense, certainly in an economic one. In spite of the global scope of Anglo-Saxon imperialism, these critics emphasized the American danger to Europe and Latin America.[89] The domination of the Americas by the United States appeared to be particularly objectionable in view of the close cultural and racial ties between Latin Americans and many Europeans. And the erection of a "Chinese Wall" between Europe and Latin America was judged to be detrimental to French economic interests.[90] The increased trade volume between France and Latin America in the final decades of the century in no way altered this view.

In a society in which diversity of opinions has long been a cherished tradition it was natural that at least a few interpretations would be somewhat more optimistic. Few Frenchmen would go so far as to say that the United States had liberated

89. Consult James Louis Whitehead, "French Reaction to American Imperialism, 1895–1908" (Unpublished Ph. D. dissertation, University of Pennsylvania, 1943), pp. 332–33; Emile Ollivier, "Les États-Unis, l'Espagne et la France," *Revue Bleue* (September 3, 1898), p. 290; Edouard Driault, "L'Impérialisme aux Étas-Unis," *Revue Bleue* (April 21, 1900), p. 505; and *Le Figaro*, August 5, 1898.

90. Whitehead, "French Reaction to American Imperialism," p. 255.

the Cubans. But, following French criticism of the United States to its logical conclusion, one commentator quite accurately described American imperialism as essentially opportunistic.[91] Applying strict business principles to their conduct of foreign affairs, Americans, he had no doubt, would not hesitate to abandon an unprofitable political project. Questions of honor and pride were not likely to hamper them as much as Europeans in matters of this kind. The appeal of this argument, later borne out by the decision to give the Philippines their independence, was at the time strengthened by the increasing anti-imperialistic sentiments of the American people. The *Revue des deux mondes* frankly acknowledged that "few other peoples resisted a policy of conquest as much as the American people."[92]

For precisely this reason many Americans were convinced that the French had unduly exaggerated the "American peril." More than that, these French fears seemed both unwarranted and unproductive. Typically characteristic of American self-reliance, the *Brooklyn Daily Eagle*[93] reacted to them by reminding the French critics of the United States that the way to meet competition was by developing the means to meet competition. But instead of strengthening and modernizing the French economy, it observed, France tried to strengthen its Russian ally through huge investments. And, adding insult to possible injury, the distinguished American intellectual, Brooks Adams, bluntly told Frenchmen that they must resign themselves to their gradual decline as a world power, which began with Napoleon's retreat from Moscow. Moreover, he added, the future belongs to "the Anglo-Saxons and whether

91. Rousiers, "L'Impérialisme Américain," p. 438.

92. Pierre Leroy-Beaulieu, "Les États-Unis—Puissance Coloniale," *RDDM* (January 1, 1902), pp. 83–85.

93. "Whither Is France Drifting?" *The Brooklyn Daily Eagle*, September 2, 1898, p. 6.

we (Americans) like it or not, we are forced to compete for
the seat of empire."[94]

7. The United States and France at the End of the Century

The French government took due notice of the results
of the Spanish-American War and adjusted its working relationship with the Americans accordingly. Through its control
of the Philippines the United States hoped to be in a better
position to influence the various powers with spheres in
China.[1] Throughout 1898 the influential *New York Journal of
Commerce* had stressed the necessity of impressing upon these
powers that the most-favored-nation principle must be applied to all products entering these spheres.[2] Napoleon-
Eugène Thiébaut, chargé d'affaires of the French Embassy in
Washington, also noted that the Senators Tilman and Mc-
Laurin of South Carolina were urging President McKinley to
protect the vital Chinese outlet for the cotton goods produced
in their state.[3] The prospect of China's disintegration as the
result of ever-widening foreign spheres of influence finally
led the United States to enunciate the principle designed to
keep the door open to international trade in China. Though
somewhat hesitant to endorse an international trade principle
couched in sweeping terms, Delcassé half-heartedly assented to
it after Great Britain and Germany had already signified

94. Brooks Adams, "The New Struggle for Life Among Nations,"
McClure's Magazine (April, 1899), pp. 561–64.
1. Achille Viallate, *Economic Imperialism and International Relations
during the Last Fifty Years* (New York, 1923), p. 34.
2. Bruwaert to Delcassé, New York, October 29, 1898, Relations Commerciales, Chine, Relations avec les États-Unis, I (AMAE).
3. Thiébaut to Delcassé, Washington, October 26, 1899, *ibid.*

their acceptance. Since in its African arrangements with Great Britain France had used the term "spheres of influence," it found itself in a rather weak position to quibble with the United States over its vagueness.[4]

America's participation in the expedition sent to put down the Boxer Rebellion and the declaration of the second Open Door principle affirming the territorial and administrative integrity of China were the first attempts of the youngest Great Power to act like one. It was encouraged in this respect by Wu Ting Fang, the Chinese envoy in Washington, who advocated the extension of the Monroe Doctrine to China.[5] Treating the United States as a Pacific power, Wu probably hoped to serve China by thus sowing the seeds of mistrust among the Western powers. Although different motivations guided them, China and the United States interpreted the Open Door principles as a barrier to the complete disintegration of China and the feared escalation of rivalries among the imperialistic powers. As a modern industrial power, the United States had good reason to assume that it would continue to be in an excellent competitive position in the world markets as long as the economic doors were being kept open. But as much as Great Britain liked seeing the United States involved in the Far East, Russia and Japan resented American interference in an area of vital interest to them. Ambassador Jules Cambon analyzed these developments with extraordinary understanding. Looking into the future, Cambon believed that a clash of interests in Asia would put an end to the nineteenth-century friendship between Russia and the United States. To him, this would be one of the great developments of the twentieth century and of far-reaching consequence to Western civilization.

Brooks Adams' arrogant and presumptuous talk elated those

4. Porter to Hay, Paris, January 6, 1900, DDFDS. See also Chambers, p. 363.

5. Cambon to Delcassé, Washington, February 23 and May 1, 1900, Relations Commerciales, Chine, Relations avec les États-Unis, I (AMAE).

Americans who were riding the wave of imperialism. Perhaps
to their amazement, the French government reacted to it in an
unexpected way. Nothing could illustrate the changing state
of affairs better than the realization of prominent Frenchmen
that their diplomatic mission in the United States would
henceforth be among the most important on our small planet.
At the beginning of the twentieth century, George Picot, of
the Institut de France, phrased it this way: "No illusion is possible; the equilibrium of the world is moving westward."[6]
And Jules Cambon's brother Paul, then French ambassador to
the Court of St. James's, emphasized the need of Frenchmen
to familiarize themselves with the American mentality and
methods in order to understand better the future arbiters of
the world. With England and Germany vying for America's
amity and Russia preferring to be on friendly terms with the
United States as long as possible, the French government took
account of the existing realities, even though Frenchmen,
looking sadly backward, found it difficult to accept them.

When Delcassé succeeded Hanotaux, he gradually shifted
the foreign political orientation of France towards a genuine
entente with Great Britain and the United States. The old colonial powers of Europe had of course a common interest in
checking Germany's international political ambitions. Within
this larger setting the Franco-American rapprochement was
both logical and expedient, following, as it did, the fairly recent improved relations between Great Britain and the
United States. Masters of the technique of studied obstruction
and procrastination, French bureaucrats suddenly ceased to
exasperate American officials. To facilitate more trade between the two countries, Delcassé agreed to the mutually advantageous commercial Convention of 1899. He also lent his
support to the Open Door principles and to the establishment

6. Jusserand, *Reminiscences*, p. 219.

of direct Associated Press services between Paris and the United States.[7] On several occasions, in speeches before the French Senate, he alluded to the desirability of ever closer bonds between the two countries whose essential interests did not clash with each other. Encouraged by the enthusiastic applause of the French legislators, Delcassé ranked his successful rapprochement with the United States among the major accomplishments of his far-flung international initiatives.[8] More than trade and sentiment dictated Delcassé's course. It evidently gave Frenchmen a greater feeling of security and satisfied their concept of a vigorous foreign policy.

In an article published in the *Gaulois,* a wishful dreamer again advanced the well-worn idea of enlarging the squares of the ancient European chessboard by the formation of a triple alliance composed of France, Russia, and America.[9] The *Figaro* stopped short of this proposal by promoting a Franco-American alliance "based not on written treaties, but on a community of sympathies; not on the eventualities of a war to be faced in common against a third power, but on a movement of ideas. . . ." At best, these vague views conveyed the broadly based desire to work with rather than against the United States.[10] How substantial Franco-American cooperation would be during the twentieth century remained to be seen.

7. Porter, *Delcassé,* pp. 154–61.

8. *Journal Officiel, Sénat* (April 3, 1900), p. 299 and (February 11, 1901), pp. 295–96. See also *Journal des Débats Politiques et Littéraires* (December 2, 1899).

9. See "France Coquettes with United States," *The Brooklyn Daily Eagle,* July 7, 1900, p. 1. The September 7, 1897, issue of *L'Éclair* carried an aricle by G. Gerville Réache, "L'Alliance Franco-Russe-Américaine," strongly pleading for such an alliance.

10. On the question of the Franco-American alliance, see also the *New York Times,* July 6 and 8, 1900; and the *Brooklyn Daily Eagle,* July 6 and 8, 1900.

8. French and American Diplomats

Even these vague notions constituted a promising change, for too often during the nineteenth century France had sent to the United States ambassadors whose pronounced prejudices tended to give their superiors in Paris wrong impressions concerning American motivations, ambitions, and civilization. The condescension and misjudgments of Genêt, Adet, Pageot, Barcourt, Sartiges, and Mercier, for instance, were not conducive to a better understanding between the two countries. By the mid-century French envoys regarded the United States as an ungrateful and unreliable power whose political morality was questionable and whose arrogant spirit of usurpation foreshadowed serious trouble for Europe.[1] Their appointment to the United States seemed to be doubly disappointing to them. It seemed to them a dead-end diplomatic assignment for it hardly offered them opportunities to demonstrate and develop their diplomatic skill. And secondly, this "dreary abode, where the law protects the rascal and leaves the honest man to take care of himself," bored the representatives of monarchical France. In Washington they missed not only a stimulating international atmosphere, but also the elegance and sophistication taken for granted among the higher levels of European society.

Usually outwardly polite, French diplomats occasionally failed to hide their social and political biases. Guillaume Tell Poussin, for instance, who before his appointment in 1848 had served in the United States Corps of Engineers and was presumed to be particularly friendly to the American republic, used such discourteous and offensive language in his corre-

---

1. A. F. de Bacourt, *Souvenirs of a Diplomat* (New York, 1885), pp. 109–10.

spondence with the State Department that his official status in America became intolerable. Secretary of State John M. Clayton deemed it necessary to inform Poussin in the late summer of 1849 that "every proper facility for quitting the United States will be promptly given you."[2] As a face-saving gesture, the American government chose this time to appoint a new minister to France. But regarding Poussin's treatment as an offense to the dignity of France, Alexis de Tocqueville, then the foreign minister of France, decided neither to send Poussin's successor to Washington nor to receive the credentials of the new American minister to France until the American government offered its apologies. In response, Clayton advised William C. Rives to leave France, if necessary, and to go to Prussia or Russia, because "diplomatic intercourse with France is not so important to us as to make it necessary to submit to indignity." Fortunately, the embarrassing impasse did not last long. As his uncle had done in 1800, early in 1850 President Louis Napoleon suddenly decided to resume relations with the United States unconditionally.

As a rule the French government displayed more restraint in its dealings with the United States than many of its envoys. Furthermore, little-known social links helped to bring about a more intimate personal relationship between prominent French political leaders and American society, particularly in the post-Civil War period. Mary King of the Rufus King family, for example, a lady raised and educated in the United States, was the charming first lady of the Quai d'Orsay when her husband, William Henry Waddington, headed the foreign ministry. Another French foreign minister, Alexandre Ribot, as well as Ambassador Jusserand and the publicist and statesman Georges Clemenceau were married to American women. The daughter of Rouher, the powerful apologist of the Second

2. See Blumenthal *Reappraisal,* p. 78. The ladies of President Taylor's family, moreover, had their serious reservations with respect to the reputation of Madame Poussin.

Empire, became the wife of American-born Samuel Wells, whose stepfather, de La Valette, was the French foreign minister in 1866.[3]

Unlike many of his predecessors, the brilliant French journalist Lucien Anatole Prévost-Paradol, a believer in constitutional monarchy and a sincere friend and admirer of the American republic, appreciated the opportunity to represent his country in the United States. When he presented his credentials to President Grant on July 16, 1870, he pledged himself to fortify the political ties between the two countries by trying to advance their industrial and commercial relations. Upon his arrival, this distinguished envoy of France found Americans well disposed toward him. If he sensed any reservations, they applied to the policies of the French emperor, an attitude that Prévost-Paradol, himself an uncompromising opponent of Napoleon's empire until its liberalization in 1869, might well have anticipated. It was nevertheless unfortunate that false rumors attributed Paradol's suicide in the early morning hours of July 20, 1870, to his "cool reception" in the United States. The scorching heat of Washington and a feeling of loneliness evidently depressed him, but two more weighty considerations seem to have driven this sensitive and melancholic intellectual to his tragic end. For some time he had pointed out the dangers France would face in a military struggle with Prussia-Germany. He had not expected the sudden turn of events in Europe he was now compelled to face helplessly. In his mind the outbreak of the Franco-Prussian War may very well have ended his usefulness to the Second Empire. His closest political friends had all along had less faith in Napoleon III than Paradol. They even regarded his

3. On these intermarriages, see Mary King Waddington, *My First Years as a Frenchwoman, 1876–1879* (London, 1914); Morgan, *Reid Diary*, p. 90; Matilda Gresham, *Life of Walter Quintin Gresham, 1832–1895* (Chicago, 1919), p. 690; Jusserand Memorial Committee, *Jean Jules Jusserand* (New York, 1937), p. 39; and G. E. Manigault, "Autobiography" (University of North Carolina MS), p. 6.

acceptance of the diplomatic post in Washington as a breach of political faith. Unable to face the impending tragedy of France and, perhaps, his misjudgment of the "Liberal Empire," he took his life. He probably did not anticipate, if he ever gave any thought to it, that his self-inflicted death would even for a moment put the United States in a compromising light.[4]

On the whole, the envoys of the Third Republic not only found life in the United States more tolerable than their monarchical predecessors, they also recognized that the development of this giant country made it an ever more important factor in the world arena. But, as already noted, Roustan, Patenôtre, and Cambon articulated views that by and large confirmed the fears of their predecessors. As far as they could judge, the United States, they reiterated time and again, posed a potential threat to the pre-eminence and civilization of Europe. They doubted, moreover, that France could rely on the United States in an emergency involving the defense of French interests. As realists, they dismissed references to the perpetuity of the historic Franco-American friendship as a romantic notion. This *Realpolitik* did not preclude, however, the promotion of Franco-American cooperation to the fullest extent possible.

Jules Cambon, an able civil servant, began his remarkable diplomatic career with his appointment in 1897 as ambassador to the United States. When he was transferred to Madrid late in 1902, he could take satisfaction in the fact that he had succeeded in convincing the American people of the community of purpose between French and American democracy. On his travels to various parts of the United States and France, this "ideal ambassador," as Elihu Root referred to him, tried

4. See Othon Guerlac, "Le suicide de Prévost-Paradol à Washington et l'opinion américaine," *Revue de littérature comparée*, VIII (1928), 100–5; Octave Gréard, *Prévost-Paradol: Étude suivie d'un choix de lettres* (Paris, 1891), pp. 708–10; and Robert Walter Reichert, *Prévost-Paradol: His Life and Work* (New York, 1949).

to interpret French and American civilization in a way designed to promote mutual understanding and to uproot lingering sentiments of mistrust.[5] When he went to Detroit he was pleasantly surprised at "being received and fêted there by descendants of . . . French" colonists of New France, and he hoped that young Frenchmen would in the future keep these close ethnic and cultural bonds alive. Cambon, however, was too much a realist and French patriot to accept, on the occasion of a banquet in honor of the departing diplomat, Archbishop Ireland's observation that "the glory of America is the continuation of the glory of France." As a matter of fact, Cambon's private and confidential correspondence during his ambassadorship in America reveals a wide gap between his public statements and his private convictions with respect to the United States. Publicly, he tried to promote friendship between France and the United States. In his confidential letters he warned his government against the economic and political perils awaiting it in the future. He thought the American octopus quite capable of ultimately reaching out for the domination of Europe. Although he naturally supported and appreciated America's cooperation with France during the First World War, the steady advance of the United States in prosperity and power merely seemed to justify his long-standing apprehension for the future of France and the European continent.

Of the French ambassadors to the United States, Jules Cambon was among the most highly respected. But none was as close to an American president as Jean Jules Jusserand, who, with his wife, enjoyed an intimate relationship with the Theodore Roosevelt family. The president and Jusserand made frequent excursions into the wooded outskirts of Wash-

5. Geneviève Tabouis, *Cambon*, pp. 117–18; and Chauncey M. Depew and James H. Hyde, *Speeches Delivered on the Occasion of a Dinner to His Excellency Jules Cambon, 15th November 1902* (New York, 1903), pp. 11–41.

ington and could frequently be seen together on the tennis court or swimming in the Potomac. So great was the president's confidence in the French ambassador that he often discussed purely American questions with him. When the health of Secretary of State Hay failed, Roosevelt suggested laughingly to Jusserand, "Well, meanwhile you will replace him without even taking the oath."[6] It was evidently no coincidence that Franco-American cooperation reached a high point during Roosevelt's administration.

In spite of the importance and prestige of the diplomatic post in Paris, American envoys were on the whole well-known and alert amateurs with a background in banking, business, journalism, and public service.[7] Usually handicapped by their inability to speak French, they managed nevertheless to be effective spokesmen. As a rule, their friendly disposition toward France was beyond question. Ever since the time of Benjamin Franklin, who enchanted French society with his charm and sophistication, American ministers to France usually came from old American families. For a long time they labored under several social handicaps. Unless they were independently well-to-do, they found it impossible to operate their country's legation and to live and entertain in a style expected of foreign dignitaries in France on their wholly inadequate budget.[8] Throughout the nineteenth century Congress showed little understanding of the special financial needs of

6. Jusserand Memorial Committee, *Jusserand*, pp. 42–43. Jusserand was awarded the Pulitzer prize for his book *With Americans of Past and Present Days*. He enjoyed, moreover, the rare distinction of having been elected to the presidency of the American Historical Association. See also Madame Saint-René Taillandier, "Silhouettes d'Ambassadeurs—IV. Jean-Jules Jusserand," *Revue d'histoire diplomatique* (1952), pp. 191–94.

7. American consulates, too, were usually entrusted to citizens for their contributions to the political party in power rather than for their international business expertise. British, French, and German consuls were usually well prepared for their posts.

8. Beckles Willson, *America's Ambassadors to France (1777–1927)* (New York, 1928), pp. 185, 237.

its envoys abroad. Indicative of this lack of understanding was Secretary of State Marcy's circular order of June 1, 1853, instructing American ministers abroad to wear "the simple costume of an American citizen." In class- and rank-conscious Europe it could be embarrassing for American officials to appear on public occasions in simple trousers and a black frock, particularly at Court receptions and soirées at which splendor and elegance symbolized power, prestige, and prosperity. Grasping the significance of this symbolism, John Y. Mason, a former Virginia judge, simply disregarded Marcy's instruction and appeared at the Tuileries in knee-breeches, silk stockings, an elegant còat, and sporting a dress sword.[9]

These apparently superficial external matters were much more keenly appreciated by Americans in Paris than by the people back home, but even they might not have liked seeing their legation in Paris located two flights of stairs above a grocery and laundry.[10] Yet when the legation was moved to more appropriate quarters in the summer of 1881, Levi Parsons Morton, the successful banker who headed it, was understandably unhappy about the new address. Even the Prefect of the Seine chuckled when Morton explained his embarrassment to him, and the municipal authorities soon graciously changed the name of the location from Place de la Bitche to Place des États-Unis.

It took much longer before a very annoying and humiliating handicap was removed. Strictly observing the decisions of the Congress of Vienna, the French treated foreign representa-

9. *Ibid.*, pp. 244–48. The diary of Albert Gallatin's son James contains the following enlightening comment: "Just been seeing the footmen, coachmen, etc., in their new liveries. For ordinary occasions, dark blue plush breeches, yellow waistcoats, and dark blue coats with silver buttons, black silk stockings; state liveries, light blue breeches, white silk stockings, yellow waistcoats, and light blue coats with broad silver braid and silver buttons. . . . Father is a little doubtful, fearing Americans may object to so much show; but he feels the Court of France requires it." *Ibid.*, p. 145.
10. *Ibid.*, p. 317.

tives in accordance with their rank. This meant that ambassadors enjoyed a priority over ministers at receptions, audiences,
and the dinner table. Diplomats were received according to
the rank they held and seated according to the amount of
time they had spent in the country of their assignment. In
1883 Levi P. Morton complained to the State Department
about the humiliation to which American ministers were consequently subjected in Europe. Any ambassador took precedence over any minister, regardless of the previously arranged
time for an interview with the French foreign minister. On
many occasions the American minister in France had to wait
patiently for hours before the foreign minister could finally
see him, because the ambassadors from other countries, who
may have suddenly arrived for an audience, could quite legitimately pull their rank on the minister.[11] About a decade later,
T. Jefferson Coolidge, the tactful Boston businessman and
diplomat, registered another complaint about this practice.
Realizing that this state of affairs did not accord the United
States the respect to which it was entitled, in 1893 Congress at
last agreed to elevate the ministers in France and Great Britain to the rank of ambassador.

Life in Paris also presented other kinds of social problems
to some American ministers and their wives. Albert Gallatin's
wife, whom Lord Bryce has described as "a typical American
Protestant and highly estimable Southerner of that time," was
shocked by the laxity in French morals during the early period of the Restoration. The ways of French ladies of the
grand monde made her very uncomfortable.[12] Instead of a
French chef, she was happy to engage a Negro cook, an es-

11. *Ibid.*, pp. 321, 347. Since each newly elected president of the United
States liked to appoint his own ministers, the term of the American ministers' service was generally rather short. On social occasions, therefore,
when length of residence determined the seating arrangements, the American representatives in France usually found themselves near the bottom
of the list.

12. *Ibid.*, p. 143.

caped American slave woman, who could cook "hominy, Maryland chicken, and buckwheat cakes." The wife of William C. Rives, who witnessed the Paris Revolution of 1830, found the introduction to the king somewhat ridiculous because, as she wrote, "I am too good a republican to be dazzled by the paraphernalia of royalty."[13] To countless American tourists, however, Court life was an attractive spectacle. Many American ministers were perplexed and amused by the endless requests of their compatriots vacationing in La Belle France to be introduced to whoever was king or emperor of France. At many royal or imperial Court parties republicans from America by far outnumbered the invited citizens of other countries. Remembering the kind treatment they had received in America in their early life, Louis Philippe and Louis Napoleon Bonaparte reciprocated this hospitality as graciously as they could.

Thomas Jefferson and William C. Rives were two highly regarded American representatives in France who, though in touch with prominent French leaders in 1789 and 1830 respectively, tried hard not to become too deeply involved in the internal affairs of France. Although leading statesmen of the Third Estate consulted the prestigious leader of the American Revolution, in 1789 Jefferson, who would have felt almost as much at home in France as in the United States, deliberately declined to take undue advantage of the influence he was in a position to exercise there. Similarly, Rives, another Virginia statesman who represented his country at the time of the July Revolution of 1830, declined to put pressure on his friend Lafayette, the famous general whose republican sympathies were well known. At that time some people back home actually accused Rives of being antirepublican because he did not energetically persuade Lafayette to establish a republic. They did not seem to understand that the aged Lafayette was then primarily concerned with finding a stable government for France, whatever its form. Rives himself thought this objec-

13. *Ibid.*, p. 169.

tive would be best accomplished by "a popular throne, surrounded by republican institutions."[14]

In spite of disclaimers to the contrary, by the mid-century the United States was willing to play a much more active role in the drafting of the Second Republic's constitution. In 1848 and 1870, moreover, the United States was the first power to recognize within a matter of days the newly proclaimed Second and Third Republics. It is also noteworthy that American ministers in France established a unique record during several crucial periods in French history. As much as Gouverneur Morris disliked the French people and the developments during the Great Revolution, he was the only foreign envoy who remained at his post during the Reign of Terror. Similarly, Elihu Washburne was the only foreign diplomat who declined to abandon Paris during the siege of 1870-71. Continuing this tradition, Robert Herrick refused to quit his post in 1914, determined not only to discharge his official responsibilities but also to do what he could to protect the precious art treasures in Paris, which to him was the "metropolis of the world."

To head the American legation in Paris was not always a pleasure. During wars, revolutions, and natural catastrophes the diplomatic assignment to France involved risks and hardships that tested the ministers' courage and endurance. Joel Barlow's attempt to overtake Napoleon during his fatal winter campaign in Russia ended in his tragic death. Though ably assisted by the astute consul general John Bigelow, William L. Dayton, the former United States senator from New Jersey who defended the Union's cause in France during the trying years of the Civil War, also died while serving his country abroad.[15]

Although the appointments of Elihu Washburne and White-

14. *Ibid.*, p. 173.
15. Another American minister to France, John Y. Mason, also died during his term of service.

law Reid were considered "vacation rewards"—the two distinguished public servants were given the opportunity to relax in the pleasant environment of Paris after many years of hard work at home—fate made unexpected demands upon both men before their assignments were completed. Washburne was surprised by the outbreak of the Franco-Prussian War and lived through the difficult months of the siege, discharging his heavy responsibilities in a manner that earned him much praise. Reid's "vacation" lasted three years. And though the Reids became known for their lavish hospitality when they entertained prominent members of French society, at the end of his "vacation" Reid's tireless and businesslike efforts helped to bring American pork back to many French dinner tables. As the minister observed at the farewell dinner in his honor, the fact that protracted negotiations on material interests "have been conducted and ended without the slightest shade of injury to cordial relations"[16] was in itself quite significant.

These farewell dinners were often more than courteous gestures to the minister and his country. They were in some instances a sincere personal tribute to ministers whose outlook, skill, and urbanity the French appreciated. As in the case of the Reids, the 1912 farewell party given for Robert Bacon, the handsome and fairly young Harvard-trained ambassador, was attended by many prominent Frenchmen, among them Premier Raymond Poincaré, the statesman Aristide Briand, and François Rodin, the famous sculptor. Bacon owed much of his popularity to the American aid he organized for the victims of the flood caused by the overflowing of the Seine in 1910. It must have been quite gratifying and reassuring to the French guests attending his farewell reception that Bacon pledged himself to be upon his return home, "in a certain sense, an unofficial ambassador of France."[17] The kind of intimate in-

16. American Citizens, Paris, "Reid Farewell Dinner," p. 16.
17. Willson, *America's Ambassadors*, pp. 384–86.

formality between officials of both countries, not at all out of order in the United States, as President Theodore Roosevelt and Ambassador Jusserand demonstrated, would have been regarded as neither proper nor customary in France. But even though the style of etiquette-conscious French officialdom was characterized by a courteous reserve, American ambassadors enjoyed the splendid hospitality and frank and friendly reception that was customary in France.

For thirty-four years, from 1875 to 1909, American envoys relied heavily on Henry Vignaud, an intellectual from Louisiana who was intimately familiar with the French language, diplomatic procedures, and the business to be conducted.[18] In his capacity as first secretary of the American Legation and as a cultured man Vignaud also enjoyed the esteem of French officials and the welcome attention of French society. Just as the bureaucracy of the Third Republic provided a certain stability and continuity amidst frequently changing ministries, so Vignaud's long experience as secretary of the American mission in Paris kept the administrative machinery in gear while inexperienced ambassadors were coming and going.

18. In his later years, however, he prevented younger men from becoming intimately familiar with the affairs of the embassy, lest he become dispensable. Allan Nevins, *Henry White: Thirty Years of American Diplomacy* (New York, 1930), p. 291. See also Mende, *Porter,* p. 192.

III

Franco-American
Diplomatic Relations

1901–14

1. French-American Economic Relations, 1901–14

In the fourteen years prior to the outbreak of the First World War trade and tariff questions continued to occupy a prominent place in Franco-American relations. In comparison with the last three decades of the nineteenth century, many changes indicated that history was catching up with both countries. The static condition of the French population, which between 1870 and 1914 increased only from 36,000,000 to 39,000,000, contrasted sharply with the rise of the American population from 40,000,000 to 99,000,000 even allowing for massive American immigration.[1] The trade volume of the two countries during the prewar years rose considerably, but the balance of trade was now mostly in favor of the United States, whose manufacturing capacity had outdistanced that of France. With 40 per cent of its population still engaged in agriculture, France remained predominantly a country of "home artistic trades, of ateliers, of small workshops."[2] Unlike the United States, it did not materially modernize its economy. Its wines, perfumes, silks, china, works of art, and other specialties were of such an attractive quality that Frenchmen engaged in their production and trade managed to maintain a comfortable, though somewhat deceptive, level of prosperity. Instead of introducing up-to-date competitive production techniques, they relied on very high tariffs as a way of protecting their domestic industries.[3] Regarding sales, they took it for granted that firms well known throughout France would be equally well known to and patronized by foreigners. Ex-

1. Gordon Wright, *France in Modern Times: 1760 to the Present* (Chicago, 1960), pp. 343–44.
2. J. P. Clapham, *The Economic Development of France and Germany, 1815–1914* (Cambridge, England, 1921), p. 258.
3. Wright, *France in Modern Times*, 346–50.

pecting Americans to come to them, few French traders would energetically promote their goods in the American market. And the French government was not disposed to assume the cost of promoting exports to the United States, as the French deputy consul general at New York had recommended in 1906.[4]

The leaders of both countries recognized not only the importance of trade per se but its political value as well. Delcassé, for instance, was at least as much motivated by his desire to woo the United States as by the prospect of desirable profits when he agreed to negotiations leading to the commercial Convention of July 24, 1899. Similarly, when two and a half years later Germany approached Delcassé for the purpose of ascertaining whether France would join in a European commercial combination to counteract America's influence upon the trade of Europe, he promptly and emphatically refused to become a party to it.[5] Basically, the Convention of 1899 provided for tariff reciprocity. In exchange for certain minimum tariff rates France conceded, the United States made a number of concessions legally authorized under the Dingley Tariff of 1897.[6] The United States Senate yielded to many pressures, particularly the strong objections from New York and New Jersey jewellers and goldsmiths when it refused to give its approval to the Convention of 1899.[7] The French Parliament not only ratified it, until September 24, 1903, it repeatedly extended its quite generous concessions to the

4. André Tardieu, *France and the Alliances—The Struggle for the Balance of Power* (New York, 1908), p. 278. He suggested the creation on Fifth Avenue in New York of a French House displaying the artistic products of France.

5. Porter to Hay, Paris, February 6, 1902, DDFDS. See also Porter, *Delcassé,* p. 155.

6. Percy Ashley, *Modern Tariff History: Germany—The United States—France* (New York, 1926), p. 336; see also American Chamber of Commerce, Paris, "Franco-American Tariff Agreement," State Department, Decimal File, 611.5131/389, Bulletin # 82, Paris, April, 1910.

7. Tardieu, *France and the Alliances,* p. 276.

United States. Thereafter occasional special agreements, such as that of January 28, 1908, provided for the reduction of import duties on French champagne wines in exchange for the minimum tariff rates France granted to articles of consumption coming from the United States and Porto Rico, with the exception of tobacco and sugar.[8]

Talk of reprisals and open tariff war reached a new high with the Payne-Aldrich tariff, which terminated all Franco-American reciprocity agreements.[9] *Le Temps*, usually quite friendly to the United States, commented on May 14, 1909, "The uncompromising protectionists of America have made the game easy for the protectionists of France." Senator Aldrich, who made a study tour of major European state banks, visited France and helped to remove some of the misunderstandings such a technically intricate document as a tariff act easily creates. At the initiative of Ambassador Henry White, the governor of the Bank of France invited Senator Aldrich, Ambassador White, the French minister of finance, and the director of the French Mint to a dinner at the Bank.[10] According to all indications, the senator's dispassionate and competent explanations succeeded in reducing the irritations the Payne-Aldrich Tariff had produced in France. Nevertheless the dissatisfaction with the framework within which Franco-American trade relations were carried on was mutual. Of the great commercial countries in the world, the United States was the only one to which French minimum tariff rates did not apply without exceptions. In this respect, France officially

8. *Ibid.*, p. 277. Late in June, 1899, Jules Cambon claimed that Algeria and Corsica should be treated as parts of France in customs matters. The American government consequently maintained that if "Algeria is France," Porto Rico is the United States, and its products, particularly its coffee, should enjoy all tariff benefits extended to the United States. A special agreement to this effect was concluded on August 8, 1902.

9. U.S. Tariff Commission, *Reciprocity and Commercial Treaties* (Washington, D.C., 1919), p. 47.

10. Chambers, *Franco-American Relations*, pp. 292–93.

classified the United States with such countries as Ethiopia, Haiti, and the Congo.[11]

On its part, France was habitually dissatisfied with American tariff rates and tried persistently to have them reduced. Furthermore, if the United States tariff rates displeased French traders and officials, the manner in which they were being administered exasperated them. After 1906 a major thrust of their complaints was directed at the Pure Food Act. The United States Customs Service rejected French goods because they were not labeled correctly, contained chemical substances such as artificial food preservers, or were packed in tin cans "sealed with a solder containing lead." The president of the Lyons Silk Manufacturers Syndicate complained about the arbitrary manner in which American Customs authorities "always applied the highest value although in the case of silks different silks of exactly the same quality may have different prices depending on whether one design is more popular than the other."[12]

On balance, it must be observed, however, that despite chronic irritations and growing international competition, Franco-American trade flourished. What experts in both countries sensed was that it could have flourished even more. The trade statistics for the period from 1900 to 1914 clearly indicate that, though significant in absolute terms, Franco-American trade remained relatively static. In the spring of 1914 the French Foreign Office expressed the desire for a new commercial treaty with the United States. President Wilson was willing to accommodate France. Indicatively, however, his coun-

11. Herrick to Bryan, Paris, April 22, 1913, DS, Decimal File, R.G. 59, 611.5131/375.

12. Herrick to Bryan, Paris, March 15, 1913, *ibid.*, 611.5131/74. Customary overvaluation on the part of the customs officials and deliberate undervaluation by exporters prompted the American Chamber of Commerce in Paris to recommend the substitition of specific for *ad valorem* duties on all dutiable imports into the United States.

Table IV. Total value of imports into France, Commerce Spécial, 1890–1914[13]

(in million francs)

From	1890	1900	1913	1914
Great Britain	627.4	675.2	1,115.1	855.8
United States	317.4	509.2	894.7	794.8
Germany	351.0	426.9	1,068.8	614.3

Table V. Total value of exports from France, Commerce Spécial, 1890–1914

(in million francs)

To	1890	1900	1913	1914
Great Britain	1,029.7	1,230.1	1,453.5	1,162.6
United States	328.8	255.2	422.6	376.6
Germany	341.6	465.1	866.7	511.1

Table VI. Percentage of total value of imports and exports, 1900 and 1913 of merchandise into and from France, Commerce Spécial

Country	Imports		Exports	
	1900	1913	1900	1913
Great Britain	14.4	13.1	29.9	21.1
Germany	9.1	12.5	11.3	12.6
United States	10.8	10.5	6.2	6.1

13. Tables IV, V, and VI are based on information contained in: (a) France, Ministère du Commerce . . . , *Annales du Commerce Extérieur, Exposé Comparatif,* 1884–1898 (Paris, 1900), pp. 126–27, 130–31, and 170–71; (b) France, Ministère du Commerce . . . , *Annuaire Statistique,* 1901 (Paris, 1902), pp. 268–71, 276; (c) France, Ministère du Travail, *Annuaire Statistique,* 1914 (Paris, 1917), pp. 254–55, 260; (d) France, Ministère du Commerce, *Annales du Commerce Extérieur* (Paris, 1908), CXXXVI, 29; and *ibid.,* (Paris, 1914), CXL, 35.

selor Robert Lansing asked one of the State Department's foreign trade advisers, "What can we offer, or what can we threaten?[14]"

Although French foreign investments amounted to about $9 billion in 1914, probably not more than $200 million had been placed in the United States.[15] Despite the improved handling of American securities in France after the organization in 1905 of the Société Financière Franco-Américaine,[16] Frenchmen were either too cautious or insufficiently informed about their opportunities in the American capital market. In the years just previous to 1914, French government leaders were, moreover, increasingly more concerned with political rather than financial dividends on French foreign investments.[17] As the prolonged economic crises in the United States of 1873 and 1893 shook the confidence of many Frenchmen in the economic stability of the United States, the sharp financial crisis of 1907 disturbed French capitalists. These crises produced their international repercussions and naturally affected the judgment of foreigners interested in foreign trade and investment. Being short of specie, the American money market applied during the crisis of 1907 to the Bank of France for assistance. Although the Bank had already sent eighty million gold eagles to New York, via the Bank of England, it was prepared to do more provided the United States Treasury would guarantee French loans to private American parties, a condition the United States government felt unable to meet on constitutional grounds.[18] It seemed to some Frenchmen that, aside from an inadequate banking system, which evidently did not satisfy the financial needs of the rapidly expanding American economy, there were too many enterprises in the United States

14. Lansing to Fleming, Washington, D.C., May 27, 1914. DS, Decimal File, 611.5131/400.
15. Feis, *World's Banker*, p. 47.
16. *New York Times*, March 23, 1905.
17. Feis, *World's Banker*, p. 123.
18. Tardieu, *France and the Alliances*, pp. 278–79.

having totally inadequate financial resources. As one writer observed in the influential *Revue des deux mondes* with respect to questionable inflationary tendencies in the United States, "Even the richest nations cannot escape sound financing, if they want to avoid crises."[19] As American power grew, France could not afford to ignore it. But it still had mixed feelings about it and trusted it only with reservations, always leaving the door open for greater cooperation in the future.

2. *The United States, France, and the Russo-Japanese War*

The various international alliances of the early twentieth century were of course symptomatic of the trouble that was brewing among the major rival powers. Although the United States was then nobody's ally, it could neither escape nor disregard the consequences of these rivalries, involving primarily France, Germany, Great Britain, Japan, and Russia. For that matter, America's resources and political orientation figured more actively in the deliberations and calculations of every one of these powers than its own traditionally passive attitude warranted.

The Franco-Russian alliance of 1894, by which either country would come to the assistance of the other in case of an attack by a European power, put an end to the uncomfortable isolation in which the Third Republic had found itself ever since its establishment.[1] Originally primarily conceived as a

19. Raphaël-Georges Lévy, "La crise économique de 1907 et les États-Unis d'Amérique," *RDDM* (December 15, 1907), p. 824.
1. Porter to Hay, Paris, January 7, 1904 (confidential), DDFDS. See also J. B. Eustis, "The Franco-Russian Alliance," *North American Review,* CLXV (July, 1897), 118.

defense against Germany, the alliance also had anti-British connotations, certainly until the Anglo-French entente in 1904.[2] Contemporaries, though, doubted its value in this respect. The American press deplored the Franco-Russian alliance because of its revival of militarism in Europe and many Frenchmen were critical of it because they saw in it a greater liability for France than an asset.[3] These Frenchmen would have preferred closer collaboration with Germany, in defense of Western Europe. As early as in the summer of 1890, the noted French historian Gabriel Monod commented, "France and Germany together can save Europe from the hegemony of Russia and can prevent the whole commerce of the world from being monopolized by England and the United States."[4]

An interlocking chain of events in the Far East during the first years of the twentieth century severely tested the Franco-Russian alliance and involved the United States in these events more deeply than might have been anticipated. Theodore Roosevelt's unwillingness to commit the United States and its navy led Great Britain to conclude the Anglo-Japanese alliance of January 30, 1902. Since Great Britain mistrusted Russia's policies with respect to China, India, and the Middle East and the interests of Russia and Japan conflicted particularly in Manchuria and Korea, the Anglo-Japanese alliance foreshadowed serious troubles for Russia. Understandably, France felt uneasy about these prospects and endeavored to delay as long as possible a showdown between Russia and Japan.[5] The Franco-Russian Declaration of March 16, 1902,

2. Pierre Renouvin, "L'Orientation de l'alliance Franco-Russe en 1900–1901," *Revue d'histoire diplomatique* (July-September 1966), pp. 193–204.

3. Thomas A. Bailey, *America Faces Russia—Russian-American Relations from Early Times to Our Day* (Ithaca, N.Y., 1950), pp. 144–45; Stuart, *French Foreign Policy*, pp. 6, 26–27.

4. William L. Langer, *The Franco-Russian Alliance, 1890–1914* (Cambridge, Mass., 1929), p. 140; see also Wright, *France in Modern Times*, pp. 385–89.

5. Vagts, *Deutschland und die Vereinigten Staaten*, II, 1110.

was a prompt response and warning on the part of these allies. Reaffirming the principles embodied in the published text of the Anglo-Japanese Treaty, including the maintenance of the status quo and the general peace in the Far East, the preservation of the independence of China and Korea, and the Open Door in China, France and Russia served notice that they reserved to themselves the right to consult "as to the means to be adopted" in case of aggression by third powers or the recurrence of disturbances in China.[6]

It was to the credit of Theodore Roosevelt that he grasped the interrelationship of the rivalries in Europe and Asia and their part in the world struggle for power. Understanding the balance-of-power concept more realistically than most American presidents, Roosevelt saw the stake the United States had in preserving an equilibrium in the world. It was during his administration that a reappraisal of Russo-American relations took place.[7] The revolting Kishinev pogroms in 1903, Russia's noncompliance with its 1902 agreement with China to withdraw its troops from Manchuria, and its disregard of the Open Door tended to drive Washington and St. Petersburg apart. While France made conscious efforts to improve its relations with the United States, America's regard for the Russian ally of France deteriorated noticeably. According to the German ambassador to the United States, this state of affairs was further aggravated by the realization of American high finance that Russia's policies in Asia ran counter to America's economic interests, particularly to the interests of its cotton and oil industries.[8] The confidential message Am-

6. See Chandler C. Anderson Papers, "Arbitration Treaties" (LC MS), Box 17.

7. See William H. Harbaugh, *Power and Responsibility—The Life and Times of Theodore Roosevelt* (New York, 1961), pp. 271–73; and Howard K. Beale, *Theodore Roosevelt and the Rise of America to World Power* (Baltimore, 1956).

8. Sternburg to Bülow, Washington, March 7, 1904, German Foreign Ministry Microfilms, 1867–1920, UC. I, Reel 118.

bassador Porter sent to Secretary of State Hay only shortly before the outbreak of the Russo-Japanese War did not improve
the trustworthiness of the Russians. In his message Porter
passed on the information then circulating in Paris "that Russia takes the ground that the Chinese Empire embraces only
eighteen provinces, and that the tributary countries of Mon-
golia, Thibet, and Turkestan, and also the territory known as
Manchuria are countries foreign to the "Chinese Empire,"
and excluded from all international agreements that Russia
had made with reference to China."[9]

When on February 8, 1904, Japan opened hostilities by at-
tacking the Russian fleet at Port Arthur without a declaration
of war, the United States took the initiative in diplomatic
soundings designed to secure respect for the neutrality of
China. Japan accepted this proposition, provided Russia, too,
would agree to it. Secretary Hay instructed Ambassador Porter
therefore to "say informally and in strict confidence to Mr.
Delcassé that our proposition is not in the interest of either
combatant, but in our own and that of the civilized world."[10]
Hay thought that prompt action by France as Russia's closest
friend would be most helpful. Delcassé adhered to the American proposition, with the proviso, however, that he thought
Manchuria, the field of military operations, ought to be ex-
cepted from the neutrality pledge. What preoccupied Delcassé
even more was his determination to steer a course that would
preserve the neutrality of France. He certainly did not want
to see France being drawn into this war and hoped that Russia would not misunderstand this attitude. The peculiar position of France was complicated by the fact that the French
had extended loans to Russia amounting to about
$1,500,000,000.[11] As at the time of the Spanish-American War,

9. Porter to Hay, Paris, January 22, 1904 (confidential) , DDFDS.
10. Hay to Porter, Washington, February 13, 1904 (most confidential) ,
FIDS. Porter to Hay, Paris, February 13, 1904 (telegram) , DDFDS.
11. *Ibid.*, February 12, 1904.

so now during the Russo-Japanese War, heavy French investments in Spain and Russia respectively exposed French investors to excessive risks. The French stake in the duration and
outcome of these wars was too great not to worry about their
consequences. The Anglo-French entente of 1904 assumed
therefore a significance going far beyond the immediate understanding regarding Egypt and Morocco. It implicitly let
Russia know that it could not expect France to join her in the
present conflict against Japan, Britain's ally.[12]

    This intimation further complicated the situation in which
Russia found itself when on October 21, 1904, one of its admirals mistook several British fishing trawlers for Japanese ships
and sank them in waters known as the Dogger Bank. The
peaceful settlement of the incident by an international commission did not distract the Russians from the realization that
the Anglo-French alliance operated against their interests in
the Russo-Japanese War. It was precisely this Russian dilemma that the kaiser tried to exploit by exploring the possibility of a Russo-German alliance. The Russo-Japanese
conflict, which started as a war of limited scope, thus opened
the door to unpredictable developments of major international
consequence. The longer the war lasted, the more the uneasiness of the French people grew. At the end of the eighth
month of the war Gabriel Hanotaux expressed the fear that
"a mere imprudence may engender a new flood of blunders in
which the whole world may be precipitated."[13] A truce and
peace equitably disposing of the pending difficulties would, he
pleaded, "call forth the cordial approval of the whole universe." Until his sudden removal from office in June, 1905, in
connection with the Moroccan crisis, Delcassé tried to find an
early peaceful solution to the Russo-Japanese War. His successor, Maurice Rouvier, was also not disposed to make sacrifices

12. Nevins, *White,* p 240.
13. "Apprehension in France," *New York Times,* November 1, 1904.

for Russia and was determined to urge St. Petersburg to agree to peace terms acceptable to Japan.[14]

The president of the United States was not a disinterested bystander: he took a keen interest in these Far Eastern developments and the increasingly anxious desire of the neutral powers for peace. Although there is no written record substantiating Theodore Roosevelt's contention that he "notified Germany and France in the most polite and discreet fashion" that the United States would side with Japan should they try to deprive Japan of the spoils of its victory, as they and Russia had done at the end of the Chinese-Japanese War in 1895, Roosevelt probably informed Ambassadors Sternburg and Jusserand to that effect.[15] At the outset of the war the president clearly favored Japan over Russia, even though he did not preclude the possibility of a future Russo-Japanese alliance which might endanger American interests in Asia. But the astounding military accomplishments of Japan and the unexpected weaknesses Russia revealed were of genuine concern to Theodore Roosevelt, for he suddenly recognized that Japan might become a much greater threat to the United States than he had heretofore estimated. With the balance of power in East Asia and the safety of the Philippines at stake, Roosevelt took the precautionary step of negotiating the Taft-Katsura Agreement, by which the United States acknowledged Japan's suzerainty over Korea in exchange for its disavowal of any aggressive designs on the Philippines.[16]

Fortunately Japan knew the limits of its power and the dangers involved in fighting a long war against Russia. At the height of their military triumph, the ingenious Japanese were

14. Robert S. McCormick to Francis B. Loomis, Paris, June 9, 1905, DDFDS.

15. See Raymond A. Esthus, *Theodore Roosevelt and Japan* (Seattle, Washington, 1966), p. 38; and Tyler Dennett, *Roosevelt and the Russo-Japanese War* (Garden City, N.Y., 1925), pp. 2, 26.

16. Sir John T. Pratt, *The Expansion of Europe in the Far East* (London, 1947), pp. 141–42.

faced with near exhaustion of their resources. On May 31, 1905, they secretly asked President Roosevelt to mediate the conflict. Roosevelt, who had helped to localize the war, now used his talents and influence to bring the two belligerents to the conference table at Portsmouth, New Hampshire. There, in August, 1905, the peace terms were settled to the greater satisfaction of the rest of the world than of either of the belligerents.

The Russo-Japanese War and the Russian Revolution of 1905 growing out of it demonstrated the financial, political, and military liability of the Franco-Russian alliance at a time when the Moroccan question cast ominous shadows over Europe's horizon.[17] Roosevelt's contributions to the settlement of both crises were therefore invaluable to France.[18]

3. *Theodore Roosevelt and the Moroccan Crisis of 1905*

Ever so often in history, what starts out as a fairly minor controversy develops into an international crisis of threatening proportions. The Moroccan crisis of 1905 is a case in point. When France tried to solidify its position in Morocco, for diplomatic rather than for local security reasons,[1] Germany manifested its objection to any unilateral changes in the Sherifian Empire.

Between December, 1900, and October, 1904, France had

17. McCormick to Root, Paris, November 17, 1905, DDFDS.
18. J. Fred Rippy, *America and the Strife of Europe* (Chicago, 1938), p. 173.
1. Kim Munholland, "Rival Approaches to Morocco: Delcassé, Lyautey, and the Algerian-Moroccan Border, 1903–1905," *French Historical Studies*, V (1968), 328–43.

concluded agreements with Italy, England, and Spain by which these powers practically granted France full freedom of action in Morocco in exchange for French concessions elsewhere. Since the International Convention of Madrid of 1880, which the United States too had ratified, provided that all powers should enjoy equal rights in Morocco, the Germans objected to these deals which put them in a disadvantageous position. Dramatically, on March 31, 1905, the kaiser delivered a saber-rattling speech at Tangier, where a German warship had carried him, proclaiming his support of the sovereign sultan of Morocco.[2]

To understand the full scope of this potentially dangerous provocation, one must keep in mind that it was made at a time when as a result of the Russo-Japanese War France's alliance with Russia had for the time being lost much of its value and weakened France on the continent. Of even greater significance, this provocation amounted to a challenge of Britain as well, since in April, 1904, Britain had agreed to French control of Morocco in exchange for French acceptance of British pre-eminence in Egypt. This meant that, regardless of the merits of the French case in Morocco, opposition to France was bound to affect British interests too.

From the beginning, Theodore Roosevelt was drawn into this delicate affair. On March 6, 1905, the German ambassador in Washington, Baron Hermann Speck von Sternburg, conveyed to the president a message from the kaiser asking him to join the German emperor in efforts to strengthen the independence of the sultan of Morocco, both by persuading him to introduce internal reforms and by promising him support against any foreign nation "which sought to obtain exclusive control of Morocco."[3] In their dealings with Roosevelt

2. Harbaugh, *Power and Responsibility*, p. 287.
3. Theodore Roosevelt to Whitelaw Reid, Washington, D.C., April 28, 1906 (absolutely private and confidential). See Elting E. Morison (ed.), *The Letters of Theodore Roosevelt* (Cambridge, Mass., 1952), V, 230. See

the Germans thought it expedient to stress the Open Door principle in Morocco, which appealed to the president. Roosevelt hesitated, however, to become at all involved in Morocco, where the interests of the United States were very small. Many related interests and by-products of the developing Moroccan crisis—the preservation of world peace, the prevention of a Franco-German war, and the probability of deteriorating Anglo-German relations—nevertheless convinced Theodore Roosevelt that the United States had much to gain by contributing to a peaceful settlement of the crisis.[4]

Repeatedly approached by Germany to help bring the Moroccan question before an international conference, the president discovered that France frowned upon giving Germany any satisfaction in this regard. Delcassé, whose strong friendship for the United States was greatly appreciated by American officials, resisted the German challenge until his dramatic dismissal on June 6.[5] Such influential American statesmen as Elihu Root and Henry Cabot Lodge also urged the president to curb the activities of the kaiser. "It would be an evil day for us," wrote Lodge to his close friend Theodore Roosevelt, "if Germany were to crush France," particularly since "the breakdown of Russia has disturbed the European equilibrium."[6] Lodge strongly favored the cultivation of the closest relations with France, "our natural ally." In a confidential letter Roosevelt sent to Ambassador Henry White from Oyster Bay, on August 23, 1905, he confessed his sympathies were at bottom with France, although he still wished to keep on good terms with the Germans.[7] His immediate objective, though,

also Eugene N. Anderson, *The First Moroccan Crisis, 1904–1906* (Chicago Ill., 1930) , pp. 205–6.

4. Nevins, *White*, p. 263.

5. "Delcassé to Remain," *New York Times*, April 23, 1905.

6. Henry C. Lodge (ed.) , *Selections from the Correspondence of Theodore Roosevelt and Henry Cabot Lodge, 1884–1918* (New York, 1925) , II, 160–63; see also Willson, *America's Ambassadors*, p. 374.

7. Nevins, *White*, p. 267.

pointed to a future war between England and Germany rather than between France and Germany. According to him, "Germany is the only potentially aggressive power in Europe, and her industrial competition is as much a threat to England's position in the world as her disciplined army and growing navy. France is only a weight between them."[14] If anything, McCormick regarded the Franco-Russian alliance and "the financial relations which sprang from this alliance" as "one of the most menacing factors in the present European situation."

A year later, he reported that England's purpose in supporting disarmament at the Second Hague Conference in 1907 was to discredit and isolate Germany, which would not consent to disarmament. France did not want to be a party to this cynical maneuver. Thoughtful Frenchmen did not wish to see their country taking the side of England against Germany and, as a result, being compelled to bear the brunt of an unjustifiable war. As they judged the future, "the practical interests of Germany and England clash in every part of the globe," those of Germany and France nowhere.[15] McCormick's observations thus kept American statesmen abreast of contemporary viewpoints with respect to major international questions. It is noteworthy, though, that, with the exception of the year 1905, in the years following the Spanish-American War and previous to World War I the United States remained relatively aloof from international politics. It refused, for instance, to be drawn into the Moroccan and Balkan crises prior to 1914. During these years it was preoccupied with trade and dollar diplomacy.

14. *Ibid.*, December 15, 1905.
15. McCormick to Root, Paris, December 21, 1906. DS, Numerical File, 1906–1910, Vol. IV, cases 40/30–31.

4. The United States in World Affairs, 1898–1914

At the beginning of the twentieth century a major effort was made to improve Franco-American cultural ties. Prominent Frenchmen came to the United States in unprecedented numbers, developing personal contacts and friendships with congenial Americans. There were lecture series on both sides of the Atlantic, designed to enlighten the public about France and the United States respectively. Many courteous gestures and exchanges of gifts studiously cultivated a friendly atmosphere between the two nations.[1] It did not follow, however, that in commercial "matters" their respective governments displayed the same amount of good will.

Altogether, the United States usually found France difficult to deal with on colonial questions. It was not until May, 1904, that a mutually satisfactory treaty was concluded in regard to Tunis.[2] Through this treaty the United States finally renounced the rights and privileges of the ancient treaties of 1797 and 1824 with the bey of Tunis. France, in turn, extended to American consuls and citizens in Tunis the advantages of all existing Franco-American treaties and conventions. Between 1905 and 1911 American economic interests in Morocco increased as noticeably as American dissatisfaction with French colonial policies, which hampered American businessmen in their drive to expand their enterprises even

1. The unveiling of the Statue of Liberty in 1886, the presentation to France of a statue of Lafayette, the presentation to the United States of the statue of Rochambeau early in the twentieth century, and the return of the body of John Paul Jones from France to America highlighted some of the most outstanding ceremonial occasions at which the friendship between the two peoples was emphasized. See Donald C. McKay, *The United States and France* (Cambridge, Mass., 1951), pp. 93–94; and Tardieu, *France and the Alliances*, pp. 270–71.

2. Chambers, *Franco-American Relations*, pp. 173–74.

further.³ Deeply concerned about the conditions in the Congo, the American government was eager to see important reforms instituted at the time the Belgian government considered the Treaty of Annexation of the Congo. When the American Ambassador in Paris broached this matter with Foreign Minister Pichon, he was evasively told that, unlike the government, French public opinion showed little interest in the Congo.⁴ Reflecting French determination to keep foreign influences out of their West African possessions, lest they open the door to agents "innocently" aiming at undermining the established authority, was an official ruling concerning the evangelization of the natives on the borders of the Upper Niger. American missionaries of the Gospel Missionary Union wished to spread the news of the gospel in the native dialects. To acquire sufficient knowledge of the native languages in order to translate the Bible into African vernaculars, these missionaries asked the French government in 1909 to grant them permission to carry on their work among tribes under French authority. The minister of colonies declined this request on the ground that "no religious missionary propaganda can receive an official sanction in the French colonies."⁵ If this decision was politically motivated, the strong influence Roman Catholic clerics exercised in French colonial administration also tended to frustrate Protestant missionaries.

Reluctantly France acquiesced in the historically special relationship between Liberia and the United States. Liberian officials had on several occasions reason to fear French designs on their territory. When in 1907 the British Colonial Office told them that it could do nothing about French designs and

3. Rippy, *America and the Strife of Europe,* pp. 68–70.
4. Henry White to Root, Paris, January 31, 1908. Private. DS, Numerical File, 1906–1910, Vol. CXCIII, Cases 1806/243.
5. See Clémenceau to Ambassador Henry White, Paris, April 13, 1909. DS, Numerical File, 1906–1910, Vol. MXXVI, Case 18091. Upon official inquiry, the State Department discovered that no existing Franco-American treaty contained clauses with respect to religious tolerance and teaching.

might even be obliged to take a slice of Liberia in case France acquired one, the Liberians turned to the United States for a guarantee of their territorial integrity—at least that is what they hoped for rather than mere friendly expressions of sympathy.[6] Although the Liberians knew that such an assurance was unlikely to be given, they sent a commission to the United States. In their meeting with Secretary of State Root on June 1, 1908, the commissioners were politely told that the United States was indeed unwilling to commit itself in Liberia too extensively.[7] In 1910, however, the United States acceded to Liberia's request for army officers to "organize and drill" its frontier force. And, in addition to financial assistance, America made its good offices available to the African state. French attempts to compare these helpful dispositions of the United States in regard to Liberia with the absolute French protectorate in Madagascar were of course wholly erroneous, but perhaps tactically useful.[8]

In a larger sense, French and American objectives in the Far East were not so far apart as to cause undue complications. French Indochina and its spheres in China obviously gave France a stronger hold on the Asian continent than the possession of the Philippines afforded the United States. But basically both countries wished to maintain the status quo and a balance of power in Asia, as well as to protect and expand their commercial relations in the Far East. Both were particularly concerned, moreover, with the attitudes and ambitions of Japan and tried to safeguard their respective interests by concluding special agreements with Japan. The Franco-Japanese Arrangement of June 10, 1907, was as much designed to remove "all cause of misunderstanding for the future"[9] as the

6. White to Root, Paris, September 27, 1907, *ibid.*, Case 3532/13–20.
7. See Philip C. Jessup, *Elihu Root* (New York, 1938), II, 60–61.
8. See Robert de Caix, "Le Libéria et les Puissances—L'Expérience Américaine," *L'Afrique Française* (March 1913), pp. 109–16.
9. See Chandler P. Anderson Papers, "Arbitration Treaties" (LC), Box 17.

Root-Takahira Agreement of November 30, 1908.[10] Thanks to
the moderating influence of Shinichiro Kurino, the Japanese
ambassador to France, the temporarily strained relations between Japan and the United States in 1906 and 1907 were
greatly toned down in France. In the case of the Japanese children who were being excluded from the public schools of San
Francisco, however, Le Figaro[11] raised the embarrassing question, "Do the Americans want to suppress the rainbow by
proscribing the red Indians, the Negroes, and the yellow races
of Asia?" Although President Roosevelt's energetic intervention settled the San Francisco school issue, the Root-Takahira
Agreement was not only welcomed in France because of its
hoped-for stabilizing effect but also because, as Le Matin[12]
commented, it "puts an end to the German Emperor's dream
of American support against the so-called Yellow Peril."
France already liked to include Japan in the anti-German
camp. With this ultimate goal in mind, as well as to discourage Japanese designs on Indochina, France made its money
markets available to Japan.[13] It truly wished to remove "all
cause of misunderstanding" which might provoke Japan.

The ill-conceived attempts at dollar diplomacy in China
during the Taft administration constituted the major area of
difference between France and the United States.[14] Secretary
Knox's proposals regarding the neutralization of the Chinese
railroads ran into strong opposition. By 1910 Great Britain,
France, and Russia had by virtue of their bilateral agreements
with Japan already recognized so many special spheres and

10. For details, see A. Whitney Griswold, The Far Eastern Policy of the
United States (New York, 1938), p. 129.
11. October 29, 1906.
12. November 30, 1908.
13. Jessup, Root, II, 38.
14. Griswold, Far Eastern Policy, pp. 133–75; Charles Vevier, The
United States and China, 1906–1913—A Study of Finance and Diplomacy
(New Brunswick, N.J., 1955), pp. 136, 148, 162–63, and 217; see also
Tien-yi-Li, Woodrow Wilson's China Policy, 1913–1917 (New York, 1952),
pp. 30;–31.

rights in China, including Manchuria, that the United States faced too many strongly entrenched vested interests there to use its financial pressures successfully. Paris and Washington also did not see eye-to-eye on the question of the recognition of the Republic of China. The Quai d'Orsay thought the United States was moving too fast in this matter and that it would be wiser to withhold recognition until the stability of the revolutionary government of China had been convincingly established. France also suggested—and this was not a mere technicality—a simultaneous recognition from several powers.[15] If any single power was to take the lead in the recognition of China, Japan felt that as an oriental power this privilege really belonged to it.

Although France ranked among the major powers with considerable possessions and influence in the Far East, its political role in the Western hemisphere was minor.[16] Early in the twentieth century, when Great Britain was gradually yielding its formidable position in Central America to the United States, a private French organization developed an ambitious scheme to counterbalance the political and economic preponderance of the United States in Latin America. The Ligue Franco-Latine, founded in Paris in 1904 and headed by Jean de-Lanessan, former minister of the marine, arranged reciprocal visits between groups of French and South American politicians and businessmen, in the hope of ultimately establishing a South American federation with France as the pivot.[17] The Ligue did not get very far, for as sympathetic as French officials might have been with the Ligue's notions, at this time their policies essentially respected the Monroe Doctrine and the "special interests" of the United States in the

15. Herrick to Knox, Paris, July 25, 1912 (telegram), DS, Decimal File, China, 893.00/1396.

16. Pierre Renouvin, *Histoire des relations internationales 1815–1871* (Paris, 1954), VI, 210.

17. "South American Federation to Offset the United States," *New York Times,* November 9, 1904.

Western hemisphere. When during the Franco-Venezuelan controversy of 1905 President Roosevelt declared that "the Monroe Doctrine could certainly not be used by Southern Republics to shield them from the consequences of their own torts," the French government felt reassured. It was perfectly willing to pledge that it would neither permanently occupy Venezuelan territory nor land troops or seize a customs house for more than a very limited period. But it desired to deal directly with financial delinquents in the Western hemisphere.[18]

In this connection, it seems appropriate to recall André Tardieu's contemporary observation that since the Spanish-American War the United States had developed a larger sense of world responsibility with singular rapidity. "It is no longer enough," he said, "not to interfere with the Americans in America. It is also necessary to be in agreement with them in other parts of the world."[19] This understanding of America's ascendency as a world power, though still in an evolutionary stage, evidently induced France to cooperate with the United States whenever possible. Soon after the Panamanian Revolution France authorized its resident consul at Panama to enter into relations with the de facto government. On November 18, 1903, Delcassé promptly recognized the Republic of Panama.[20] In 1913 the French government showed its friendliness towards the United States by doing its utmost to prevent any assistance to the Huerta government.[21] Nevertheless, among such other countries as Great Britain and Germany, which had financial stakes to defend in Mexico, France recognized the Huerta regime. The unusually hostile tone of the French press in its disapproval of President Wilson's Mexican policy, however, did not reflect official French policy. It seems to have

18. Memorandum of an interview between the president, the secretary of state, and the French ambassador, December 14, 1905, FNTDS.
19. Tardieu, *France and the Alliances*, pp. 283–86.
20. Porter to Hay, Paris, November 11 and 19, 1903, DDFDS.
21. Herrick to Bryan, Paris, October 31, 1913, DS, Decimal File, Mexico, 812.00/9646.

been "inspired" by British and German capital and, most likely, also by the agents of Huerta in France.[22]

To the extent that German activities in Latin America aroused the suspicions of the United States, France was destined to benefit from such apprehensions. With the international rivalries, the alliance systems, and the immense outlays for armaments foreshadowing a conflict of major proportions, Secretary of State Elihu Root, anxious to reduce world tensions, concluded as many as twenty-five arbitration treaties. The first of these treaties was made with France.[23] Root signed it on February 10, 1908, and it was extended for another five years in 1913. This treaty provided for arbitration in accordance with the recommendations of the Hague Conference, subject to considerable qualifications insisted upon by the United States Senate. It was not a substitute for disarmament, which the "realists" among the military strategists in France, as well as elsewhere, regarded as dangerous to their country's safety. But it showed the concern felt in both countries for mechanisms potentially capable of contributing to the reduction, if not elimination, of international frictions. It was therefore a psychological mistake on the part of Germany to refuse to become a party to a similar arbitration treaty with the United States. A disappointed Root charged in a letter to Andrew Carnegie, dated April 3, 1909, that "Germany, under her present government, is the great disturber of the peace of the world."[24] He singled out Germany as the main obstacle to all rational attempts to lessen the chances of war.

22. *Ibid.*, April 25, 1914, Mexico, 812.00/11723.

23. Scott, "Elihu Root," in Bemis, *American Secretaries of State*, IX 225–26; see also Charles C. Tansill, "The United States and International Arbitration, 1872–1914," *Thought, Fordham University Quarterly*, XVI (December 1941), 716. As far back as 1888, 112 members of the French Chamber of Deputies proposed international arbitration treaties. "La France et les États-Unis," *Courier des États-Unis*, May 2, 1888.

24. Jessup, *Root*, II, 310.

If nothing else, these arbitration treaties were America's symbolic announcement to the world that it had a stake in the preservation of world peace. From the French point of view, the recognition that, as Colonel House phrased it, "the factors, upon which American traditions rested had disappeared," was a welcome initial step the United States had taken in the world arena. But it did not go far enough. Lewis Einstein, an American diplomat in Paris, pleaded two years prior to the outbreak of the First World War for greater American participation in European affairs.[25] In his judgment, the breakdown of the European balance of power would gravely endanger the security of the United States and most likely intensify the frictions between Germany and the United States. This minority viewpoint was as yet not acceptable to the large mass of the American people and its political leaders. As future events were to demonstrate, Einstein was less ahead of his time than his compatriots had been behind it. When the guns of August ushered in a new age, American public opinion, though favoring neutrality, clearly sided with France. As the *New Republic* commented late in 1914, "This is not France's war. She has been necessarily involved in it; but she did not want it."[26]

25. Rippy, *America and the Strife of Europe*, pp. 77–79.
26. December 5, 1914.

Conclusion

A summary view of Franco-American diplomatic relations in the nineteenth century runs the risk of many oversimplifications because both countries changed so much that at different times they represented quite different entities. At the beginning of the century France ranked among the truly leading powers in the world and exercised a profound influence on the civilization of the modern world. At the end of the century, its relative power had declined. But in spite of Waterloo and Sedan and its failure to industrialize as fast as Germany, Great Britain, and the United States, its genius left its impressive imprint on modern civilization.

Starting as a small and only recently colonial country, the United States gradually overtook France in many material and physical respects, proving by 1900 to be a colonial empire of major consequence. Although France and the United States naturally had their differences during the long period from 1789 to 1914 and at times went to the brink of war, it was remarkable that, with the exception of the undeclared naval war in the closing years of the eighteenth century, they never took up arms against each other. By the turn of the twentieth century, these two politically and institutionally revolutionary societies were devoting their energies to the more peaceful industrial and cultural revolutions also designed to benefit mankind. Even their restrictive trade policies, particularly since the last third of the century, did not prevent them from trading profitably with each other, regardless of the political system currently operating in France. Ideological preferences on both sides produced few provocations and no insurmountable obstacles. Altogether, America's steady institutions, its preoccupation with hemispheric affairs, and its defense of the freedom of the seas permitted it to follow a fairly simple and constant course until the end of the nineteenth century. Although the United States did not interfere with French policies in Europe, its restraining influence on French colonialism in Africa and Asia seemed somewhat inconsistent to Frenchmen who witnessed the steady territorial expansion of the American republic.

The course of French policy with respect to the United States was much more complex and erratic. It amounted to a strange mixture of opposition to the American rival and propositions to him as a potential ally, of a certain distance and relative familiarity, of condescension and restrained admiration. This ambivalence can be traced as far back as the American Revolution. Louis XVI and Napoleon Bonaparte acted "generously" toward the United States for the sake of France. They were more motivated by their determination to deliver a blow against Britain than by their eagerness to aid the United States. If the obligations of the United States towards France seem therefore to have been limited, the question must nevertheless be raised: What would have been the fate of the United States without French assistance in the War of Independence and without Napoleon's decision to sell the Louisiana Territory? Since Napoleon I French governments, monarchical and republican alike, treated the United States as a friend whose shadow always frightened them. How tall would the American giant grow? Would he merely dwarf France or absorb Europe by the mere force of his upward momentum, if not by intent? Perceptive Frenchmen worried about these prospects and ever so often wished to halt and break this momentum, not so much out of hatred for the United States as of concern for the safety and independent future of their own country.

In a peculiarly frustrating and unproductive fashion France developed the habit of annoying the United States with its allusions to interferences that usually did not materialize. In the 1840's Guizot would have liked to organize Europe to prove to America that there was nothing "manifest" in its destiny. In the 1850's Empress Eugénie pleaded for the formation of a European league against the republican pretensions of the United States. In the 1860's Napoleon III appeared to be ever ready to take the initiative in European moves to keep the United States divided. At the height of the American Civil War Alphonse Lamartine addressed a letter to the monarchs of Europe asking them to join forces in a move that would make certain, once and for all, that no nation would in the future become a victim of America's commercial despotism. In the final years of the century this concern did not abate. On the contrary, Pan-Americanism, Secretary of State Blaine's ambitious dream, sounded to many Frenchmen like a euphemism for economic imperialism and Europe's total exclusion from the New World.[1] Even worse, to protect Europe itself against America's overwhelming financial and commercial power, Jules Cambon advocated the creation of a European league. To the disillusionment of France, moreover, the Teutons and Anglo-Saxons seemed to be closing ranks against the Latins. There was little that France could effectively do about the United States. Surely, its restrictive economic measures, particularly during the 1880's, blocked the advancing American economy as little as its earlier vain attempts at checking the territorial expansion of the United States.

In 1880 the renowned philologist Émile Littré shocked his compatriots, particularly, of course, legitimists, imperialists, and clericals, when he went as far as to draw the premature conclusion from the fall of Sedan that France had really become a second-class power.[2] Its rising empire, its alliances, its roles as international banker and brilliant art center in the late nineteenth century simply did not justify this dethronement from the rank of the great powers. But the meteoric rise of the United States did pose a challenge and Frenchmen were divided as to how it should be met. Proponents of one school

1. Roustan to Challemel-Lacour, Washington, May 27, 1883, CPEU, CLX; see also Claudio Jannet, *Les États-Unis Contemporains* (Paris, 1889), pp. 144–49.

2. "French Foreign Policy," *New York Times*, January 27, 1880, p. 4.

of thought proposed an expansion of the Franco-Russian alliance into a triple alliance, with the United States as the third party which would send ships, arms, munitions, foodstuffs, and other supplies in case of a long war between France and Germany.[3] Jules Patenôtre, French ambassador to the United States, advised Gabriel Hanotaux, on the other hand, that the tradition of noninvolvement in strictly European wars was too strongly rooted to be discarded by the American people.[4] For other reasons too Patenôtre was pessimistic about the feasibility of a Franco-American alliance. Although by 1897 the United States navy occupied the fourth or fifth place among the navies of the world, the French diplomat quite realistically assumed that the defense of America's long coast lines would take precedence over any European needs. Considering, moreover, the practical nonexistence of an American army, the disappointing attitude of the United States during the calamitous war of 1870, and the fact that national interests rather than sentimental memories form the basis for alliances, Patenôtre discounted the United States as a possible ally. Though moral obligations might take a back seat in history, however, profitable trade, he thought, would always find open channels. Jules Cambon came to the same conclusion. In essence, in addition to immensely important cultural influences, the trade relations between the two countries occupied the central place in Franco-American relations of the nineteenth century.

It took France a long time to recognize the positive aspects of the Franco-American relationship. France could have badly hurt the United States during the period of its mid-century territorial expansion, the Civil War, and probably during the Spanish-American War. Whatever the reasons for the hesita-

3. G. Gerville-Réache, "L'Amérique et l'Europe," *L'Éclair*, October 3, 1897.

4. Patenôtre to Hanotaux, Washington, October 14, 1897 (confidential), Politique étrangère, États-Unis, Relations avec la France, 1897–1900 (AMAE).

tions of France, its failure to act decisively then almost eliminated its chances of checking the constantly rising power of the United States later on. By the turn of the twentieth century France could, in a material and political sense, do little to or for the United States. Even if traditional and cultural ties, however, had not linked the two countries closely together, in matters of trade and navigation they developed mutual interests. For that matter, the stability and prosperity of France was an essential feature in the maintenance of continental and global balance which both countries strove to preserve. Much more exposed to challenge and aggression by rival powers than the insulated United States, France had, in a material and political sense, much to gain from Franco-American cooperation, for in that sense, the United States had much to offer France.

Great Britain had long ago recognized the valuable contribution the United States could make to its existence. In addition to common cultural and racial bonds and close association in trade and finance, Britain and the United States on the whole also cooperated in political questions of mutual concern. In spite of many frictions and controversies, ever since the Peace Treaty of Ghent the two countries had managed to settle their differences peacefully. The experiences of the American Revolution and the War of 1812 apparently deeply impressed upon the British the increased danger they faced whenever their Old World rivals and their New World relatives challenged them either jointly or simultaneously. To avoid this kind of confrontation in the future, Britain went to great lengths to cultivate as friendly a relationship with the United States as its own interests would tolerate. Occasionally it was tempted to teach the Yankees a wholesome lesson, but it did not seriously interfere with American expansion. Particularly after the Civil War it was resigned to accepting the United States as the leading power in the Western hemisphere. Although Great Britain's Civil War policy irritated and disappointed many contemporary Americans, on balance Britain's nonintervention helped to preserve the Union. Its willingness to arbitrate and adjudicate many Anglo-American disputes in the final decades of the nineteenth century and its friendly attitude during the Spanish-American War clearly indicated its desire to keep on good terms with the United States.[5]

World politics of course had a great deal to do with this outlook. Influenced by history and existing realities, Great Britain continued to regard France as its traditional rival and it watched with concern the growing Russian menace to its interests in Asia and the Near East. In view of this attitude, the Franco-Russian alliance of 1894 assumed a rather ominous significance from the British point of view. The British were fully aware, moreover, that the addition of Germany, Japan, and the United States to the circle of world powers meant at least the relative decline of their own power. What was under these circumstances more natural than the decision to solidify Anglo-American relations? By 1904 the British Admiralty had come to the conclusion that a war with the United States would be the supreme folly. Moreover, "no combination of Powers could successfully invade and conquer the United States—and the contest if persisted in could only result in the destruction of the British Empire and the downfall of the English-speaking race." This was also the conclusion to which Theodore Roosevelt had come in 1905. Believing as he did that the interests of the two countries in the Western hemisphere and the Orient were "identical," he took it for granted that the United States could readily cooperate with Great Britain in world affairs.

Geography, outlook on life, and primary political interests separated France and the United States to the extent that on

5. See Bourne, *Britain and the Balance of Power in North America*, pp. 340–41, 380–81, 409; and Chessman, *Roosevelt*, pp. 110–11.

the whole they went their own ways up to 1914. Controversies and contradictions in their relations were the norm rather than the exception. Still, in the perspective of history, the two countries always managed to build bridges that assured the continuity of their friendly contacts and the protection of their vital interests. Although by the turn of the twentieth century the United States was preoccupied with Germany and Japan and more actively involved with Great Britain in affairs of mutual concern than it was with France, its people and government continued to feel a special closeness to France. And although France's theater of operations in world affairs differed greatly from that of the United States, France, too, reserved special sentiments for the United States. America's lingering obligation toward France and its potential contribution to the security of France induced both nations to forget many mutual disappointments. Historically, the Franco-American vision of Napoleon I, dormant and disregarded at times, survived the test of time. The United States did inherit Britain's mantle of power and responsibilities, and France and the United States did maintain a fairly steady working relationship. But by the early twentieth century the cooperation of these two republics was no longer directed against Great Britain. It had become more positive, promoting direct mutual benefits in a changing world arena.

Appendixes, Bibliography,
and Index

Appendix A

"WAR WITH SPAIN"
Excerpts from Lt. Kimball's Report of June 1, 1896*

United States naval operations in European waters might be very effective if the matter of coal supply could be satisfactorily solved. . . . A small U.S. squadron properly constituted for the work might coal in any one of several unfortified anchorages in the Balearic Islands that are sufficiently secure as regards weather, if the colliers were sent from England under the British Flag. . . .

The matter of chartering openly or confidentially would to a small degree depend upon the attitude of the British Government in regard to coal, but it should be as secret as possible in order to prevent complications. Of course, the same system of providing coal for the fleet might be applied to France or Italy, but it could probably be more easily arranged in England than elsewhere. . . .

With flying coaling bases as above, a flying squadron might accomplish much. . . .

As the ammunition supply would be scant, the commanding officer would have to husband it with care, but even so he could strike at Spanish trade in the Mediterranean heavily, could put many unfortified towns under ransom. He could operate in both the Atlantic and Mediterranean coasts of Spain, but the greater part of his work should be done along the latter because he could there better harass the Spanish trade afloat, and towns ashore, and because a U.S. squadron appearing off Barcelona, Valencia, and Cartagena would probably result in a demand for naval protection by the eastern provinces and thus produce strains upon the Ministry it could illy [sic] bear.

*This report (Record Group 313, Entry 43, Office of Navy Intelligence) was declassified by the Naval Intelligence Command of the Department of the Navy on January 8, 1968.

Appendix B

THE DEATH OF LINCOLN*
by Edouard Grenier
Translated by Mrs. Anne C. L. Botta

I.

To chant thy dirge in fitting, worthy words,
Our time is too perturbed, our souls too vain;
Where may we find, O Lincoln, accents strong
Wherewith to paint thy rugged, wondrous traits?
Can our own tongue, nursed at the seat of kings,
On whom it pours unceasing flatteries,
Can it in verse plebeian and robust
Sing the death-song of a great citizen?
Let me essay—thy virtue be my theme;
Inspire me thou with accents worthy her,
In which, without or pomp or splendor vain,
Simplicity shall into grandeur rise.

II.

Ere yet an age had passed the Atlantic saw
The new America born on her shores
Springing to life and growth, the arena vast,
Fruitful and free—free to all human kind,
Where the old world her swarming millions sent,
And where in Nature's bosom man again
Returned to freedom, as the metal grows
Pure in the crucible. Now striding on
With rapid bounds did the young nation reach
The great Pacific, there to set a bound
To the Colossus of the frozen North,
Who casts, his threatening shadow over us,
Whom icy feet tread on three continents.
Thus to despotic power God seemed to say,
"No farther go!" Eternal justice now
Holds its divine balance o'er the globe,

*This poem, published in *Harper's Weekly*, October 19, 1867 (p. 658) ,
obtained the prize at the Concours de Poésie of the French Academy.

Making this free young land to rise and bloom,
And show the astonished world the spectacle
Of a great State self-governed, self-sustained.
But in her greatness lurked the germ of death,
A deep devouring canker gnawed her breast;
Slavery most hideous all her laws deformed;
She whose foul chains outrage two souls at once,
Victor and victim bind in one dread bond,
Branding the master deeper than the slave,
The nation saw the curse that grew with time,
Tend onward to its fatal end, and knew
That she must cast it off or perish there;
Then, like a hero, with firm hand and sure
She plucked the iron from her dreadful wound,
And bravery washed away the stain in blood—
Alas! how freely and how pure it flowed!

III.

When Lincoln to the helm of State was called,
America was drifting toward the rocks,
Like a disabled, storm-tossed ship at sea;
The day of dreadful reckoning had come,
The winds of discord whistled through the sails,
And rent the flag of stars; doubt and dismay
Seized on the gallant ship about to plunge
Into the yawning gulf which opened wide.
He came, sad and alone—God his sole guide—
With firm, intrepid gaze saw the dire ill;
Without reproach or fear he seized the helm,
And through four years, four dark, tempestuous years,
Calm in defeat as calm in victory,
He saw at length the fearful storm subside
The waves retire, lulled by his sovereign voice,
The sound of discord stifled dies away,
And the brave pilot sights the distant port.
To him the slave holds forth his unbound arms,
And peace and mercy wait on all his steps.
But the grand drama has a bloodier act,
Blind hatred now to the vast hecatomb
Of martyrs slain the last great victim adds—
Lincoln falls bleeding at the assassin's feet.

IV.

Die then, but die content, since ere they closed
Thine eyes beheld the day of Justice dawn,
And at thy bidding a whole race oppressed
Rise up and gain the dignity of man,
Of family, of citizen, of law.
A nation's crime to expiate thy life
Thy great soul offered as a sacrifice,
And God accepted it. Oh! happy thou
The glory of thy country, thy great name
The legacy to our degenerate age,
Supplanting the false grandeur of the Past;
A model rare with moral beauty crowned,
Gentleness, justice, and simplicity.
Hero and Christian, Child of Liberty,
Our age is proud of thee, great honest man!—
Honest and dear! The heroes of old Rome
Thou dost not pale before. Democracy
Shall to thy virtues point, and say with pride,
I too my Cincinnatuses can boast!
Upward and onward was thy course of life,
Whose every step was nearer to the goal:
The hewer of wood, the unlettered laborer,
Self-taught, set his firm foot on the first round.
Ardent and eager on he took his way,
Higher and higher, to a wider field:
Up from the forum to the height of State,
Made by the people's love Chief Magistrate.
But not enough—one higher step remains,
One glory still—the palm of martyrdom!
'Tis his; and now, O Lincoln, thou canst die,
Earth and its grandeur has no more for thee.

V.

Thus didst thou die; but why did mocking Fate
Reserve for thee a Caesar's destiny—
Scorner of freedom and of human kind?
Upon what sacred right hadst thou laid hand?
When didst thou seek thine own wrongs to avenge?
When did thy covetous lust of power lead thee,
In the State's name, to trample on the weak?

Thou didst not blight nor vail fair Liberty,
Type of a nation's head, great citizen!
Good, simple, grand, thou only knewest it not.
Alas! when thou didst fall, at that dread stroke
Evil had done its work, the hour had come
Of triumph for thy heart's great clemency,
The crowning glory of all conquerors.
Oh, with what filial care, what tenderness,
Wouldst thou thy bleeding country have raised up,
And in her bosom, rent with nameless wounds,
Have poured oblivion, pardon, and peace.
How gentle was the soul in thy rude form,
What hidden sweetness lay in thy great strength;
How simple, childlike, guileless was thy heart,
Thou gentle statesman—lion nursed with milk!

VI.

For thee, thou mime fired with the assassin's part,
Blind criminal, whom Ravaillac awaits
Among the parricides, didst thou not know
That step by step does vengeance follow crime?
That thought, immortal thought, no word can harm,
No power can conquer not like it divine;
That who would slay it only aids its growth?
Did the blow struck by Brutus save the world
From the oppressor's chain? No; Caesar's blood
The royal purple of Octavius dyed;
In Plato Socrates still lived and spoke;
Luther, Melanchton, Huss bequeathed his foes;
Joan of Arc, upon her funeral pyre
Transformed, became the angel of the land:
And Christ, in dying on the shameful cross,
Saved a lost world, that henceforth hailed his God!

VII.

Lincoln, sleep now in peace! Thy memory
Girt with a double halo, will remain:
In good men's hearts thy name will ever live,
And toil's poor sons, soldier to duty vowed,
The lowly, simple, meek ones of the earth,
Shall find in thee the hero of their dreams.

The worship of those ancient ravagers
Of states and cities, whose triumphant feet
Trampled to dust alike the child and sire,
Scourges of God, in history now shall pale
Before the growing splendor of thy fame.
O gentle hero, wise and great plebeian,
Sleep thou in peace! we bless thee! sleep thou well!
The great good man lives for all time, all men,
And when he dies his country not alone,
But all the world his memory inherits.
To thee man owes the slave's dissevered chain,
Thrones the example of a duty done;
Thy country owes to thee peace, strength restored.
Europe an ideal grand and undefined;
And future ages shall thy name inscribe
Higher than Caesar's—next to Washington.

Bibliography

Archival materials have necessarily been the main sources systematically consulted for this study. In France, the collections of the Archives du Ministère des Affaires Étrangères, both the Correspondence politique, États-Unis, and the Correspondence consulaire et commerciale contain the essential data. The political correspondence, arranged chronologically up to 1896, has thereafter been processed by topics. At times, as in the case of the Spanish-American War, French archival materials relating to Austria, Great Britain, Russia, and Spain have been consulted. Among others, Delcassé's papers, only fairly recently made available to the public, have proved to be a rich, indeed revealing, source. Alfred Maury's unpublished memoirs, in the archives of the Institut de France, are enlightening with respect to certain aspects of the diplomacy of Napoleon III.

In the United States, the records of the State Department deposited in the National Archives constitute the main body of the information incorporated in this study. The diplomatic Instructions and Dispatches to and from the United States Mission in France to 1906 are readily accessible. For 1906–14 the decimal system guides the researcher to his appropriate source. The Notes to and from the French Legation/Embassy in the United States serve as a useful supplement. And the Consular Dispatches from France usually contain valuable information on economic and cultural questions. It was considered advisable, moreover, particularly with respect to the wars in which the United States has been engaged, to consult also the Instructions and Dispatches to and from the American Missions in Austria, Germany, Great Britain, Mexico, Russia, and Spain.

As far as secondary sources are concerned, no over-all study deals specifically with Franco-American diplomatic relations from 1789 to 1914, either in English or in French. In fact, until the end of the nineteenth century, few French diplomatic studies as much as mentioned the United States. In modern times, Claude Fohlen, Pierre Renouvin, and René Rémond, to cite only a few outstanding French scholars, have made valuable contributions to Franco-American history to 1914. Fohlen's comments about the cotton crisis during the American Civil War, Renouvin's *Histoire des relations inter-*

nationales, 1815–1914, and Rémond's *Les États-Unis devant l'opinion française, 1815–1852,* offer valuable insights and interpretations. For the early period, students may consult the following with profit: Ulane Bonnel, *La France, les États-Unis et la guerre de course (1797–1815),* Paris, 1961; Jacques Godechot, *L'Europe et l'Amérique à l'époque napoléonienne,* Paris, 1967; and Alfred Schalck de la Faverie, *Napoléon et l'Amérique,* Paris, 1917. In the mid-century, the critic Émile Montégut followed the American scene very closely. For a good summary of his penetrating views, see his article, "Les États-Unis en 1852, *Revue des deux mondes* (July 15, 1852), pp. 322–54. H. D. Barral-Montferrat, in "La doctrine de Monroe et les évolutions successives de la politique étrangère aux États-Unis," *Revue d'histoire diplomatique* (1903), pp. 594–619, reflected the critical attitude of many Frenchmen who resented and feared the external "go ahead" policy of the United States. Two French dissertations deal with this middle period. St. J. Pincetl, Jr. discusses the relations between the United States and the Second French Republic in his "Relations de la France et des États-Unis pendant la Seconde République, 1848–1851," Université de Paris, 1950. Richard Korolewicz-Carlton analyzed French policy during the first two years of the war in his "Napoléon III, Thouvenel et la guerre de sécession," Université de Paris, 1951. George Charles Mitchell's doctoral dissertation, "La presse française et la guerre hispano-américaine en 1898," Paris, 1949, shows the diversity of French opinion concerning the Spanish-American War. Alberic Neton's *Delcassé (1852–1923),* Paris, 1952; Jean Jules Jusserand's *What me Befell—Reminiscences of J. J. Jusserand,* Boston, 1933; and André Tardieu's *Notes sur les États-Unis—La Société, La Politique, La Diplomatie,* Paris, 1908, reflect the views of three leading French statesmen who were friendly toward the United States.

Several American studies concentrate on certain aspects of Franco-American relations. For the period of the American Revolution, Samuel Flagg Bemis, *The Diplomacy of the American Revolution,* New York, 1935, and Richard Morris, *The Peacemakers: The Great Powers and American Independence,* New York, 1965, represent the best background studies. An excellent discussion of the final decade of the eighteenth century can be found in Alexander De Conde's two volumes, *Entangling Alliance—Politics & Diplomacy under George Washington,* Durham, N.C., 1958, and *The Quasi War—The Politics and Diplomacy of the Undeclared War with France, 1797–1801,* New York, 1966. In his book, *Jefferson and France: An Essay on Politics and Political Ideas,* New Haven, 1967, and in several articles, cited in the bibliography below, Lawrence S. Kaplan discusses with authority Jefferson's and Madison's foreign policy in relation to France. R. A. McLemore, in *Franco-American Diplomatic Relations, 1816–1836*, Baton Rouge, 1941, focuses on the Restoration period and treats in particular the spoliation claims episode. For a detailed discussion and bibliography of the middle period, see Henry Blumenthal, *A Reappraisal of Franco-American Relations, 1830–1871*, Chapel Hill, N.C., 1959. The merits of Lynn M. Case's *French Opinion on the United States and Mexico, 1860–1867*, New York, 1936, remain undiminished. And Donald C. McKay's survey, *The United States and France*, Cambridge, Mass., 1951, emphasizes Franco-American history in the early twentieth century. Finally, Crane Brinton's latest book, *The Americans and the French*, Cambridge, Mass., 1968, offers background information and stimulating insights.

Several American doctoral dissertations are worthy of mention: John W. McCleary, "Anglo-French Naval Rivalry, 1815–1848," Johns Hopkins University, 1947; Warren F. Spencer, "Edouard Drouyn de Lhuys and the Foreign Policy of the Second Empire," University of Pennsylvania, 1955; Francis X. Gannon, "A Study of Elihu Benjamin Washburne: American Minister to France during the Franco-Prussian War and the Commune," Georgetown University, 1950; Richard Montgomery Packard, "The French Pork Prohibition in American Diplomacy, 1881–1891," Harvard University, 1954; Samuel Tinsley Chambers, "Franco-American Relations, 1897–1914," Georgetown University, 1951; and James Louis Whitehead, "French Reaction to American Imperialism, 1895–1908" University of Pennsylvania, 1943.

Among the studies dealing with public-opinion aspects of Franco-American diplomatic relations, the following offer valuable information: E. M. Carroll, *French Public Opinion and Foreign Affairs*, 1870–1914, Hamden, Conn., 1964; Lynn M. Case, *French Opinion on War and Diplomacy During the Second Empire*, Philadelphia, 1954; Simon J. Copans, "French Opinion of American Democracy, 1852–1860," unpublished Ph.D. dissertation, Brown University, 1942; Francis X. Gerrity, "American Editorial Opinion of French Intervention in Mexico, 1861–1867," unpublished Ph.D. dissertation, Georgetown University, 1952; John de Witt McBride, Jr., "America in the French Mind During the Bourbon Restoration," Ph.D. dissertation, Syracuse University, 1954; W. Reed West, *Contemporary French Opinion on the American Civil War*, Baltimore, 1924; Elizabeth Brett White, *American Opinion of France from Lafayette to*

Poincaré, New York, 1927; and Beckles Willson, *America's Ambassadors to France (1777–1927)*, New York, 1928. John G. Gazley's *American Opinion of German Unification, 1848–1871*, New York, 1926, contains two detailed chapters on American opinion on the French and on the Franco-German War.

Several biographical studies of American and French diplomats help to round out the Franco-American picture of the period to 1914. They include: Margaret Clapp, *Forgotten Citizens John Bigelow*, Boston, 1947; Egon Caesar Corti, *Die Tragödie eines Kaisers* (a biography of Emperor Maximilian), Wien, 1949; Pierre Guiral, *Prévost-Paradol, 1829–1970*, Paris, 1955; J. Lucas-Dubreton, *Lamartine*, Paris, 1951; Robert McElroy, *Levi Parsons Morton—Banker, Diplomat and Statesman*, New York, 1930; Elsie Porter Mende, *An American Soldier and Diplomat—Horace Porter*, New York, 1927; J. H. Powell, *Richard Rush: Republican Diplomat, 1780–1859*, Philadelphia, 1942; Maurice Reclus, *Jules Favre, 1809–1880*, Paris, 1912; Robert Walter Reichert, *Prévost-Paradol: His Life and Work*, New York, 1949; G. Roux, *Thiers*, Paris, 1948; James Brown Scott, *Robert Bacon: Life and Letters*, New York, 1923; and Geneviève Tabouis, *The Life of Jules Cambon* (translated from the French by C. F. Atkinson), London, 1938.

Finally, on the period of modern imperialism, the following studies contain pertinent information: Henri Brunschwig, *French Colonialism, 1871–1914: Myths and Realities*, New York, 1960; Jules Ferry, *Le Tonkin et la mère patrie*, Paris, 1890; Thomas F. Power, Jr., *Jules Ferry and the Renaissance of French Imperialism*, New York, 1944; Stephen H. Roberts, *History of French Colonial Policy, 1870–1925*, Hamden, Conn., 1963; and Edward H. Zabriskie, *American-Russian Rivalry in the Far East—A Study in Diplomacy and Power Politics, 1895–1914*, Philadelphia, 1946.

The reader's attention should furthermore be called to a significant work by Lynn M. Case and Warren F. Spencer, *France and the American Civil War*, Philadelphia: University of Pennsylvania Press, 1969.

I. MANUSCRIPT SOURCES

A. Official Papers

1. Material in the Archives du Ministère des Affaires Étrangères

Correspondance politique
Angleterre, 1844–47, 1861–64, 1898.
Autriche, 1861–62, 1866, 1898.
Espagne: Cube, Porto Rico, les Philippines, 1898.
États-Unis, 1812–96.
Prusse, 1861–62, 1870–71.
Russie, 1861–64, 1898.
Politique Étrangère, Canada, Relations avec la France, 1897–1904.
Politique Étrangère, États-Unis, Relations avec la France, 1897–1900.
Relations Commerciales, Chine, Relations avec les États-Unis, 1898–1904.

Correspondance consulaire et commerciale
Baltimore, 1875–86.
Boston, 1861–96.
Charleston, 1854–65.
Chicago, 1890–1901.
New York, 1853–99.
New Orleans, 1841–64, 1897–99.
Philadelphia, 1863–99.
Washington, D.C., 1831–73.

Mémoires et documents
Papiers Delcassé.
Papiers Jules Favre.
Papiers Thouvenel.
Papiers Waddington.

Documents diplomatiques
"Affaires de Chine et du Tonkin, 1884–1885."
"Affaires du Congo, 1884–1895." Conférence africaine à Berlin.
Correspondance et Protocoles.

2. Material in the Archives Nationales

Papiers Eugène Rouher, 45 AP.

3. State Department Diplomatic and Consular Correspondence

Instructions to U.S. ministers in all countries, 1801–29.
Dispatches from U.S. ministers to Austria, 1898.
Instructions to U.S. ministers in France, 1829–1906.
Dispatches from U.S. ministers to France, 1789–1906, 1906–14.

Dispatches from U.S. ministers to Germany, 1870–71, 1898.
Dispatches from U.S. ministers to Great Britian, 1848–64, 1898.
Dispatches from U.S. ministers to Mexico, 1859–67.
Dispatches from U.S. ministers to Russia, 1853–56, 1898.
Dispatches from U.S. ministers to Spain, 1897–98.
Notes to and from the French Legation in the U.S., 1800–1906.
Consular Dispatches from Bordeaux, 1882–1900.
Consular Dispatches from Le Havre, 1870–75, 1897–1906.
Consular Dispatches from Lyons, 1870–78, 1889–1904.
Consular Dispatches from Marseilles, 1885–1901.
Consular Dispatches from St. Petersburg, 1854–56.
Consular Dispatches from St. Pierre, Martinique, 1897–1902.
Consular Dispatches from St. Pierre, St. Pierre and Miquelon, 1898.

4. U.S. Naval Records (in National Archives)

Correspondence Relative to Observance of International Law by
    Vessels of the U.S. Navy, VI—Box I, 1861–65.
Journal of the U.S. Sloop *Peacock*, April 15—August 30, 1814.
Office of Navy Intelligence. Lt. Kimball's Report of June 1, 1896:
    "War with Spain." Record Group 313, Entry 43.

    B. *Private Papers*

Anderson, Chandler P. (LC).
Avenel Family (Tulane University).
Balch, Edward Swift: Journal, 1859–1906 (University of Virginia).
Bancroft, George (LC).
Bigelow, John (New York Public Library).
Brookes, Iverson L. (Duke University).
Dayton, William L. (Princeton University).
Everett, Edward (Massachusetts Historical Society).
Eyma, Xavier: Correspondance (Bibliothèque Nationale, Paris).
Fish, Hamilton: "Dairy" (LC).
Hincks Family (Tulane University) .
Manigault, Gabriel E.: "Autobiography" (University of North
    Carolina).
Marcy, William L. (LC).
Maury, L. F. Alfred: "Souvenirs d'un homme de lettres." 4 vols.
    (Institut de France, MS. 2650).
Miles, William P. (University of North Carolina).

Moore, Frank: "Letter Book, Paris, July 1870–July 1873" (New York Historical Society).
Niles, Nathaniel (LC).
Polk, James (LC).
Reid, Whitelaw: "General Correspondence" (LC).
Rives, William C. (LC).
Rush, Richard: "Family Letters" (Princeton University).
Russell, Jonathan (Brown University).
Seward, William H. (Rochester University).
Ticknor, George: "Letters" (Massachusetts Historical Society) .
Vignaud, Henry (Louisiana State University) .
Washburne, Elihu B. (LC).
Webb, James Watson (Yale University) .
Welles, John: "Diaries" (Columbia University).

II. GOVERNMENT PUBLICATIONS, PUBLISHED COR-RESPONDENCE, SPEECHES, AND GUIDES

A. United States

Compilation of Reports of the Committee on Foreign Relations, 1789–1901. 8 vols. Published as *U.S. Senate Doc.,* 56th Cong., 2d sess., No. 231. Washington, D.C., 1901.
Congressional Globe, 1853–54, 1870–71.
Congressional Record, 1880–1900.
House Ex. Doc., 48th Cong., 1st sess., No. 1, Part 3. Communication of Rear-Admiral Ammen, U.S.N., on the subject of Marine Rams. August 8, 1883.
Sen. Ex. Doc., 40th Cong., 1st sess., No. 20. Correspondence relating to the Maximilian affair.
Sen. Ex. Doc., 45th Cong., 3d sess., No. 58. International Monetary Conference, 1878.
Sen. Ex. Doc., 49th Cong., 1st sess., No. 196. Correspondence in relation to the affairs of the Independent State of the Congo. Washington, D.C., 1886.
Sen. Doc., 61st Cong., 2d sess., No. 467. March 25, 1910. Report on affairs in Liberia.
Sen. Doc., 62d Cong., 2d sess., No. 353. The General Arbitration Treaties with Great Britain and France, 1911.
Sen. Misc. Doc., 37th Cong., 3d sess., No. 38. Concurrent Resolution of February 28, 1863, relating to foreign intervention in the Civil War.

U.S. Census Bureau. *The Foreign Commerce and Navigation of the United States, 1901 and 1914.* Washington, D.C., 1902 and 1915.

U.S. Treasury Department. *Annual Report and Statements of the Chief of the Bureau of Statistics on the Foreign Commerce and Navigation of the United States, 1892. Washington, D.C., 1893.*

U.S. Tariff Commission. *Reciprocity and Commercial Treaties.* Washington, D.C., 1919.

Nasatir, A. P. *French Activities in California: An Archival Guide.* Stanford, Calif., 1945.

Richardson, J. D. (ed.) *A Compilation of the Messages and Papers of the Presidents.* 10 vols. Washington, D.C., 1896.

Wellesley, H. R. C. *Secrets of the Second Empire: Private Letters from the Paris Embassy,* ed. F. A. Wellesley. New York, 1929.

Wellesley, V., and Sencourt, R. *Conversations with Napoleon III.* London, 1934.

B. France

Assemblée Nationale. *Discours et Débats, 1872–1914.* (Journal Officiel).

Ministère du Commerce. *Annales du Commerce Extérieur, 1884–98, 1913.* Paris, 1900 and 1914.

———. *Annuaire Statistique, 1901.* Paris, 1902.

Ministère du Travail. *Annuaire Statistique, 1914.* Paris, 1917.

Favre, Jules, *Discours parlementaires.* 4 vols. Paris, 1881.

Thiers, Adolphe. *Discours parlementaires.* Paris, 1880–81.

Thouvenel, L. *Le secret de l'empereur—correspondance confidentielle et inédite échangée entre M. Thouvenel, le Duc de Gramont et le Général comte de Flahaut, 1860–63.* 2 vols. Paris, 1889.

C. Germany

Die Grosse Politik der Europäischen Kabinette, 1871–1914. 40 vols. Berlin, 1922–27.

D. Great Britain

Gooch, G. P., and Temperley, H. (eds.). *British Documents on the Origins of the War, 1898–1914.* 2 vols. London, 1927.

III. NEWSPAPERS AND PERIODICALS

A. Newspapers

1. American (in LC)
Atlanta Constitution, 1870–98.
Brooklyn Daily Eagle, September, 1898—July, 1900.
Daily Picayune (New Orleans), 1852 .
New York Times, 1870–1914.
New York Tribune, 1894–1898.
New York *Courier des États-Unis,* 1848–62.
Washington, D. C. *National Intelligencer,* 1835–65.

2. French (in the Bibliothèque Nationale, Paris)
Le Constitutionel, 1835–66.
Continental Gazette (American journal, Paris), 1878–82.
Journal des Débats, 1835–70.
Le Figaro, 1861, 1870, 1898.
Le Matin, 1898.
Messager Franco-Américain, 1850.
Le Patrie, February-March, 1848; November-December,
    1861; October-November, 1862.
Le Patriote, September, 1870.
La Presse, 1846–60.
La Révolution, July-August, 1830; September-December, 1851.
La Vérité, November, 1870.
Le Temps, 1861–1900.
L'Univers, 1848–54.

B. Periodicals

1. American
American Journal of International Law.
American Historical Review.
De Bow's Review.
French Historical Studies.
French-American Review.
Harper's Magazine.
Journal of American History.
Journal of Modern History.
Mississippi Valley Historical Review.

The Nation.
North American Review.

2. French
Le Correspondant.
Études d'histoire moderne et contemporaine.
Journal des économistes.
Revue des deux mondes.
Revue d'histoire diplomatique.
Revue d'histoire moderne et contemporaine.
Revue historique.
Revue de Paris.
Revue des sciences politiques.

IV. MEMOIRS, THESES, BOOKS, AND ARTICLES

A. Period 1789–1815

Andrews, Edward L. *Napoleon and America.* New York, 1909.

Bemis, S. F. *John Quincy Adams and the Foundations of American Foreign Policy.* New York, 1950.

Bowman, Albert Hall. "The Struggle for Neutrality—A History of the Diplomatic Relations Between the United States and France, 1790–1801." Unpublished Ph.D. dissertation, Columbia, University, 1954.

Braman, Isaac. "Union with France a Greater Evil Than Union with Britain." Sermon, April 5, 1810. Rowley, Mass., 1810.

Brant, Irving. *James Madison, Secretary of State, 1800–1809.* Indianapolis, 1953.

———. *James Madison, The President, 1809–1812.* Indianapolis, 1956.

Brown, Kenneth L. "Mr. Madison's Secretary of the Navy," *U.S. Naval Institute Proceedings,* LXXIII (1947), 967–75.

Brown, Roger H. *The Republic in Peril: 1812.* New York, 1964.

Burt, A. L. *The United States, Great Britain and British North America—From the Revolution to the Establishment of Peace After the War of 1812.* New York, 1961.

Channing, William Ellery. "Sermon Preached in Boston, April 5, 1810." Boston, 1810.

Corvin, E. S. *French Policy and the American Alliance of 1778.* Princeton, N.J., 1916.

Darling, Arthur Burr. *Our Rising Empire, 1763–1803.* New Haven, Conn., 1940.

Echeverria, Durand. "Antoine Jay and the United States," *American Quarterly,* IV (Fall, 1952), 235–52.

———. "L'Amérique devant l'opinion française, 1734–1870: Questions de méthodes et d'interprétations." *Revue d'histoire moderne et contemporaine,* IX (1962), 51–62.

Faÿ, Bernard. *The Revolutionary Spirit in France and America.* New York, 1927.

Gallatin, Count (ed.). *The Diary of James Gallatin, Secretary to Albert Gallatin—A Great Peacemaker, 1823–27.* New York, 1924.

Gershoy, Leo. *The French Revolution and Napoleon.* New York, 1961.

Giddens, Paul H. "Contemporary Opinion of Napoleon," *Journal of American History,* XXVI (1932), 189–204.

Glover, Richard. "The French Fleet, 1807–1814; Britain's Problem; and Madison's Opportunity," *Journal of Modern History,* XXXIX (1967), 233–52.

Golder, F. A. "The Russian Offer of Mediation in the War of 1812," *Political Science Quarterly,* XXXI (1916), 380–91.

Hazen, Charles D. *Contemporary American Opinion of the French Revolution.* Gloucester, Mass., 1964.

Hyde de Neuville, Jean Guillaume. *Mémoires et Souvenirs.* 2 vols. Paris, 1892.

Hyneman, Charles S. *The First American Neutrality—A Study of the American Understanding of Neutral Obligations.* Urbana, Ill., 1934.

Kaplan, Lawrence S. "France and Madison's Decision for War, 1812," *Mississippi Valley Historical Review,* L (1964), 652–71.

———. "Jefferson's Foreign Policy and Napoleon's Idéologues," *William & Mary Quarterly,* 3rd ser., XIX (1962), 344–59.

———. "Jefferson, the Napoleonic Wars, and the Balance of Power," *William & Mary Quarterly,* 3rd ser., XIV (1957), 196–217.

Ketcham, Ralph L. "France and American Politics, 1763–1793," *Political Science Quarterly,* LXXVIII (1963), 198–223.

Lyon, E. Wilson. "The Directory and the United States," *American Historical Review,* XLIII (1938), 514–32.

Mahan, A. T. *Sea Power in Its Relations to the War of 1812.* 2 vols. London, 1905.

Malone, Dumas (ed.). *Correspondence Between Thomas Jefferson and Pierre Samuel du Pont de Nemours, 1789–1817.* Boston, 1930.

Morris, Anne Cary (ed.). *The Diary and Letters of Gouverneur Morris.* 2 vols. New York, 1888.

Nevins, Allan (ed). *The Diary of John Quincy Adams, 1794–1845.* New York, 1951.

O'Donnell, William Emmett. *The Chevalier de La Luzerne, French Minister to the United States, 1779–1784*. Bruges, 1938.

Perkins, Bradford. *Prologue to War: England and the United States—1805–1812*. Berkeley, Calif., 1963.

Rice, Howard C. "James Swan: Agent of the French Republic, 1794–1796," *New England Quarterly*, X (1937), 464–86.

Richmond, Arthur A. "Napoleon and the Armed Neutrality of 1800: A Diplomatic Challenge to British Sea Power," *Royal United Service Institution Journal*, CIV (1959), 186–94.

Stourzh, Gerald. *Benjamin Franklin and American Foreign Policy*. Chicago, 1954.

Thiers, Adolphe. *The History of the French Revolution*, trans. Frederick Shoberl. 4 vols. Philadelphia, 1848.

Troude, O. *Batailles Navales de la France*. Paris, 1868.

Turner, Frederick Jackson. "The Policy of France Toward the Mississippi Valley in the Period of Washington and Adams," *American Historical Review*, X (1905), 249–79.

Vagts, Alfred. "The United States and the Balance of Power," *Journal of Politics*, III (1941), 401–49.

Van Tyne, Claude H. "French Aid Before the Alliance of 1778," *American Historical Review*, XXXI (1925), 20–40.

———. "Influences Which Determined the French Government to Make the Treaty with America, 1778," *American Historical Review*, XXI (1916), 528–41.

Washington, H. A. (ed). *The Writings of Thomas Jefferson*. Vol. VI. Washington, D.C., 1854.

B. Period 1815–1871

Acomb, Evelyn M., and Brown, Marvin L., Jr. *French Society and Culture Since the Old Regime*. The Eleutherian Mills Colloquium, 1964. New York, 1966.

Adams, E. D. *Great Britain and the American Civil War*. 2 vols. New York, 1925.

Aldis, O. F. "Louis Napoleon and the Southern Confederacy," *North American Review*, CXXIX (1879), 342–60.

Amann, Petter H. "Writings on the Second French Republic," *Journal of Modern History*, XXXIV (1962), 409–29.

Ames, Mary Lesley (ed.). *Life and Letters of Peter and Susan Lesley*. 2 vols. New York, 1909.

Baldensperger, F. "L'initiation américaine de Georges Clémenceau," *Revue de littérature comparée*, VIII (1928), 127–54.

Barbier, Jean-Baptiste. *Outrances sur le Second Empire.* Paris, 1956.
Barker, Nancy Nichols. *Distaff Diplomacy: The Empress Eugénie and the Foreign Policy of the Second Empire.* Austin, Texas, 1967.
———. "France, Austria, and the Mexican Venture, 1861–1864," *French Historical Studies,* III (1963), 224–45.
Belperron, Pierre. *La guerre de sécession, 1861–1865.* Paris, 1947.
Bernstein, Samuel. *Essays in Political and Intellectual History.* New York, 1955.
Bigelow, John. *France and the Confederate Navy, 1862–1868.* New York, 1888.
Blue, George Vern. "France and the Oregon Question," *Oregon Historical Quarterly,* XXXIV (1933), 39–59, 144–63.
Blumenthal, Henry. "Confederate Diplomacy: Popular Notions and International Realities," *Journal of Southern History,* XXXII (1966), 151–71.
———. "George Bancroft in Berlin: 1867–1874," *New England Quarterly,* XXXVII (1964), 224–41.
Cambriaire, Célestin-Pierre. *Le rôle de la France dans l'expansion des États-Unis.* Paris, 1935.
Carrey, Émile. *Grandeur et Avenir des États-Unis. Paris, 1863.*
Case, Lynn M. "La France et l'affaire du 'Trent'," *Revue Historique* (1961), 57–86.
Chambrun, Charles A. de. *Impressions of Lincoln and the Civil War—A Foreigner's Account.* New York, 1952.
Chevalier, Michael M. *France, Mexico, and the Confederate States,* trans. Wm. H. Hurlbut. New York, 1863.
Chinard, Gilbert. *L'Amérique d'Abraham Lincoln et la France.* Washington, D.C., 1945.
———. "L'Amérique et la révolution de 1848," *French-American Review,* I (1948), 264–72.
Claussen, M. P. "Peace Factors in Anglo-American Relations, 1861–65." *Mississippi Valley Historical Review,* XXVI (1940), 511–22.
Courmont, Félix de. *Des États-Unis, de la Guerre du Mexique et de l'Ile de Cube.* Paris, 1847.
Curti, Merle E. "The Impact of the Revolutions of 1848 on American Thought," *Proceedings of the American Philosophical Society,* XCIII (1949), 209–15.
———. "The Reputation of America Overseas (1776–1860)," *American Quarterly,* I (1949), 58–82.

Curtis, Eugene N. *The French Assembly of 1848 and American Constitutional Doctrine.* New York, 1918.

Dansette, A. *Deuxième République et Second Empire.* Paris, 1942.

———. *Explication de la Deuxième République.* Paris. 1942.

Debidour, A. *Histoire Diplomatique de l'Europe (1814–1878)* Paris, 1891.

Deschanel, Louis P. *Histoire de la Politique Extérieure de la France, 806–1936.* Paris, 1936.

Domenech, The Abbé Emmanuel. *Missionary Adventure in Texas and Mexico.* London, 1858. (Translated from the French).

Droz, Jacques. *Europe Between Revolutions, 1815–1848.* New York, 1967.

Duberman, Martin B. *Charles Francis Adams, 1807–1886.* Boston, 1961.

Duniway, Claude A. "Reasons for the Withdrawal of France from Mexico," *AHA Annual Reports,* I (1902), 315–28.

Durham, A. L. "The Development of the Cotton Industry in France and the Anglo-French Treaty of Commerce of 1860," *Economic History Review,* I (1928), 281–307.

Duveau, Georges. *1848: The Making of a Revolution,* trans. Anne Carter. London, 1967.

Einstein, Lewis. "Napoléon III et les préliminaires diplomatiques de la guerre civile aux États-Unis," *Revue d'histoire diplomatique* (1905), pp. 336–48.

Evans, Thomas W. *Memoirs—The Second French Empire.* New York, 1905.

Farmer, Paul. "Some Frenchmen Review 1848," *Journal of Modern History,* XX (1948), 320–25.

Fasel, George W. "The French Election of April 23, 1848—Suggestions for a Revision,"*French Historical Studies,* V (1968), 285–98.

Favre, Jules. *Gouvernement de la défense nationale.* Paris, 1871.

Ferri-Pisani, Colonel Camille (aide de camp de S.A.I. Le Prince Napoléon). *Lettres sur les États-Unis d'Amerique.* Paris, 1862.

Fisch, Georges. *Les États-Unis en 1861.* Paris, 1862.

Fohlen, Claude. "La Guerre de Sécession et le Commerce Franco-Américaine," *Revue d'histoire moderne et contemporaine,* VIII (1961), 259–70.

Fröbel, Julius. *Amerika, Europa, und die politischen Gesichtspunkte der Gegenwart.* Berlin, 1859.

———. *Theorie der Politik, Als Ergebnis einer erneuten Prüfung demokratischer Lehrmeinungen.* 2 vols. Vienna, 1864.

Galbraith, John S. "France as a Factor in the Oregon Negotiations," *Pacific Northwest Quarterly*, XLIV (1953), 69–73.

Gasparin, Agénor Étienne de. *Après la Paix—Considérations sur le Libéralisme et la Guerre d'Orient*. Paris, 1856.

———. *L'Amérique devant l'Europe*. Paris, 1879.

Gavronsky, Serge. "American Slavery and the French Liberals: An Interpretation of the Role of Slavery in French Politics During the Second Empire," *Journal of Negro History*, LI (1966), 36–52.

Gershoy, Leo. "Three French Historians and the Revolution of 1848," *Journal of the History of Ideas* (January, 1951), pp. 131–46.

Golder, F. A. "Russo-American Relations during the Crimean War," *American Historical Review*, XXXI (1926), 462–76.

Goyau, Georges. *La France missionnaire dans les cinq parties du monde*. 2 vols. Paris, 1948.

Graebner, N. A. *Empire on the Pacific—A Study in American Continental Expansion*. New York, 1955.

Guichen, E. de. *Les grandes questions européennes et la diplomatie des puissances sous la seconde république française*. Paris, 1925.

Guizot, François. *Histoire parlementaire de France*. Paris, 1864.

Hanna, K. A. "The Role of the South in the French Intervention in Mexico," *Journal of Southern History*, XX (1954), 3—21.

Huntley, Stephen McQueen. *Les rapports de la France et la Confédération pendant la guerre de sécession*. Toulouse, 1932.

Johnson, Douglas. *Guizot: Aspects of French History, 1787–1874*. London, 1963.

Joinville, Prince François de. *Notes sur l'état des forces navales de la France*. Paris, 1844.

Jomini, A. G. *Diplomatic Study on the Crimean War (1852 to 1856)*. 2 vols. London, 1882.

Jones, Russell M. "The Flowering of a Legend: Lafayette and the Americans, 1825–1834," *French Historical Studies*, IV (1966), 384–410.

Lafond, Georges. *L'effort français en Amérique latine*. Paris, 1917.

Lally, Frank Edward. *French Opposition to the Mexican Policy of the Second Empire*. Baltimore, 1931.

Landes, D. S. "French Entrepreneurship and Industrial Growth in the Nineteenth Century," *Journal of Economic History*, IX (1949), 45—61.

Lorin, Henri. "L'Évolution de La Doctrine de Monroe," *Revue des deux mondes* (June 15, 1915), pp. 818–47.

Lynch, Sister M. Claire. *The Diplomatic Mission of John Lothrop Motley to Austria, 1861–67.* Washington, D.C., 1944.

Mahieu, Robert G. *Les Enquêteurs français aux États-Unis de 1830–37.* Paris, 1934.

Mange, Alice E. *The Near Eastern Policy of the Emperor Napoleon III.* Urbana, Ill., 1940.

Mazade, Charles de. "Cinquante Années d'Histoire Contemporaine, M. Thiers," *Revue des deux mondes* (April 15, 1881), pp. 826–61.

McLemore, R. A. "The Influence of French Diplomatic Policy on the Annexation of Texas," *Southwestern Historical Quarterly,* XLIII (1940), 342–47.

Merk, Frederick. *Manifest Destiny and Mission in American History—A Reinterpretation.* New York, 1963.

———. *The Monroe Doctrine and American Expansionism, 1843–1849.* New York, 1966.

———. *The Oregon Question—Essays in Anglo-American Diplomacy and Politics.* Cambridge, Mass., 1967.

Millman, Richard. *British Foreign Policy and the Coming of the Franco-Prussian War.* Oxford, England, 1965.

Montalembert, Le Comte de. *La Victoire du Nord aux États-Unis.* Paris, 1865.

Montégut, Émile, "Les États-Unis en 1852," *Revue des deux mondes,* XV (July 15, 1852), 322–54.

———. *Libres Opinions—Morales et Historiques.* Paris, 1888.

Montgéry, Jacques Philippe Mérigon de. *Notice sur la vie et les travaux de Robert Fulton.* Paris, 1825.

Moreau, Henry. *La Politique Française en Amérique, 1861–1864.* Paris, 1864.

Pingaud, A. "La politique extérieure du Second Empire," *Revue historique,* CLVI (1927), 41–68.

Poujade, E. *La diplomatie du Second Empire.* Paris, 1871.

Pouthas, Charles. *Les révolutions de 1848 en Europe.* Paris, 1952.

Prévost-Paradol, L. A. *Quelques Pages d'Histoire Contemporaine Lettres Politiques.* Paris, 1864.

Ray, Jean. *Un précédent à la question des dettes—La liquidation d'une dette de guerre de la France envers les États-Unis: Le conflict de 1834–1836.* Paris, 1933.

Renouvin, Pierre. *La question d'Extrême Orient, 1840–1940.* Paris, 1946.

———. *La politique extérieure du Second Empire.* Paris, 1940.

Robertson, William Spence. *France and the Latin-American Independence*. Baltimore, 1939.

————. "French Intervention in Mexico in 1838," *Hispanic American Historical Review*, XXIV (1944), 222–52.

Rothfels, Hans. "1848—One Hundred Years After," *Journal of Modern History*, XX (1948), 291–319.

Rush, Richard. *Residence at the Court of London, Recollections of the Court of Louis Philippe and the French Revolution of 1848*. London, 1872.

Schéfer, Christian. *La grande pensée de Napoléon III: Les origines de l'expédition du Mexique, 1858–62*. Paris, 1939.

Schnerb, Robert. *Rouher et le Second Empire*. Paris, 1949.

Sencourt, R. *Napoleon III: The Modern Emperor*. London, 1933.

Simpson, F. A. *The Rise of Louis Napoleon*. London, 1950.

Snoy, J. Charles. "Les répercussions internationales de la guerre de sécession, 1861–1865," *Revue générale* (September 15, 1929), pp. 284–300.

Soltau, Roger. *French Political Thought in the Nineteenth Century*. New Haven, Conn., 1931.

Spencer, Ivor D. *The Victor and the Spoils: A Life of William L. Marcy*. Providence, R.I., 1959.

Spencer, W. F. "Drouyn de Lhuys et les Navires Confédérés en France . . . ," *Revue d'histoire diplomatique* (1963) , pp. 314–41.

Stanton, Theodore. "Le général Grant et la France," *Revue de Paris* (November 1, 1894), pp. 183–202.

Stock, Leo Francis. "Catholic Participation in the Diplomacy of the Southern Confederacy,' *Catholic Historical Review*, XVI (1930) , 1–18.

Stolberg-Wernigerode, Otto zu. *Germany and the United States of America During the Era of Bismarck*. Philadelphia, 1937.

Tarsaidze, Alexandre. *Czars and Presidents*. New York, 1958.

Ticknor, George. *Life, Letters and Journals*. 2 vols. Boston, 1876.

Tocqueville, A. de. *Souvenirs*. Paris, 1893.

Van Deusen, Glyndon G. *William Henry Seward*. New York, 1967.

Washburne, E. B. *Recollections of a Minister to France, 1869–1877*. 2 vols. New York, 1887.

Webster, C. K. "British Mediation Between France and the United States in 1834–36," *English Historical Review*, XLII (1927), 58–78.

Weed, Harriet (ed.) . *Autobiography of Thurlow Weed*. 2 vols. Boston, 1884.

Weill, Georges. "L'idée républicaine en France pendant la Restauration," *Revue d'histoire moderne*, II (1927), 321–48.

Welles, E. T. (ed.). *The Diary of Gideon Welles.* 3 vols. Boston, 1911.

Welschinger, Henri. *La guerre de 1870—Causes et responsabilités.* 2 vols. Paris, 1910.

Whitridge, Arnold. *Men in Crisis: The Revolutions of 1848.* New York, 1949.

C. Period 1871–1900

Adams, Brooks. *America's Economic Supremacy.* New York, 1900.

———. "The New Struggle for Life Among Nations," *McClure's Magazine*, XII (1899), 558–64.

American Citizens, Paris. *Mr. Whitelaw Reid in France— 1889— 1892.* Paris, 1892.

Anderson, M. S. *The Eastern Question—1774–1923.* New York, 1966.

Ashley, Percy. *Modern Tariff History—Germany, United States, France.* New York, 1926.

Auxier, George W. "Middle Western Newspapers and the Spanish-American War, 1895–1898," *Mississippi Valley Historical Review*, XXVI (1940), 523–34.

Bacon, Nathaniel T. "American International Indebtedness," *Yale Review*, IX (November, 1900), 265–85.

Bacourt, Adolphe de. *Souvenirs d'un Diplomate, Lettres sur l'Amérique.* Paris, 1891.

Bailey, Thomas. *America Faces Russia—Russian-American Relations from Early Times to Our Day.* Ithaca, N.Y., 1950.

Barrows, Chester L. *William M. Evarts—Lawyer, Diplomat, Statesman.* Chapel Hill, N.C., 1941.

Battistini, Lawrence H. *The Rise of American Influence in Asia and the Pacific.* East Lansing, Mich., 1960.

Baxter, James Phinney. *The Introduction of the Ironclad Warship.* Cambridge, Mass., 1933.

Beisner, Robert L. *Twelve Against Empire: The Anti-Imperialists, 1898–1900.* New York, 1968.

Benton, Thomas H. *Thirty Years' View.* 2 vols. New York, 1879.

Bérard, Victor. "Questions extérieures—Panama," *Revue de Paris* (January 15, 1902), pp. 423–44.

Bigelow, John. *Retrospections of an Active Life.* Vol. III. New York, 1909.

Blake, Nelson Manfred. "Ambassadors at the Court of Theodore

Roosevelt," *Mississippi Valley Historical Review,* XLII (September, 1955), 179–206.

Bourne, Kenneth. *Britain and the Balance of Power in North America, 1815–1908.* Berkley, Calif., 1967.

Boutellier, Paul. "Les États-Unis—Leur expansion économique et mondiale," *Le Monde Économique,* (December 10 and 17, 1904), pp. 739–40, 776–78.

Brooks, John G. *As Others See Us—A Study of Progress in the United States.* New York, 1908.

Bury, J. P. T. *France, 1814–1940.* London, 1962.

Cady, John F. *Thailand, Burma, Laos, Cambodia.* Englewood Cliffs, N.J., 1966.

———. *The Roots of French Imperialism in Eastern Asia.* Ithaca, N.Y., 1954.

Cameron, Rondo E. *France and the Economic Development of Europe, 1800–1914.* Princeton, N.J., 1961.

———. "L'Exportation des capitaux français, 1850–1880," *Revue d'histoire économique et sociale,* XXXIII (1955), 346–53.

Chadwick, French E. *The Relations of the United States and Spain.* New York, 1909.

Chamber of Commerce, San Francisco. *Franco-American Commerce.* San Francisco, 1879.

Church, William Covant. *Life of John Ericsson.* 2 Vols. New York, 1890.

Clapham, J. P. *The Economic Development of France and Germany, 1815–1914.* Cambridge, England, 1951.

Clough, Shepard B. *France: A History of National Economics.* New York, 1939.

Constant, Paul Henri Benjamin Baron d'Estournelles de. *La Politique en Tunisie—Le protectorat et ses origines 1854–91.* Paris, 1891.

Coolidge, T. Jefferson. *Autobiography of T. Jefferson Coolidge, 1857–1900.* Boston, 1902.

Cortissoz, Royal. *The Life of Whitelaw Reid.* 2 vols. New York, 1921.

Dennis, Albert L. P. *Adventures in American Diplomacy, 1896–1906.* New York, 1928.

Depew, Chauncey M., and Hyde, James H. *Speeches Delivered on the Occasion of a Dinner for His Excellency Jules Cambon, 15th November, 1902.* New York, 1903.

Dislère, P. "Notes sur la marine des États-Unis," *Revue maritime et coloniale,* XXII (January, 1868), 261–301.

Driault, Édouard. *Les problèmes politiques et sociaux à la fin du XIX*ᵉ *siècle*. Paris, 1900.

———. "L'Impérialisme aux États-Unis," *Revue Bleue* (1900), 502–5.

Dudley, Thomas H. "Three Critical Periods in our Diplomatic Relations with England During the Late War," *The Pennsylvania Magazine of History and Biography*, XVII (1893), 34–54.

Duncan, Bringham. "Protectionism and Pork: Whitelaw Reid as Diplomat: 1889–1891," *Agricultural History*, XXXIII (1959). 190–95.

Dyer, B. *The Public Career of William M. Evarts*. Berkely, Calif., 1933.

Edgar-Bonnet, G. "Ferdinand de Lesseps et les États-Unis," *Revue d'histoire diplomatique* (1956), pp. 289–322.

Eyre, James K. Jr. "Russia and the American Acquisition of the Philippines," *Mississippi Valley Historical Review*, XXVIII (1942), 539–62.

Falkner, Roland. "The United States and Liberia," *American Journal of International Law*, IV (1910), 529–45.

Feis, Herbert. *Europe—The World's Banker, 1870–1914*. New Haven, Conn., 1930.

Gignilliat, John L. "Pigs, Politics, and Protection: The European Boycott of American Pork, 1879–1891," *Agricultural History*, XXXV (1961), 3–12.

Glazebrook, G. P. de T. *A History of Canadian External Relations*. Toronto, 1950.

Golob, Eugene Owen. *The Méline Tariff: French Agriculture and Nationalist Economic Policy*. New York, 1944.

Gottschalk, Louis, and Lach, Donald. *The Transformation of Modern Europe*. Chicago, 1954.

Gréard, Octave. *Prévost-Paradol—Élude suivie d'un choix de lettres*. Paris, 1894.

Grenville, John A. S. *Lord Salisbury and Foreign Policy—The Close of the Nineteenth Century*. London, 1964.

———. and Young, George B. *Politics, Strategy, and American Diplomatic Studies in Foreign Policy, 1873–1917*. New Haven, Conn., 1966.

Gresham, Matilda. *Life of Walter Quintin Gresham, 1832–1895*. Chicago, 1919.

Guerlac, Othon. "Le Suicide de Prévost-Paradol à Washington et l'Opinion Américaine," *Revue de littérature comparée*, VIII (1928), 100–12.

Haight, Frank A. *A History of French Commercial Policies*. New York, 1941.

Jannet, Claudio. *Les États-Unis Contemporains*. Paris, 1889.

Keenleyside, Hugh Ll., and Brown, Gerald S. *Canada and the United States: Some Aspects of Their Historical Relations*. New York, 1952.

Kindleberger, Charles P. *Economic Growth in France and Britain, 1851–1950*. Cambridge, Mass., 1964.

Lafeber, Walter. *The New Empire: An Interpretation of American Expansion, 1860–1898*. Ithaca, N.Y., 1967.

Langer, William L. *The Franco-Russian Alliance, 1890–1894*. Cambridge, Mass., 1929.

Leclerc, Max. *Choses d'Amérique: Les crises économique et religieuse aux États-Unis*. Paris, 1895.

Le Fur, L. *Étude sur la Guerre Hispano-Américain de 1898*. Paris, 1899.

Leroy-Beaulieu, Paul. "Conditions for American Commercial and Financial Supremacy," *The Forum*, XX (December, 1895), 385–400.

Leroy-Beaulieu, Pierre. "Les États-Unis—Puissance Coloniale," *Revue des deux mondes* (January 1, 1902), pp. 77–112.

Levasseur, E. "The Concentration of Industry and Machinery in the United States," *Annals of the American Academy of Political and Social Science* (February 23, 1897), pp. 178–97.

Livezey, William E. *Mahan on Sea Power*. Norman, Okla., 1954.

Mahan, A. T. *The Influence of Sea Power upon the French Revolution and Empire, 1793–1812*. 2 vols. Boston, 1898.

———. *The Interest of America in Sea Power, Present and Future*. Boston, 1898.

Mars, V. de. "La Marine en France et aux États-Unis en 1865," *Revue des deux mondes* (August 15, 1865), pp. 777–819.

Maureau, Auguste. "La Maîtresse de la Mer—Les Théories du Capitaine Mahan," *Revue des deux mondes*, XI (October 1902), 681–708.

May, Ernest R. *American Imperialism: A Speculative Essay*. New York, 1968.

———. *Imperial Democracy: The Emergence of America as a Great Power*. New York, 1961.

McCormick, Thomas. "Insular Imperialism and the Open Door: The China Market and the Spanish-American War," *Pacific Historical Review*, XXXII (1963), 155–69.

McGann, Thomas F. *Argentina, the United States, and the Inter-American System, 1880–1914.* Cambridge, Mass., 1957.

Medlicott, W. N. *The Congress of Berlin and After—A Diplomatic History of the Near Eastern Settlement, 1878–1880.* Hamden, Conn., 1963.

Mérignhac, A. "La doctrine de Monroe à la fin du XIXᵉ siècle," *Revue du droit publique et de la science politique en France et à l'étranger,* V (1896), 201–78.

———. "La Paix Hispano-Américaine," *Revue du droit publique,* XI (1899), 229–63.

Mitchell, Donald W. *History of the Modern American Navy: From 1883 Through Pearl Harbor.* New York, 1946.

Molloy, Leo Thomas. *Henry Shelton Sanford, 1823–1891: A Biography.* Derby, Conn., 1952.

Montague, L. L. *Haiti and the United States, 1714–1938.* New York, 1966.

Moore, John Bassett. *History and Digest of the International Arbitrations to Which the United States Has Been a Party.* 6 vols. Washington, D.C., 1898.

Morgan, H. Wayne. *William McKinley and His America.* Syracuse, N.Y., 1963.

———. (ed.). *Making Peace with Spain—The Diary of Whitelaw Reid, September–December 1898.* Austin, Texas, 1965.

Neale, R. G. *Britain and American Imperialism, 1898–1900.* Brisbane, Australia, 1965.

Noël, Octave. "Le Péril Américain," *Le Correspondant* (March 25, 1899, and April 10, 1899), pp. 1083–1104 and 116–44.

Ollivier, Émile. "Les États-Unis, l'Espagne et la France," *Revue Bleue* (September 3, 1898), pp. 289–93.

Pearce, Haywood J., Jr. "Georges Clemenceau: Chronicler of American Politics," *South Atlantic Quarterly,* XXIX (October, 1930), 394–401.

Pisani-Ferry, Fresnette. *Jules Ferry et le partage du monde.* Paris, 1962.

Pletcher, David M. *The Awkward Years—American Foreign Relations Under Garfield and Arthur.* Columbia, Mo., 1962.

Priestley, H. I. *France Overseas: A Study of Modern Imperialism.* New York, 1938.

Puleston, W. D. *Mahan: The Life and Work of Captain Alfred Thayer Mahan, U.S.N.* New Haven, Conn., 1946.

Rainey, H. Dr. *Thomas W. Evans—America's Dentist to European Royalty.* Philadelphia, 1956.

Reclus, Maurice. *Grandeur de "La Troisième" de Gambetta à Poincaré.* Paris, 1948.

Reeves, Jesse S. *The International Beginnings of the Congo Free State.* Baltimore, 1894.

Richards, E. W. "Louis Napoleon and Central America," *Journal of Modern History,* XXXIV (1962), 178–84.

Rippy, J. Fred. "The European Powers and the Spanish-American War," *The James Sprunt Historical Studies,* XIX (1927), 22–52.

Roberts, Adolphe. *The French in the West Indies.* New York, 1942.

Roberts, Stephen H. *History of French Colonial Policy, 1870–1925.* 2 vols. London, 1929.

Ropp, Theodore. "Continental Doctrines of Sea Power," in E. M. Earle, *Makers of Modern Strategy.* Princeton, N.J., 1944. Pp. 446–56.

Rouquette, Louis. *La France aux États-Unis—Comment concurrencer le commerce allemand.* Paris, 1915.

Rousiers, Paul de. "L'Impérialisme Américain," *Revue de Paris* (March 15, 1899), pp. 424–42.

Savard, Pierre. *Jules-Paul Tardivel, La France et Les États-Unis, 1851–1905.* Quebec, 1967.

Say, Léon. *Les finances de la France sous la troisième République.* 4 vols. Paris, 1898.

Scott, John A. *Republican Ideas and the Liberal Tradition in France, 1870–1914.* New York, 1966.

Sears, Louis Martin. "French Opinion of the Spanish-American War," *Hispanic-American Historical Review,* VII (1927), 25–44.

Sée, Henri. *Histoire économique de la France.* 2 vols. Paris, 1942.

Sée, Paul. *Le Péril Américain.* Lille, 1903.

Spetter, Allan B. "Harrison and Blaine: Foreign Policy, 1889–93." Unpublished Ph.D. dissertation, Rutgers University, New Brunswick, N.J., 1967.

Sprout, Harold, and Margaret. *The Rise of American Naval Power, 1776–1918.* Princeton, N.J., 1946.

Stolberg-Wernigerode, Otto zu. *Germany and the United States of America during the Era of Bismarck.* Reading, Pa., 1937.

Taillandier, Madame Saint-René. "Silhouettes d'Ambassadeurs: IV. J. J. Jussserand," *Revue d'histoire diplomatique* (1952), 191–94.

Taylor, A. J. P. *The Struggle for Mastery in Europe, 1848–1918.* Oxford, England, 1954.

Thomson, David. *Democracy in France since 1870.* London, 1964.

———. *Democracy in France, The Third and Fourth Republics.* London, 1960.

Tyler, Alice Felt. *The Foreign Policy of James G. Blaine*. Hamden, Conn., 1965.

Waddington, Mary King. *My First Years as a Frenchwoman, 1876–1879*. London, 1914.

Warner, Donald F. *The Idea of Continental Union—Agitation for the Annexation of Canada to the United States, 1849–1893*. Lexington, Ky., 1960.

Wolf, John B. *France: 1814—1919—The Rise of a Liberal-Democratic Society*. New York, 1963.

Wright, Gordon. *France in Modern Times: 1760 to the Present*. Chicago, 1960.

D. Period 1900–1914

American Chamber of Commerce, Paris. *Franco-American Tariff Agreement*. Bulletin No. 82, State Department Decimal File 611.5131/389. Paris, April, 1910.

Anderson, Eugene N. *The First Moroccan Crisis, 1904–1906*. Chicago, 1930.

Bailey, Thomas A. *America Faces Russia: Russian-American Relations from Early Times to Our Day*. Ithaca, N.Y., 1950.

Beale, Howard K. *Theodore Roosevelt and the Rise of America to World Power*. Baltimore, 1956.

Bemis, Samuel Flagg (ed.). *The American Secretaries of State and Their Diplomacy*. Vol. IX. New York, 1958.

Bishop, Joseph B. *A Chronicle of One Hundred and Fifty Years—The Chamber of Commerce of the State of New York, 1768–1918*. New York, 1918.

Cambon, Jules. "The Permanent Bases of French Foreign Policy," *Foreign Affairs*, VIII (1930), 173–85.

Chessman, Wallace G. *Theodore Roosevelt and the Politics of Power*. Boston, 1969.

Dennett, Tyler. *Roosevelt and the Russo-Japanese War*. Garden City, N.Y., 1925.

Dennis, Albert. *Adventures in American Diplomacy, 1896–1906*. New York, 1928.

Dunn, Robert W. American Foreign Investments. New York, 1926.

Einstein, Lewis. *A Diplomat Looks Back*. New Haven, Conn., 1968.

———. "The United States and Anglo-German Rivalry," *Living Age*, CCLXXVI (1913), 323–32.

Esthus, Raymond A. *Theodore Roosevelt and Japan.* Seattle, Wash., 1966.

Eustis, J. B. "The Franco-Russian Alliance," *North American Review,* CLXV (July 1897), 111–118.

Hanotaux, Gabriel. *Études Diplomatiques: La Politique de l'Équilibre 1907–1911.* Paris, 1914.

Harbaugh, William H. *Power and Responsibility: The Life and Times of Theodore Roosevelt.* New York, 1961.

Jessup, Philip C. *Elihu Root.* 2 vols. New York, 1938.

Lévy, Raphäel-Georges. "La crise économique de 1907 et les États-Unis d'Amérique," *Revue des deux mondes* (December 15, 1907), pp. 805–28.

Lodge, Henry C. (ed.). *Selections from the Correspondence of Theodore Roosevelt and Henry Cabot Lodge, 1884–1918.* 2 vols. New York, 1925.

Lorin, Henri. "L'Évolution de la doctrine de Monroe," *Revue des deux mondes* (June 15, 1915), pp. 818–47.

Morison, Elting E. (ed.). *The Letters of Theodore Roosevelt.* 6 vols. Cambridge, Mass., 1951–54.

Munholland, Kim. "Rival Approaches to Morocco: Delcassé, Lyautey, and the Algerian-Moroccan Border, 1903–1905," *French Historical Studies* V (1968), 328–43.

Nevins, Allan. *Henry White: Thirty Years of American Diplomacy.* New York, 1930.

Porter, Charles W. *The Career of Théophile Delcassé.* Philadelphia, 1936.

Pratt, Sir John T. *The Expansion of Europe in the Far East.* London, 1947.

Renouvin, Pierre. "L'Orientation de l'Alliance Franco-Russe en 1900–1901," *Revue d'Histoire Diplomatique* (July–September, 1966.), 193–204.

Rippy, J. Fred. *America and the Strife of Europe.* Chicago, 1938.

Scott, James Brown. *The Hague Peace Conferences of 1889 and 1907.* 2 vols. Baltimore, 1909.

Steed, Henry Wickham. *Through Thirty Years, 1892–1922.* New York, 1924.

Stuart, Graham H. *French Foreign Policy: From Fashoda to Sarajevo (1898–1914).* New York, 1921.

Tardieu, André. *France and the Alliances: The Struggle for the Balance of Power.* New York, 1908.

Tien-yi-Li. *Woodrow Wilson's China Policy, 1913–1917.* New York, 1952.

Vagts, Alfred. *Deutschland und die Vereinigten Staaten in der Weltpolitik.* 2 vols. New York, 1935.

Vevier, Charles. *The United States and China, 1906–1913: A Study of Finance and Diplomacy.* New Brunswick, N.J., 1955.

Viallate, Achille. *Economic Imperialism and International Relations During the Last Fifty Years.* New York, 1923.

Index